DELTA THEORY AND PSYCHOSOCIAL SYSTEMS

Delta Theory establishes the foundation for a true scientific applied psychology, a theory of how human influence induces change in others. Delta Theory is unified and universal, applying to all cultures, historical periods, and goals for change. It integrates concepts and research from psychology, sociology, anthropology, evolution theory, philosophy, psychoneurology, cognitive science, and Cultural-Historical Activity Theory. Yet Delta Theory is clear, economical, and elegant, with a full exposition of tactics for its practices. Rich examples are drawn from professional practices, but also from the creation and operations of criminals, healing ceremonies of indigenous peoples, and cross-species comparisons. This book ultimately seeks to describe how influence works, how it could be improved, and how it can be resisted.

Roland G. Tharp is Emeritus Professor of Psychology at the Universities of Hawaii, Manoa, and California, Santa Cruz. He has also taught at University of Arizona, Stanford University, and the University of Greenland. Tharp is the director of the national Center for Research on Education, Diversity, and Excellence. He has done extensive fieldwork with indigenous people, including Mayan, Polynesian, Navajo, Zuni, and Inuit. Tharp is the author or coauthor of the books *Behavior Modification in the Natural Environment*, *Rousing Minds to Life*, *Teaching Transformed*, and *Self-Directed Behavior*. His articles have appeared in such journals as *American Psychologist*, *American Anthropologist*, and *Psychological Bulletin*, among others. He is the laureate of the Grawemeyer Prize in Education and the Hopwood Award (Major, in Poetry) from the University of Michigan and has held the Frost Fellowship of the Bread Loaf School of English, Middlebury College.

Delta Theory and Psychosocial Systems

THE PRACTICE OF INFLUENCE AND CHANGE

Δαß

Roland G. Tharp

Emeritus Professor
Universities of California and Hawaii

CAMBRIDGE
UNIVERSITY PRESS

CAMBRIDGE
UNIVERSITY PRESS

University Printing House, Cambridge CB2 8BS, United Kingdom

Cambridge University Press is part of the University of Cambridge.

It furthers the University's mission by disseminating knowledge in the pursuit of education, learning and research at the highest international levels of excellence.

www.cambridge.org
Information on this title: www.cambridge.org/9781107531734

© Roland G. Tharp 2012

First published 2012
First paperback edition 2015

A catalogue record for this publication is available from the British Library

Library of Congress Cataloguing in Publication data
Tharp, Roland G., 1930–
    Delta theory and psychosocial systems : the practice of influence
    and change / Roland G. Tharp.
        p.   cm.
    Includes bibliographical references and index.
    ISBN 978-1-107-01491-6 (hardback)
    1. Behavior modification.   2. Adjustment (Psychology)   3. Social
    psychology.   I. Title.
    BF637.B4T43   2012
    153.8′5–dc23   2011025631

ISBN 978-1-107-01491-6 Hardback
ISBN 978-1-107-53173-4 Paperback

To my first and primary psychosocial system:
Ila and George, Berma and Oswald, Carol and Gail

CONTENTS

List of Figures   *page* xii

Preface   xiii

Acknowledgments   xix

SECTION ONE: THE THEORY OF INFLUENCE AND CHANGE

1. Introduction and Overview   3

   Influence and Change: Intended, Adventitious,
       Inadvertent, and Incompetent   3
   Delta: An Overview of the Domain   5
   The Scope   7
   Delta Theory ($\Delta\alpha\beta$): A Summary   7

2. Psychosocial Systems and the Exercise of Influence   10

   Psychosocial Systems   10
   The Organization of Social Relationships   11
   Psychosocial Systems: The Dynamics of Formation and Change   12
       Propinquity   12
       Joint Activity   14
       Intersubjectivity   15
       Affinity   17
   The Phases of Psychosocial Systems: Beta, Alpha, and Delta   20

3. The Zone of Proximal Development, Activity, and Semiotics   24

   Overview of Social Influence on Development   24
   The Zone of Proximal Development   27

Influence and the Zone of Proximal Development   28
   Stage I: Where Performance Is Assisted by More
      Capable Others   30
   Domain Knowledge and Professional Expertise   32
   Stage II: Where the Self Assists Performance   33
   Stage III: Where the Performance Is Developed,
      Automatized, and Fossilized   34
   Stage IV: Where De-Automatization of Performance
      Leads to Recursion back through the Zone of Proximal
      Development   36

4. The Means of Influence   38
  Influence, Assistance, Regulation   38
  "Scaffolding"   39
  Means of Influence: The List   40
    Task Structuring   43
    Propping/Nudging   44
    Modeling   45
    Contingency Management   48
    Instructing   48
    Questioning   49
    Cognitive Structuring   50
    Feeding back against a Standard   51

5. The Organization of Activity   54
  The Concept of Activity Settings   55
  Motive and Meaning in Activity Settings   56

6. Unifying the Study of Culture and Psychology:
  Philosophical and Scientific Issues   59
  The Game and the Candle   60
  Relationships between Studies of Culture and Psychology:
    A Brief Retrospect   61
    Anthropological Perspectives   61
    Psychological Perspectives   64
  Foundational Considerations, Philosophical and Scientific,
    for a Unified Perspective   65
  The Four Levels of Human Development   66

Understanding the Cultural through *Background*   69
    Subprimate Asides   71
    Background Resumed   72
   An Empirical Example   74
   Culture and Ecology   79

SECTION TWO: THE PRACTICE OF INFLUENCE AND CHANGE

7. Influencing and Change: Delta Theory of Practice   85

   Introduction   85
   The Spread of Obesity   85
   Intended Influence, Intended Change, Subject To   87

8. A Natural History Museum of Influence
   and Change: Dioramas   90

   Introduction   90
   Aboriginal Americans vs. the United States of America   90
    Education and the Cherokee Syllabary   91
    Retention and Conversion of Captives   93
   Malign-Purposed Influence   95
    Recruitment and Socialization of Underage Prostitutes   95
    The Creation of Dangerous Violent Criminals   97
    Military Training   101
    Reichstag Death Squadrons   101
    Universalism: Disciplinary and Cross-Disciplinary   103
   Culture-Based Deltas   103
    Hoʻoponopono   103
    Navajo "Sings"   104
   A Notable Historical Failure. American School Desegregation   107
   Primary Socialization   108
    Among the Nso   108
    "But I Am Your Mother ..."   110

9. Who Influences? The Triadic Model of Influence and Change   111

   Organizing for Influence and Change: Dyadic Deltas   111
   Organizing for Influence and Change: A Triadic Model
    of Assistance   113

Triadic Deltas   113
Field-Vectored Deltas   114
Self as Source of Influence in Practice   115
Influence, Power, and Organizational Structure   117
Activity Settings: Not Only Who, but What They Do   120

10. Basic Tactics and Strategy in Designing Influence   123

Principles and Protocols for Designing Influence and Change   124
    Units of Analysis   125
    Design Protocol   126
Basic Tactics of Influence and Change   127
    Tactic 1: Agent Influences Subject Directly   128
    Tactic 2: Agent Influences Subject through Mediator(s)   131
    Tactic 3: Agent's Influence Is Directed to Subject's
        Psychosocial System   131
    Tactic 4: Agent Curtails Subject's Participation in Competing
        Psychosocial Systems   133
    Tactic 5: Agent Creates or Enlists Additional or Alternate
        Psychosocial Systems for Subject   133
Strategies Involving Multiple Tactics   135
    A Strategy Involving Tactics 1, 2, and 3   135
    A Strategy Involving Tactics 1, 4, and 5   136
    A Strategy Involving All Five Tactics: The Delta Classroom   136

11. Cultural Patterns in the Practice of Influence   139

Indigenous Formal Activities of Influence   139
Professional Activities of Influence Practiced with Cultural
    Accommodations   141

12. Challenges, Research, and Future Development   149

Delta Theory and Other Sciences: Relationships and
        Opportunities   149
    Issues of Causation   149
    The Example of Synchrony   151
Fads, Failures, and Futures: Prediction and Postdiction
        by Delta Theory   152
    Traditional Therapies   152
    Predictive Analysis: Tango Therapy   154

Exploring the Cognitive and Neural Bases of Influence
    through Joint Activity 157
The Future Development of Delta 160

Appendix: Criteria, Standards, and Guidelines necessary for
a Unified, Universal Theory 163
    General Requirements 163
    Requirements Specific to a Unified Theory 163
    Desirable Qualities 164
    Methodological Implications of a Unified Theory 165

References 167
Index 181

FIGURES

2.1. The cycle of social sorting   *page* 13

3.1. Progressions through the zone of proximal development
     and beyond   29

6.1. The funnel of human development   67

9.1. Agent influences Subject directly   112

9.2. The basic triadic model: Agent influences Subject indirectly
     through Mediator   114

9.3. A psychosocial system as Mediator   120

10.1. Agent influences only Subject with little or no shared activity   128

10.2. Agent directly influences Subject in their shared
      psychosocial system   130

10.3. Through activity settings involving Agent and Mediator(s),
      the Mediator is influenced to use activity settings with Subject
      to influence Subject toward change   131

10.4. Agent influences by participation in Subject's existing
      psychosocial system(s)   132

10.5. Agent influences Subject by preventing Subject's psychosocial
      interactions in existing competing psychosocial systems   133

10.6. Agent influences Subject into new activity groups   134

PREFACE

This book's work was not conducted in isolation but was intensely psycho-social. It could not have been otherwise, as its domain of inquiry is the acquisition of behavioral and attitudinal patterns, the building of the mind, and the building of consciousness itself – which results from intensely social processes, processes that do not cease during life.

However, as a young man, I had a period of exclusively self-directed learning. Like most autodidacts, I no doubt developed some idiosyncrasies. A decade of formal education thereafter would seem sufficient to correct them, nevertheless the author of a theory purporting to unify across such a large domain can hardly deny some measure of peculiarity. The autodidact is subject to a society of authors who do not engage him in dialogue. In formal education, some dialogue is provided, and although never enough, interpretation of facts received and activities endorsed is subject to negotiation, explanation, and socialization. Not so for the autodidact.

Some years ago, two young students in an audience with the revered Buddhist spiritual leader, the Dalai Lama, asked him the following:

> STUDENTS: I wonder if you have in your past any people who were important ... teachers ... or a kind of master that you think about now?
> THE DALAI LAMA: Those Indian pundits! Many centuries back ...
> STUDENTS: No, I mean someone who influenced you when you were a child or a younger man, who was a master to you, and you his disciple.
> THE DALAI LAMA: Yes ... the great Indian pundits of the past many centuries.
> STUDENTS: But no one living? I mean, not an actual person?
> THE DALAI LAMA: No. You see, those living persons, they are just carrying the messages of the great Indian pundits ... (Hilgers & Molloy, 1981, p. 195, quoted in Tharp & Gallimore, 1998)

I do not liken myself to the Dalai Lama – quite the reverse. In his formal monastic education between the ages of six and twenty-three, he would have been immersed in the school's intensely social patterns of interaction, in which interpretation of text and application to life are dramatically disputed in a pattern very close to "debate" in the Western tradition, or to the "drum-dance" contest of ideas among traditional Inuit. In all likelihood, he reached his private dialogue with books and authors in his later life.

As a young autodidact, I made what I could of readings alone under a night-light: broad, sweeping surveys – Fraser's *Golden Bough*, Toynbee's *Study of History*, the many volumes of *The Story of Civilization* and *The Story of Philosophy* by Will and Ariel Durant, Freud, Einstein, a set of books about the biological-medical researchers who pioneered disease theory. I suppose attempting a simulacrum of survey courses was an economical way of understanding how knowledge is organized and of what categories it consisted. However, as I will emphasize further in this work, *more is learned than is taught*. Mentors teach disciplines and craft; but learners absorb them as models. Not that those "pundits" seemed infallible, any more than a reader will find this author so. Yet it still seems to me that building toward a unified theory is what scholars are supposed to do.

Only recently have I attempted such a thing myself. An accumulation of concepts has developed along with a kind of sorting and stacking, so after a long career there seem enough blocks in my shed to attempt some kind of edifice.

A PERSONAL JOURNEY

As an undergraduate at the University of Houston, I had a rat and a Skinner Box. In graduate school at the University of Michigan, I studied field theory, systems theory, social psychology, and anthropology; I used sociological theory in my dissertation. At the Palo Alto Veterans' Administration Hospital, I was further trained in applied behaviorism, community psychiatry, and the social therapies for families and institutions. As a young faculty member of the University of Arizona, in 1961, I designed the first graduate degree program in Community Psychology. Many of the building blocks of my personal intellectual structure came from these fields. I continue to find value in them, and all reverberate in Delta Theory.

Delta Theory's central concepts also include three of Lev Vygotsky's (1978) concepts, which I have expanded and published previously: the zone of proximal development (Tharp & Gallimore, 1969); the developmental domains, particularly his cultural-historical domains (Tharp, 1994);

and, by asserting the strong case, an extension of the age range of applicability of ZPD-assisted performance principles (e.g., Watson & Tharp, 2006). These expansions are made possible by decades of data accumulated since Vygotsky's death. The Cycle of Social Sorting (Tharp, Estrada, Dalton & Yamauchi, 2000) is an amalgam of Cultural-Historical Activity Theory concepts and some from sociology. Other Delta material has other sources, from cognitive behaviorism to cognitive science to brain studies. A concept vital to Delta is drawn from the philosopher John Searle (see Chapter 6). My method is to accrete domain-specific data and explanations to the structure of Delta concepts and dynamics, and thereby articulate a unified scientific theory explaining influence and change.

A "UNIFIED" THEORY

In Delta Theory, what is being unified? My purpose is to bring together a number of theoretical and research domains *insofar as they treat influence and change*. Thus I draw together explanatory concepts and research findings from (as examples) cognitive science, sociology, anthropology, philosophy, Cultural-Historical Activity Theory, behaviorism, observational learning, evolution theory, criminology, and history. I do not purport or aspire to unify these entire disciplines, but rather to propose a theory of influence and change that unites and interweaves contributions from each. A secondary aspiration is that Delta Theory serve as a demonstration or proof of concept of the feasibility of unifying many small domain theories – not to refute or remove them, but to offer a system of more basic processes to enrich their own theorizing and research.

"Modern physics began with a sweeping unification: In 1687 Isaac Newton showed that the existing jumble of disparate theories describing everything from planetary motion to tides to pendulums were all aspects of a universal law of gravitation. Unification has played a central role in physics ever since.... In addition to predicting new physical effects, a unified theory provides a more aesthetically satisfying picture of how our universe operates" (Lisi & Weatherall, 2010, p. 55–56). I quote these two ambitious theorists in physical science to emphasize that unification is necessary to progress. Likewise in the human sciences: We will unify or stultify. There will be unifiers. There will be unification.

In speaking to colleagues about this aspiration, I meet some sardonic smiles and perhaps will now receive a great deal more. Yet also encouragement: It is not unique to suppose that the task of scientists is to contribute discoveries pertinent to theory or challenging to current theory, thereby participating in theory building itself. Pecking away at it and sometimes attempting a reach: This is the calling of science and indeed of the intellectual life.

I feel far from my autodidactic youth, having had a professional life of intense collegiality. Virtually all of the concepts used here are the result of work and dialogue with a set of extraordinary collaborators, through whose influence this work has developed. Delta Theory is *synthesis* in another sense, being an integration of concepts that emerged during my long study of various forms of influence and change in the settings of many cultures. Readers of my previous writings, many of them decades prior to my exposure to Vygotskian concepts, will meet again some familiar terms and threads of thought but will perhaps see them anew in this whole-cloth attempt.

A last personal note: In critiquing the professional practice of influence and change, every shortcoming I strive to influence and change I too have committed.[1] Of practitioner errors, I write with the bona fides of frustrated experience, not disdainfully but with empathy.

IS DELTA COMPLETE?

The question may arise: Is Delta a finished theory or a draft of a work in progress? My hope is that Delta will never be "finished," unless or until it is refuted. Absent that, any theory with power will accrete, expand, modify, and gradually incorporate into accepted science, especially a universalist theory for which there is a built-in process of modification. As this book will emphasize, the basic discipline of any universal theory is the Method of Universals, characterized most frequently as William James's "one white crow" test, in which any universal proposition (such as "all crows are black") is upset by a single exception. Thus instances of exceptionality are followed by a modification of the specific proposition. The discipline of the universalist requires vigilance in searching for white crows.

---

[1] My career has been in many specific domains of influence and change: research and practice in marriage and family counseling; group and individual psychotherapy (office based and home based); formal education from preschool to graduate school; community psychology; and coaching (athletic, personal, and professional development). This has brought regular collaboration with nursing, psychiatry, occupational therapy, public health, rehabilitation, group homes both open and closed, mental hospitals, and community mental health centers. I have also had the common human experiences of influencing children, in my case as the parent of five. Working for a unified therapy for these domains was less a choice than being driven to solve the problems of Babel.

Thus any universal theory is only provisionally complete; it is ever open to necessities for greater precision until the community of scientists is satisfied that some propositions require no further searching and are declared accepted science.

DELTA?

I have appropriated the word *delta* from calculus, Δ denoting a change, as the result of a specifiable relationship between one variable and others it affects. The name's obvious appeal is as the metaphor for change, but its mathematical association also invokes standards of disconfirmability and the potential for quantification of relationships among concepts as variables. I choose to fly the flag of Δ not as a claim of territory occupied, but as an idealistic symbol. Throughout the work assembled here into Delta Theory, I have taken care only to use concepts potentially quantifiable and their relationships disconfirmable. If any should prove not to be so, they must be refined or replaced.

Efforts through quantitative research to test theoretical propositions are expensive in resources and effort. The warrants for such work lie in the plausibility of the theoretical ideas, plausibility sufficient to justify prudent investment. I have attempted to test the Delta assertions against plausibility at every stage of the theory's construction. Using the one white crow test, I have not found exceptions. A further test is to continually ask at each stage of theory development: Among the interdependencies of the central concepts, is the weave tight enough to hold complex phenomena without spillage? When it is not, the strands must be further tightened.

Of course, plausibility is a criterion requiring judgment, and that judgment will now be the reader's to make.

A NOTE ON "NATURAL" AND "NATURE"

Forty years ago, in *Behavior Modification in the Natural Environment* (Tharp & Wetzel, 1969) our use of the word *natural* was much remarked, in the tone of "What's more natural about school and home than the laboratory?" Nevertheless, I retain the idea of natural, because the strongest evidence for the validity of Delta Theory is its correspondence with successful human practices of influence as they occur naturally (as opposed to professionally), but also in a more foundational sense. The theoretical processes of Delta Theory are natural because they occur *by and through the nature* of *Homo sapiens.* Thus grounding in science – physical, biological, and social – is essential to my criteria for a valid theory of human behavior. Successful influence processes are successful *because* they operate through natural processes – those that are phylogenetically laid down, historically conditioned, and socially influenced toward development.

ACKNOWLEDGMENTS

Ronald Gallimore and Clifford O'Donnell insisted that I attempt this unification. I am indebted to Elias Ali, Justin Wiley, and Michael Tharp for their assistance in clarifying the Delta metaphor. For critical reading of the manuscript and suggestions, I thank Bert van Oers, Ronald Gallimore, Lisa Tsoi Hoshmand, Stephanie Stoll Dalton, Karl Kristian Paartoq Olsen, Robert Rueda, and Ann Bayer. Julie Tharp gave patient and tireless bibliographic assistance and introduced me to the work of Temple Grandin. My seminar students Marianna F. Valdez and Susan Mrazek contributed important ideas to the breadth of Delta Theory. Natalie Crespo talked with me for hours, enriching my understanding of her original and invaluable research, so important to the exposition in Chapter 8. For their early interest and sponsorship ten years ago, I thank Montserrat Castelló Badia and her colleagues at Ramon Llull University, Barcelona; and César Coll, University of Barcelona. For decades of shared activity and dialogue, producing many of the concepts in this book, I have had the great good fortune of intersubjectivity and friendship with Ronald Gallimore, Clifford O'Donnell, Ralph Wetzel, David Watson, and Karl Kristian Paartoq Olsen.

SECTION ONE

THE THEORY OF INFLUENCE AND CHANGE

1

Introduction and Overview

Most attempts to influence others do not succeed. In general, it is a good thing that subjects reject and resist, and that successful influence requires sustained, thoughtful, and purposeful effort. Even among sustained, thoughtful, and purposeful attempts, many are simply incompetent, and the effects, if any, are inadvertent. A classic example is the reinforcing power of negative attention, by which a scolding teacher increases the mischief of children who could better be ignored (Gallimore, Tharp, & Kemp, 1969). The "law of unintended consequences," which has historically plagued public policy, is of this nature – that is, unintended consequences resulting from ignorance, incomplete analysis, or inadequate theory. Adventitious effects are unplanned and unexpected, perhaps disappointing, and often truly unpredictable. Although not a result of inadvertence in planning, adventitious effects in complex systems are common. Overlapping and interacting psychosocial systems are no exception.

Beyond the intellectual satisfaction of a unified theory of influence and change, there is wide potential utility. Better professional practice should flow from richer theoretical understanding. Personal lives may be more satisfied if we are able to influence others for their own good, just as our own lives will improve if we understand how to be better parents, lovers, pastors, or accountants. Further, there is another use of the knowledge of how influence changes us. I hope the ideas of Delta Theory will come to the attention of general readers as well as social scientists, because there is no human who is not under social influence, much of which is not benign. The world is awash with attempts to influence: blandishments of advertisers; twists of politicians; systematic campaigns of conversion, seduction, or trickery.

Knowledge of how influence works will allow us better to resist it. A fuller understanding of how influence leads to change can help us defend against unwanted influence while providing effective influence for those we foster and protect.

The domain of discussion here is *influence and change*. Influence and change is practiced in many settings and professions and, indeed, by us all. Who does not attempt to exert influence and hope for change? Educators, psychotherapists, coaches, and parents do; but so do seducers, political spinmeisters, and gang bosses. Members of the latter groups will have little interest in this intellectual construction, but I am suggesting that professional practitioners might attend, if warily, to a theory purporting to unite our separate and too-often competitive disciplines.

Influence and change is professionally practiced as a set of discipline-specific techniques and is not guided by a general theory. Convincing evidence for the efficacy of those techniques is scarce. Most human service professionals work in multidisciplinary case conferences, a theoretical Tower of Babel. It is a difficult matter, this practice of influence and change, and it is perhaps even more difficult to achieve *sustainable* change. Yet there is no resource to most practitioners beyond disciplinary techniques, no general theory based on *Homo sapiens'* nature, societies, and cultures.

Further, a fundamental misunderstanding handicaps many professional practitioners of influence. We objected to it forty years ago:

> [T]he *treater* is rarely a psychiatrist or psychologist or social worker, but is rather the individual's parent or teacher or spouse or ward attendant or sibling or friend or employer.... If the environment [setting of the intervention] is the hospital, these people are the nurses, doctors, or other patients; if ... the school, they are the principal, teachers, or other pupils; if ... the family, they are siblings, the spouse, or the parents.

> The traditional alternative is to build a new and artificial relationship between the *treater* and the individual.... *This procedure is patently wasteful, if there is indeed an alternative form of intervention, which mobilizes the potential power of [an individual's existing social relationships].* (Tharp & Wetzel, 1969, pp. 3–4, emphasis added)

Forty years later it has become obvious that any professional Agent's first task is to analyze Subject's psychosocial field and then devise an influence plan using existing psychosocial systems, disrupting or extracting Subject from the destructive ones and creating new ones when necessary. This is what the masters of influence do, from good mothers to organized criminals. The default choice should not be Agent directly and individually relating to Subject; that should be a temporary and, indeed, the last choice, taken only in the absence of anything more effective.

A unified theory *will* some day soon be accepted. Physical science's galloping pursuit of a unifying theory has glamorized the search for a "theory of everything," so in social science unification may take on a reflected legitimacy. Delta is not an attempt at a theory of everything. My aspirations are only for a theory of everything in one field – a large field, but one with clear boundaries: intentional influence and change in behavior, thoughts, emotions, and values. Only by going toward a goal can we hope to get beyond the present, and then only by the orderly interpretation of accumulating evidence – the activity we call science, in which there is a permanent vector of *toward*.

I write from the general orientation of developmental psychology, which has been vigorous in recent decades. If there is a synonym available for *influence and change*, it may be *intentional development*. Yet no single discipline or domain of knowledge can satisfy universalistic criteria. If a unified theory is possible, it will be construed from and in the languages of many disciplines. Thus Delta Theory draws together explanatory concepts and research findings from (as examples) cognitive science, sociology, anthropology, philosophy, cultural-historical activity theory, behaviorism, observational learning, evolution theory, criminology, and history, *insofar as they treat influence and change*.

DELTA: AN OVERVIEW OF THE DOMAIN

Delta Theory reveals the principles and dynamics by which change is effected, yet it simultaneously shows why change occurs so infrequently. *The foundational proposition of Delta Theory is that influence and change operate primarily, indeed almost exclusively, within and through psychosocial systems – that is, affiliated persons organized into systems that share values, purpose, and activity.* The theory and practice require a valid description of how social systems are formed and the internal processes that account for their continuation, particularly those involving the challenges of change. The practice of Delta *mobilizes the potential power of an individual Subject's social relationships, either preexisting or created by the Agent*. Professional Agents understand this at the first level: They attempt to create a new psychosocial system consisting of him- or herself and the Subject. The core of Delta Theory is that every Subject of influence is embedded in complex psychosocial systems whose tendency toward inertia is directly analogous to Isaac Newton's First Law of Motion. Any Agent of influence must perforce change those psychosocial systems – a far more complex task than presumed by the one-to-one counselor.

The burden of Delta Theory is to explain how *change* (both learning and development) is brought about by *influence.* Influence is social. To begin with the end of the argument, each *Agent* of influence and *Subject* of change interact under known phylogenetically provided restrictions, conditioned by historically provided cultural values and expectations, which are re-created and sustained by small psychosocial systems loosely articulated into social networks. *Every successful action of intended influence takes place in species, cultural, life-historical, and technical human-science validities.*

That prescription sounds daunting, but the doing need not be. Many of those validities flow naturally from the nature of *Homo sapiens.* Humanity's existence depends on influencing one another, by fostering the young and defending against the depraved. Successful influence can be seen all around us, sometimes benign, sometimes malign. The most effective change Agents are the crafty – the good mother, the gang boss, the leader – who *feel* the intricacies of influencing. Less often successful are we professional practitioners, who are restricted by incomplete theory and must, in the vacuum, take guidance from our guilds.

My task now is to guide a walk through the processes by which we have become ourselves and through which our becoming continues. This complex field of forces is intellectually comprehensible through a small number of concepts.[1] Perhaps some readers will say as I did: *Aha.* Accepting the strictures of settled science, we will consider what we know from relevant developmental and social science and then contextualize that knowledge within levels of phylogenesis, historical-ethnogenesis, and the ontogenesis

---

[1] In common sense, we over-attribute effects to "persuasion." For example, the recruitment of underage girls into prostitution (see Chapter 8) is not by persuasion, except perhaps for the acceptance of a first date with the young man who is actually the crime syndicate's pimp, working to protocol. Thereafter, even during that very date, Delta theory explains. Thus I exclude persuasion from this theoretical analysis. As we will see, influence makes for change only after Subject has been persuaded to engage in Agent's prescribed activities. Persuasion's objective is to induce Subjects to agree to actions or beliefs. I have been persuaded by Aristotle to adopt his expository structure: Delta Theory's *Means of Influence* will be defined, then their dynamics clarified through illustrations, just as Aristotle does in his *Rhetoric*, which identifies his Means of Persuasion and, through examples, clarifies their dynamics. We scientists and thinkers attempt to persuade and engage one another. But for Delta processes to produce change, persuasion is either prior or irrelevant. *Influence,* a more complex psychosocial process, begins after persuasion is achieved. Author influences reader only if and when reader begins to act in a different way.

of life histories. I will attempt to sever the knot that has prevented a unification of psychological and cultural studies, that last hindrance to a universal theory. That exposition is replete with examples.

We will then turn from the science and theory of influence and change to its practice, design, and engineering principles, with special attention to cross-cultural contexts. We conclude with some considerations of the future prospects of Delta Theory's own further development.

THE SCOPE

The scope of a *unified* theory of influence and change includes, at least, the following: primary socialization of the young; formal schooling; psychological and social therapies; counseling; public health; civic public education; restricted residential environments; family intervention; home-based social-service treatments; correctional programs; criminology; social casework; community development; organizational development; professional development; on-the-job training; mentoring; rehabilitation; occupational therapy; all coaching – personal, cognitive, and athletic; self-help groups and programs; self-directed behavior change; all twelve-step programs; and all training of all practitioners, from philosophers to soldiers.

The scope of a *universal* theory of influence and change includes and applies equally to all cultures and historical periods.

The theory must fit not only the "engineered" operations of formal institutional and professional services, but also the processes by which humans have successfully socialized and developed one another informally, currently and historically, and across cultures, including the primary socialization of child rearing.

A unified theory of change and influence must account for unsuccessful and successful instances – both institutional and informal, and both benign and malign in purpose or outcome. That is to say that the theory must be equally effective in accounting for socialization into convents as into criminal gangs. And it will reveal why change is so often very hard to do.

DELTA THEORY (Δαß): A SUMMARY

The foundational proposition of Delta Theory is thus: Influence and change operate primarily, indeed almost exclusively, within and through *psychosocial systems,* that is, groups of persons that tend toward stability of affiliation. I call this theory *Delta,* but it might be better labeled Δαß, or *Delta/*

Alpha/Beta, in respect of the three *phases* of psychosocial systems. In the simplest terms, for psychosocial systems:

ß The *Beta* phase is one of behavioral and social equilibrium and stability.
α The *Alpha* phase is characterized by disequilibrium and instability.
Δ The *Delta* phase is organized for enhancing influence and change.

The phases are not explanatory concepts. They constitute a descriptive typology only. Most psychosocial systems, even those with stable membership, move from phase to phase in predictable response to processes and forces that operate uniformly in all three phases. Just as ice, water, and vapor are three phases of H_2O, each responsive to variable temperature and pressure, Delta, Beta, and Alpha psychosocial systems may be seen as phases, their transitions resulting from the variables discussed in the next chapter. The phases are also in a predictable dynamic with one another: Everything trends toward Beta's homeostasis; change is resisted; a Delta condition of purposeful change is infrequent and usually temporary; and the discomforts of Alpha provoke maneuvers for return to Beta.

Consideration of the phases is vital for understanding and planning influence and change. By analogy, consider the design (and the experience) of a roller coaster. At any point on the roller coaster's track, its efficiency or safety or thrill can be understood through the same set of forces and particles – friction, gravity, inertia, and so forth. These scientific forces and elements function lawfully at all points of the course and in all forms of cars: rail, cogwheel, automobile, or spacecraft. However, different design challenges inhere in, let us say, three roller-coasting conditions: whether the cars are rising, falling, or coasting flat. These three conditions organize the physical forces and particles quite differently, and the human experiences of the three are breathlessly disparate.

Likewise, there are three phases of psychosocial organization: Recognizing the differences among Delta, Beta, and Alpha is necessary for successful design and planning, as well as for appreciation of the experience of the changer and the changed.

We will consider the processes of formation and maintenance of psychosocial systems and how they continue as if in response to Newton's First Law of Motion (something in motion tends to stay in motion with the same speed and direction unless acted upon by an unbalanced force). We will also consider the launching of "unbalanced forces," an analogy for weakening, creating, or otherwise influencing psychosocial systems in which change goals are implicated.

Most pages in this book will be devoted to discussing the processes and forces that influence psychosocial systems from without and within, with particular attention to the processes by which Subjects are influenced, changed, and developed. The processes are themselves psychosocial and occur within psychosocial systems. The *means* by which influence is exercised will be seen as a short but open list, operating universally in all influence and change.

At this point in the argument (Chapter 6), we pause to confront the most serious intellectual challenge to any possibility of a universal theory. Cultural differences are pervasive and powerful and on the surface would appear to require quite different procedures for influence and change. The resolution of this challenge will reveal a deeper level of unity of concepts and suggest further guidance for designing influence interventions.

The chapters of Section Two, devoted to the practice of Delta, are analyses of designs for intentional behavior change. In the service of testing the capacity of the Delta Theory proposal to explain, predict, and guide, illustrations of a variety of influence and change operations are included, some benign, some reprehensible, some successful, [and]some failed. The last chapter looks toward the current horizon, anticipating arenas of research that offer promise for the continued development of Delta.

Finally, the Appendix provides an outline of the standards and guidelines used by the author in the developmental work of the propositions and cited evidence for Delta Theory. In brief, these standards and guidelines require that theoretical propositions be valid within the boundaries of settled science; that inquiry be conducted, and data evaluated, within the strictures of mathematical and symbolic logic; and that the theory must be held to the standards of science, including generativity, testability, discomfirmability, simplicity, and elegance.

2

Psychosocial Systems and the Exercise of Influence

The source nexus of influence has long been attributed to social groups. Cooley (1962, 1909) defined the *primary* group by *intimate face-to-face association and cooperation*, which he considered as foundational for the creation of an individual's ideals and social nature. A century ago he argued that the very self is constituted by the shared life and purposes of the primary group. More recently, Athens (1992) has elaborated and clarified the definition of the primary group as the following:

> a group characterized by regular face-to-face interaction and intimate familiarity between its members, such as a family, gang, or clique, whereas a secondary group can be characterized by the absence of the quality of intimacy, such as a large school's graduating class (p. 28).

These and other sociologists have long observed that the primary group – far more than the secondary – has great impact on the development of values, repertoires, and identity of the individual. That there may be more than one highly influential group renders the primary label less useful; in these and other ways the dynamics of influential social groups (both in their creation and functioning) can now be more elaborately described. Thus I will refer to these influential groups as *psychosocial systems*.

PSYCHOSOCIAL SYSTEMS

Two great challenges face the viability of a unified theory of influence and change. The most obvious is to preserve the goal of universal explanatory concepts while assuring that manifest and powerful cultural differences are acknowledged and incorporated. Before facing that issue in Chapter 6, there is a prior challenge. There can be no unified theory until the divide is bridged between approaches that primarily employ psychological constructs as explanations for influence and those that employ primarily *social* constructs. I will suggest a way to unify these two approaches by adopting psychosocial constructs. This is more than a ruse of words, because the phenomena of influence and change themselves do not manifest socially and psychologically as separated elements; rather, they are *unified* – although a better term might be *preseparated*. The designata of concern in influence appear as reflected facets – psychological and social – but the facets are in our spectacles, not in nature.

As we observe the roiling world, rife with attempts to influence and change others, most intellectuals of my age find it is almost impossible to keep a steady focus on one actual event; our attention flicks between social and psychological perceptions, perceptions conditioned by more than a century of social sciences. For progress toward a unified theory, concepts that engage an existential unity of social and psychological phenomena are needed.

They are at hand, ready for use.

The foundational proposition of Delta Theory is that influence and change operate primarily, indeed almost exclusively, within and through psychosocial systems – that is, affiliated persons organized into systems that share values, purpose, and activity. This proposition is asserted as a universal.[1] Such an assertion requires a valid description of the processes of formation and continuation of psychosocial systems as well as of their internal processes, particularly those involving the challenges of behavior change.

THE ORGANIZATION OF SOCIAL RELATIONSHIPS

Social relationships are organized and predictable. Who interacts with whom? Who are they who choose to be together? Who influences whom? People have family, neighbors, friends, associates, colleagues, cliques, gangs, clubs, churches, rivals, and a myriad of other relationships, and it is only among these relationships that joint activity occurs. These relationships are restricted to a tiny proportion of those on planet Earth who might well provide satisfying interaction. So, a first principle of the organization of relationships is that they are restricted.

The second principle is that relationships are not random, but are sorted primarily along social class and its components: income, education, race, culture, and language. Sociologists have made it clear that social systems tend

---

[1] This, like all universalist propositions, will be refined through the seeking of exceptions (see Appendix, §**m**.)

to coalesce around certain predictable variables, and these are primarily the following: (1) amount of education; (2) amount of income; (3) neighborhood of residence; (4) culture and race; and (5) language spoken.

The third principle is that psychosocial relationships are highly stable. This massive sorting out of people into all their complicated patterns of social relationships is actually orderly, predictable, and highly conservative in that these psychosocial systems tend to maintain, reproduce, and repeat themselves, absent the introduction of some opposing force.

In the next section, we will examine how social relationships are formed and changed.

PSYCHOSOCIAL SYSTEMS: THE DYNAMICS OF FORMATION AND CHANGE

Relationships arise only between people proximal enough to know each other. Sociologists refer to a group restricted by proximity as a *pool of eligibles*: those out of the world population from which relationships can actually be drawn. What are the factors that qualify members for a pool of eligibles? Common sense, in this instance, is dead right. Ego's pool of eligibles includes only those close enough to be met.[2] So it is fitting to begin an analysis of social sorting with the issue of physical proximity and then examine how from the pool of eligibles a psychosocial system emerges.

Figure 2.1 is a graphic account of the processes operating to form and maintain psychosocial systems. The Cycle of Social Sorting describes the vital dynamism of almost all psychosocial groups by the use of four concepts: propinquity, joint activity, intersubjectivity, and affinity.[3]

Propinquity

Propinquity refers primarily to physical proximity between people. In social psychology, propinquity has been much studied for half a century, particularly as to its effects on interpersonal attraction, such as social networking, assortative mating, and friendship selection. In the early classic

---

[2] Will the explosion in distance communication develop "virtual propinquity" by electronic means? Early indications are that virtual propinquity is frequent enough to induce joint activity, but lacking much of the richness and subtlety inherent in face-to-face communication, intersubjectivity develops less reliably.

[3] A discussion of the Cycle of Social Sorting was previously presented (Tharp et al., 2000), to which this section is indebted. The earlier discussion was illustrated by phenomena associated with social cliques in schools.

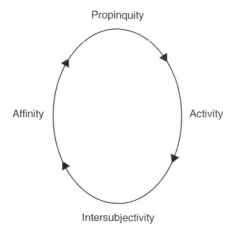

FIGURE 2.1. The cycle of social sorting.

study, residents of an urban apartment complex were found to have 90 percent of their friends from their same building and 42 percent within one door (Festinger, Schachter, & Back, 1950).

Propinquity effects extend beyond closeness of residence. Individual human *mobility* patterns are also stable and predictable. Studied through cell phone use by 100,000 users, "human trajectories show a high degree of temporal and spatial regularity, each individual being characterized by a time-independent characteristic travel distance and a significant probability to return to a few highly frequented locations" (Gonzalez, Hidalgo, & Barbási, 2008, p. 2). People spend the preponderance of their time in very few locations and the remaining time, less frequently and irregularly, in five to fifty places. With both residence and motion highly stable and restricted, propinquity is the most powerful force in limiting pools of eligibles for any psychosocial system.

Some writers have defined propinquity to include *psychological* "closeness" (similarity) as well as geographical proximity. I will not do so, although such an impulse is understandable. Socioeconomic class sorting – or sorting by race, culture, and/or language – has an enormous effect on propinquities, because streets, neighborhoods, districts, and even cities are sorted by these variables: People of the same class, race, or culture – those most alike on the psychological plane – are those who live next door to one another. Thus geographical sorting produces pools of eligibles with similar experiences, tastes, values, and expectations. Now, out of the pool of eligibles, established so strongly by propinquity, the crucial choices are made and actual relationships are chosen. However, the processes by which the social and psychological come together should not be confounded. Psychological alikeness (intersubjectivity) is separated from physical propinquity by two major processes, an issue that if ignored will lead to misfortune.

In fact, the initial formation of relationships is determined, in overwhelming degree, by this simple variable of propinquity, which virtually controls the formation of pools of eligibles. Propinquity allows some simple selective criteria to come into play so that further development of a social relationship may occur. In a study demonstrating this phenomenon, professors randomly assigned students to seats and rows on the first day of class. Students then immediately introduced themselves to the entire class. Students then rated likeability of each classmate. Repeating the rating scale one year later, greater intensity of feelings of friendship were present between students sitting close together (Back, Schmukle, & Egloff, 2008). Miller and Beer (1977) reviewed research on effects of proximity in nursing homes for the elderly. Generally these effects on friendship are positive, as differentiated by distances of only twenty to thirty feet. Thus the "propinquity effect": the tendency for people to develop relationships with those whom they are most likely to encounter.

Yet even within the pool, those who are mutually attracted may well never develop any feelings of affinity or choose to relate. Two people who commute on the same train every day, even if they both appreciate the other's appearance, will most likely never move to friendship – not unless there is shared activity.

Joint Activity

The power of propinquity does not lie within itself (it is, after all, a static concept) but has its effects by *increasing the likelihood of joint activity.* Joint activity – although it does not guarantee it – is the most reliable and potent force influencing the development of affinities.

When people work together toward a common objective or to produce something together, *common motives* are created, at least within the bounds of the shared situation. When the theater company mounts a play, when the new software version is under team design, when the Volunteers for Cleaner Beaches are recruiting and planning, no one succeeds unless all succeed. Individual goals are subordinated – the play itself is the thing. When a Polynesian crew builds another voyaging canoe, it must be seaworthy and admired by the community or no individual participant will be satisfied. When individual priorities are subordinated to shared priority, conflict is replaced by harmony.

That transformation from conflict to harmony is almost certainly medi-ated by the creation of Subject-Subject relationships rather than Subject-Object relationships (Leont'ev, 1989). Because you and your coworker have the same desires, empathy is easy; it is easy for him to imagine that you want as he wants. Feeling together the pleasures of progress and the disappoint-ments of setbacks is radically different from experiencing the other as an object to be manipulated for one's own purposes. Joint productive activity

> allows a participant to understand and experience the other as one much like the self, a fellow worker, one with feelings and aspirations like one's own. Thus working together for a common objective is not one among an infinite and casual variety of social arrangements, it is an existential condition with unique powers for human transformation (Tharp et. al, 2000, p. 58).

Shared transformations of understanding and valuing create intersubjec-tivity; and even when the project is complete and the stage is struck, there will remain the ramifying consequences of intersubjectivity – increased felt affinity resulting from those social relationships.

We have understood for decades that affinity is increased by frequent interaction (Zajonc & Marin, 1967). Now we also understand that affinity does not flow directly from interaction, but rather is mediated by the con-dition of intersubjectivity (meanings, understandings, and values held in common) developed through joint productive activity.

Intersubjectivity

Intersubjectivity as a term suffers from a variety of usage. In this discussion, I mean to hold to the simple, surface meaning of the prefix "inter," which denotes *between or among people, shared*; "subjectivity," denotes *the world-as-experienced, perceptions, interpretations, meanings, and values.* This subjective world is to be understood as different from the "objective" world, presumed to exist independent of human interpretation – the "scientific" level that exists independent of anyone's individual perceptions or values. Intersubjectivity is present when people perceive things in the same way, interpret them in the same way, use the same categories for understanding them, value them in the same way, respond to them in the same way, and expect the same response back from the world.

During joint productive activity, these shared meanings, understand-ings, and expectations arise by using common cognitive strategies and problem solving and by developing a shared language to discuss the activity, which in turn establishes its subjective purposes and meanings. This process is enabled by the condition of Subject-Subject relationships and thus the receptivity toward a developing common language.

I have emphasized that joint productive activity in the natural world is most often accompanied by language exchanges, which carry the interpretation, meaning, and valuation of activity – the very essence of intersubjectivity. However, as has been insisted since the time of Lev Vygotsky, other semiotic systems can carry that same function. Communication systems have been shown in the laboratory to emerge in the context of joint activities. Galantucci's (2005) findings showed that a task's requirement for interpersonal coordination between two experimental subjects can drive the creation of nonverbal symbolic communication systems that help establish common ground between coactors. As Cultural-Historical Activity Theory has insisted, such symbolic exchange systems are not tied specifically to language; in the natural world of joint activity, symbolic exchanges of other sorts accompany activity and language: song, gesture, visual inscriptions, and symbols. All contribute to the common ground of intersubjectivity.

During joint productive activity, members that are more knowledgeable about the task and/or context use their own language and visual symbols as they assist novices. Negotiated terms develop during conversation, of course, and peers develop word meanings and discourse routines during their cooperative work:

> The denotative, connotative and affective components of word meaning are acquired in discourse accompanying action. Thus words, flags, badges, gestures, images, tunes and the full panoply of symbols are the "stuff" of subjectivity, and accepted common meaning of word, sign and symbol among people is the condition of intersubjectivity. In working together, and talking about the purposes and meanings of the activity, strategizing and problem solving together – all these aspects of interaction influence each participant, and foster emotional and cognitive commonalty.... The process of socialization into school or into criminal gangs or a religious community (Rubin, 1991) or any community, consists of an increasing intersubjectivity mediated by the appropriation of the new code of language, sign and symbol (Tharp, Estrada, Dalton, & Yamauchi 2000, p. 59).

For Delta Theory, this is the primary proximal process by which influence is exercised: the development of intersubjectivity through influence during joint activity.

With intersubjectivity – when the world is taken in the same way – the conditions for felt kinship are created. In fact, intersubjectivity is the direct, proximal determinant of affinity. The flow of effects begins with joint productive activity accompanied by shared language, allowing participants to interpret the world in the same ways, to express that understanding in mutually understood symbols, and to respond to the world in the same ways. With these developments, the pool of eligibles is further screened, and first steps are often taken toward the formation of a sustained psychosocial system.

Because of emerging intersubjectivity, participants tend to develop more differentiated and pronounced feelings toward one another, which, if positive and reciprocal, are likely to enhance development (Bronfenbrenner, 1979). The development of intersubjectivities is a consequence of profound importance for individual development, for a satisfying community life, and for the perpetuation of culture. For the explication of Delta Theory, note that a good measure of intersubjectivity is a necessary condition for the continuation of all psychosocial systems, particularly in the Delta phase, where influence and change is an important goal of the system itself.

Intersubjectivity is not a dry intellectual condition. If there is a single dominant dimension of intersubjectivity, it is *shared feeling*. Crucial elements of intersubjectivity are the emotional charges attached to events and perceptions. Emotions are primordial capacities, but their attachments are influenced and learned for every behavioral nuance. As a quantitative variable, *emotional arousal* affects the potency of all influence. In its dependent mode, emotion is roused in the psychosocial system by signs and symbols learned through sharing and thus permeates intersubjectivity. Emotion intertwines with values, so as language interprets how to think about activity and outcomes, it influences how the Subject feels about them. In its causal mode, emotional arousal, positive and negative, is induced directly by contagion or provocation; however influenced, it enters the behavioral and psychological repertoires of individuals and of psychosocial units, and it affects the dynamics of the delta, beta, and alpha phases.

Contrariwise, when a psychosocial system sees some members as deviant, alienated, or nonparticipating, this signals a lack of intersubjectivity – a failure to define the situation in the same way, a failure to accept the same process for problem solving, or a failure to accept the same goals, values, and feelings of the psychosocial system. This is the alpha phase.

Affinity

Thus does intersubjectivity increase the likelihood of felt affinity among members of an existing, expanding, or potential psychosocial system. By *affinity* I mean a liking, a feeling of being alike, a felt kinship, and an inclination toward relationship. Affinity is not always a factor in the development of relationship, and indeed some work, community, and even family relationships proceed with no sense of this felt kinship or even of liking. However, the choosing of another for inclusion in psychosocial systems is made more likely by affinity. When affinity is present, relationship formation and maintenance are facilitated (Berscheid, 1998). What people experience as friendship – liking, love, feelings of "us" – feels like the definitive determinant of relationship choices.

So affinity is not only the end of the great circle of relationship development, but it may also be its beginning, because affinity leads to further propinquity. When walking into a hall, people are more likely to choose a seat among those with whom no complex discussion is necessary, because a nudge in the ribs and a roll of the eye communicates. Those related to each other by inclination will find ways to bring themselves close enough together to maintain relationships and thus do things together.

Thus the looping force line of psychosocial sorting intensifies and stabilizes. In childhood and adolescence, affinities are often volatile, but even when short lived they are powerful organizers of activity and sources of powerful influence. Thus affinity produces a new round of propinquity, with its activity, intersubjectivity, intensified affinity, and still more concentrated propinquity: The great conservative Cycle of Social Sorting rolls on and on.

Psychosocial systems that are purpose-built for influence and change are not exceptions to these processes. The social-sorting dynamic described here is perhaps most dramatically visible in educational institutions, formal and informal. The psychosocial systems of teacher/students and students/peers often arrive at schools already formed through associations of propinquity determined by social-class sorting of neighborhoods. Further, school-directed propinquities determine the patterns of joint activity, intersubjectivity, and affinity. To whom a learner attaches is first a matter of propinquity. Which teacher is assigned? Which other children are in the Blue Group? Who rides the bus? Who is on the vocational track? Who are in the pool of eligibles from which relationships will develop?

Affinity can be used to bring a teacher and a student together. In graduate and professional schools, the sorting out of advisees and advisors, mentees and mentors depends to some measure on felt affinities. In many traditional cultures, affinity is allowed to work as a major sorting principle. Young Pueblo Indian girls observe potters from a distance until the natural attraction of a potter to child and of the child to potter (or her pots!) results in a voluntary mentorship pairing (John-Steiner & Osterreich, 1975). In primary and secondary schools today, teacher shopping is limited for students. However, in other teaching-learning relationships, particularly with peers, affinity is the basis of almost every voluntary association. Yet those affinities must be understood as the consequence of the rolling force line: propinquity, activity, intersubjectivity, affinity, and so on.

Absent specific organized intervention, friendship psychosocial systems (cliques, "crowds") determine the groupings for school-based activity, both academic and social. Students move toward others with whom they feel affinity, choosing whenever possible to group themselves in existing psychosocial systems. If there is no teacher-directed differentiation of activities in classrooms (if there is only a whole-group organization, if grouping is only by performance levels, or if students themselves choose activity partners), then beta phases of existing systems will perpetuate, stabilize, and further strengthen year after year. Influence for behavior change and development will continue primarily within existing psychosocial systems. The Cycle of Social Sorting is highly conservative, and it ramifies into the cognitive processes and development through which social class perpetuates into families of the next generation.

We will return to these topics later in Chapter 10's discussion of strategies for improved intentional influence. For now, some general conclusions can be drawn from the analysis of the four cyclical processes of social sorting into psychosocial systems.

First, influence operates through and within psychosocial systems. This is true for purpose-developed systems as well as natural ones.

Second, a viable psychosocial system requires sufficient propinquity to allow joint activity.

Third, a frontal attack on intersubjectivity is likely to be a poor tactic. The development of intersubjectivity in joint activity can be guided and strengthened by the influence of a change Agent, who provides explanations, values, and interpretations of events. This change Agent may be a parent, a teacher, or a professional behavior changer. Success will depend on imbedding the influence into joint activity as interpretations of shared experiences.

Fourth, affinities do not generally yield to direct influence. Indeed it is almost impossible to affect affinities directly, as every teacher or parent knows who has tried to talk a young person out of one felt affection or into another.

Finally, only one conclusion is left: It is *joint activity* that provides the condition through which influence and change can be expected to operate directly on psychosocial system(s) and their members.

THE PHASES OF PSYCHOSOCIAL SYSTEMS: BETA, ALPHA, AND DELTA

To recapitulate: In Delta Theory, at the systemic level, the basic unit of analysis is the psychosocial system in which joint activities occur. Psychosocial systems are of many types: familial, institutional, economic, educational, ideological, social, and so forth, including those organized purposefully for influence and change. All psychosocial systems develop through the cyclic processes of propinquity, activity, intersubjectivity, and affinity. All function to maintain psychosocial stability in contexts that are continually changing. With respect to influence and change, psychosocial systems manifest themselves in different phases, a reflection of changing dynamics resulting from context instability and developmental changes in members. To understand or effect influence and change, phase changes must be considered, as most people are involved in multiple psychosocial systems, each moving from one phase to another, often affecting one another. In this section, phases and their dynamics are described.

ß The *beta* phase: behavioral and social equilibrium and stability.

I define beta phase as the psychosocial system that is equilibrated and stable, highly resistant to change, and self-perpetuating. Joint activity is regularized, and accompanying language and symbolic exchanges serve to further develop intersubjectivity, repair misunderstandings, reinforce affinities, and provide mutual influence that modulates and coordinates behavior changes of the members.

Stability is the hallmark of a smoothly functioning social system. All stable human functioning groups operate in some version of it, and every change Agent had best assume that client Subjects live in psychosocial systems either in beta phase or seeking to maximize beta-like stability.

However, caution is in order. The dynamics of the universe are governed by competing forces whose influence varies with scale, thus local forces can override universal forces in discrete regions. In cosmological studies, at great distances the attraction between two galaxies may be too small to have a significant effect. However, within a galaxy's "local neighborhood," if more densely packed with elements, the gravitational attraction among them can be very significant and the interactions more complex and consequential (Davis, 2009). By analogy, the dynamic forces of the Great Cycle are basic and universal, but in densely packed local social environments, psychosocial systems collide and interact, which does not negate the Cycle of Sorting's homeostatic tendencies toward beta condition but does disrupt simple progress and prediction.

Observers and analysts of densely packed social organizations can expect to find attracting and repelling local forces, such as ambition, sexual attraction, competition, or conflicting emotion, which obscures the fundamental cycle dynamic and leads to homeostasis. Some such forces are ever-present and available for enlistment or intervention by Agent. This issue will be further clarified in the discussion in Chapter 10 of Influence/Change strategies.

α The *alpha* phase: disequilibrium and instability.

As an equilibrated force field, beta phase requires a major bombardment of external force to break in or break it down. Yet it does happen; in rare instances relationships leap across the Great Cycle. War, sexual intoxication, natural disasters, and "miracles" of accident can bring people together in vital relationships that violate the predictability and stability of beta and the regularities of social sorting itself. It is the rarity of these exceptions that make them of such interest in literature, film, and fantasy. Yet all beta systems are in fact continually bombarded by unforeseen events – disruptions ranging from growth developments to death, collisions between competing psychosocial systems, rising and falling fortunes, and withdrawals and loss of resources.

Thus the beta phase becomes alpha. Alpha phase is volatile, disequilibrated, unstable, deteriorated from a beta or delta, and manifested by psychological and social discord. This condition is the trigger for most instances of professional intervention for influence and change, that is, interventions constructed to restore stability. Whether through restorative natural developments or by influence engineering, alpha is not permanent; homeostatic forces will eventually establish a new equilibrium, as inexorably as the sea flows in through a rupture in a dyke. Casualties may ensue, but eventually stable, self-organized social systems will emerge.

Δ The *delta* phase: enhancing influence and change.

In delta phase, the psychosocial system enhances influence and change. Some psychosocial units are organized specifically to provide influence and change and so are in a semipermanent delta phase. Longevity of the delta phase is variable. The paradigmatic delta condition is that of the family. In a family, for example, child (and adult) development provides a flowing necessity for change, such as continuing alteration of activity settings, goals, and means of influence. The essential dynamism of delta operates to regulate itself into responsive and changing patterns. To provide influence for change is one of its primary purposes; the dynamism of the processes is a constant re-equilibration, but it is a stability of the delta phase that is sought, because families have the goal of seeing that inevitable developmental processes and changes are seen through to good outcome. All members of a psychosocial system age and develop, and the ideal family continues to assist each other through and for those changes.

Delta phases are found in social systems that are small or large, weak and adjustable, powerful and guarded, and lifelong or ad hoc.[4] At opposite poles from the family, traditional psychotherapy is also a small psychosocial system in delta phase but designed to be impermanent and containing only the changer (Agent) and the client (Subject). This is not limited to psychotherapy: In the course of this exposition of Delta Theory, we will examine both naturally occurring and professionally designed influence efforts. In all cases influence operates in delta-phase psychosocial systems. Intentional, self-conscious plans for influence and change (professional or amateur) has the first task of organizing one or more delta-phase psychosocial systems in which to affect the influence.

An illustrative example is as follows: Agent (such as a consulting psychologist) may come into a situation on referral from the family or the school because of an acting-out adolescent member of a prominent clique; Agent then decides whether the Subject of influence is to be the one member or the whole clique. Agent's goal might be better school performance, cessation of drug use, or defusing tensions among peer groups. In any event, Agent has limited options: to create a purpose-built delta-phase psychosocial system, to use an existing one, or to turn existing beta-phase system(s) into delta(s). Thus, Agent might design influencing activities in the delta of a clients' family; or attempt to create a new small delta, beginning with a one-to-one counseling relationship between Agent and Subject; or attempt to work with the clique as system by inducing it to adopt a delta-phase change goal.

In each tactic, Agent may make the best available predictions of the effects on one another of some members of the systems, such as whether the effect of William on John is desirable, or whether William will energize Mary and/or Susan. However, Agent will also know that some systemic

---

[4] One might expect schools also to be categorically delta phase organizations, organized for the purpose of influence and change. Instead, schools ordinarily operate like other beta-phase organizations, that is, in the service of stability and continuation.

effects can be predicted. For example, Agent will expect each system to tend toward stability, in which intersubjectivities, affinities, and activities will again become congruent.

That, of course, is only the first stage of a change intervention. In the counseling instance, one mid-term goal might well be to influence the young person to broaden her activities to include a set of companions more likely to assist the strengthening of new repertoires, thus widening the delta condition beyond the planet-moon system of therapist-client. As all would-be influencers know, an improved Subject's return to her continuing psychosocial beta is a sure prescription for relapse and recidivism. On the other hand, once the change goals have been met, a beta condition becomes a desirable condition so long as its stabilities support the maintenance of the new goal repertoire.

Many illustrative examples of influence and change through alpha, beta, and delta systems will follow. However, before going further with the exposition of psychosocial system intervention, it is prudent to consider fully the micro-processes of influence that operate within these psychosocial systems. These micro-processes are uniform, universal, and easily understood. They are the processes by which psychosocial systems achieve flexibility, mutual influence, and stability; they are the interpersonal acts by which system members influence.

3

The Zone of Proximal Development, Activity, and Semiotics

OVERVIEW OF SOCIAL INFLUENCE ON DEVELOPMENT

The foundational concept for this theoretical effort has come from the work of L. S. Vygotsky, the Russian psychologist active in the 1920s whose work began to influence thought worldwide some sixty years later. Although Vygotsky invoked concepts from phylogenetic formulations and other theoretical levels, the setting of his work was primarily in a pedagogical institute, and the problems he experienced practically and theoretically arose in issues of child development, both normative and pedagogical.

Vygotsky generated students, they generated students, and this line has now reached at least the fifth generation. This theoretical orientation has been called neo-Vygotskian, sociocultural, and Cultural-Historical Activity Theory (CHAT); it now has international associations, scholarly journals, and worldwide influence on social science research and theory. The majority of phenomena addressed by these groups continues to be early development, early socialization, and pedagogy. Of course there are notable exceptions; in the context of Delta Theory, there come to mind the programs of organizational behavior and development by Engeström (e.g., Engeström & Middleton, 1996) as well as a few forays into psychological treatment (Miltenburg & Singer, 1999; Tharp, 1999; Portes, 1999).

My own empirical work is no exception, so much of it having focused on formal education. The pertinence of Vygotsky's thought was obvious to me on first reading. As I began to use his conceptual tools to attempt reorganization of ill-functioning educational systems, it also became apparent that his foundational thought was applicable to far more than early development and pedagogy. Indeed, I will argue that his basic concepts, sufficiently elaborated, are universal in utility and extend to all influence and change. That assertion and those elaborations are among the foundations of Delta Theory.

In the formal requirements of a unified theory, proposition §b (see Appendix) asserts, "the theory must be as parsimonious of concepts as pertinent phenomena will allow." Thus a small range of Vygotskian/CHAT concepts will be discussed here, that is, those I consider indispensable for this stage of this theory development. The criterion for excision is parsimony, not potential for eventual enrichment.

To clarify my extension of concepts that were specifically applicable to early socialization to universal applicability, some important original quotations from Vygotsky and others will be presented, whereas my own statements will often imply an extension from the child-as-Subject to any-person-as-Subject.

Through mundane activities and interactions, each child develops cognitive and communicative tools and skills from interactions with parents and teachers. This insight of Vygotsky's (1978) has the most profound implications for how we think of development and influence:

> From the very first days of the child's development his activities acquire a meaning of their own in a system of social behavior and, being directed towards a definite purpose, are refracted through the prism of the child's environment. The path from object to child and from child to object passes through another person. This complex human structure is the product of a developmental process deeply rooted in the links between individual and social history. (Vygotsky, 1978, p. 30)

Psychological and behavioral development thus must be understood not only by a focus on the Subject, but also by examining the world of people and objects in which that individual life has developed and will continue to develop. For any Subject, we must examine not only the current persons and their world, but also their historical social aspects, carried by those people who assisted and explained, who participated with the learner in shared functioning and thus provided influence. It is likewise in the present: Those who participate in a person's life represent the world through interpretations projected through their own social and historical screens:

> [A]ny function in the child's cultural development appears twice, or in two planes. First, it appears on the social plane, and then on the psychological plane. First it appears between people as an interpsychological category, and then within the child as an intrapsychological category. This is equally true with regard to voluntary attention, logical memory, the formation of concepts, and the development of volition. (Vygotsky, 1981, p. 163)

Vygotsky explained how the social becomes the psychological by a process called internalization: "[T]he process of Internalization is not the transferal of an external activity to a preexisting, internal 'plane of consciousness': It is the process in which this plane is formed" (Leont'ev, 1981, p. 57). Individual "planes of consciousness" (i.e., higher cognitive processes) are communicated to learners by others in speech, social inter-action, and the processes of cooperative activity. Thus individual conscious-ness arises from actions and speech of others.

However, people – even the youngest children – reorganize and recon-struct their experiences of the external plane of action and speech. A child learns to speak by hearing others speak – indeed children learn to think through hearing others speak. Yet as private speech sinks "underground" into thought, it is abbreviated, becomes telegraphic, and eventually autom-atized. At this point, it bears little resemblance to speech itself.

So no one, not even a young child, is a merely passive recipient of influ-ence and assistance, but the developing person transforms or reinvents the world as represented to him through the influence of others. The concept of "guided reinvention"

> acknowledges the social learning theorists' insistence that social guid-ance is ubiquitous. It also acknowledges, however, the Piagetian insight that to understand is to reconstruct. Thus, guided reinvention elaborates the theme that normal cognitive development must be understood as a collaborative process involving the child and the environment. (Fischer & Bullock, 1984, pp. 112–113)

In summary, cognitive and social development – not only of the child – unfolds through the reciprocal influence of person and social environment. Higher mental functions move from the social plane – the social and cultural heritage as represented by social influence – to the psychological plane, that is, from the intermental to the intramental and from the socially regulated to the self-regulated. Through the regulating actions and speech of others, each child is guided into independent action and speech. In the resulting inter-action, the individual performs, through assistance and cooperative activity, at levels beyond his or her individual level of competence. In the begin-ning of the transformation to the intramental plane, the person – not only the child – need not understand the activity as the influencer understands it. For behavior development to develop into an internalized, self-regulated capacity, all that is needed is performance through the influence of assisting interaction. Through this process, the person acquires not only the "plane of consciousness" of the influencing society, including behavior repertoires, but also a system of understanding and values that supports and justifies them.

THE ZONE OF PROXIMAL DEVELOPMENT

For every developing person, there is a zone between what can be done alone and what can be done with assistance of others. For Vygotsky, the contrast between assisted and unassisted performance identified the fundamental nexus of development and learning, which he called the zone of proximal development (ZPD) and is defined as follows:

> The distance between the actual developmental level as determined by individual problem solving and the level of potential development as determined through problem solving under adult guidance or in collaboration with more capable peers ... The zone of proximal development defines those functions that have not yet matured but are in the process of maturation, functions that will mature tomorrow but are currently in an embryonic state. These functions could be termed the "buds" or "flowers" of development rather than the "fruits" of development. (Vygotsky, 1978, p. 86, italics original)

Among contemporary theoreticians, that quotation is understood to mean performance in specific domains of competence. There is no single zone for each individual. For any domain of performance, merely beginning an effort to perform it with available assistance can open a zone of proximal development. This idea is crucial to a unified theory of influence and change. It implies that for each goal of change, the influencer and Subject must open a zone of proximal development. Whatever the activity, in the zone of proximal development assistance is provided by someone who has more expertise in the performance domain. This in turn implies that organizing the most effective social system of influence is a requirement for an influence plan. Through this assistance, "learning awakens a variety of internal developmental processes that are able to operate only when the child is interacting with people in his environment and in cooperation with his peers. Once these processes are internalized, they become part of the child's independent developmental achievement" (Vygotsky, 1978, p. 90). Distinguishing the proximal zone from the developmental level by contrasting assisted versus unassisted performance has profound implications for the delivery of all human services. It is in the proximal zone that influence may be defined as assisting development. In Vygotskian terms, influence is good only when assistance "awakens and rouses to life those functions which are in a stage of maturing, which lie in the zone of proximal development" (Vygotsky, 1956, p. 278, quoted in Wertsch & Stone, 1985, italics original).

By whom performance is influenced is less important than that performance is assisted by a more competent other. To the extent that peers can assist performance, learning will occur through that assistance. In terms of human services, assistance should be offered in those interactional contexts most likely to generate joint performance, because that will maximize available assistance.

Vygotsky's own available work principally discusses children, but identical processes can be seen operating in the learning adult. Developmental processes arising from assisted performance in the zone of proximal development can be observed not only in the ontogenesis of the individual, but in the microgenesis of discrete capacities as they develop throughout the life course. Recognition of this fact allows a principled creation of effective programs for all human services and offers guidance for organizational management of systems of influence and assistance. Explication of that point requires a discussion of the zone of proximal development in an elaborated model of four stages.

INFLUENCE AND THE ZONE OF PROXIMAL DEVELOPMENT

Before children can function as independent agents, they must rely on adults or more capable peers for regulation of task performance – it is likewise for any beginners in any domain, although the dynamics are more obvious for children. The vocabulary of *regulation* is appropriate in discussing behavior of the young and vulnerable. The amount and kind of *other-regulation* a child requires depends on the child's age and the nature of the task: that is, the breadth of and progression through the zone of proximal development for the activity at hand. Regulation points to the locus of control; regulated behavior indicates that over which some agent has control. However, the acts to which regulation refers are those acts designated in Vygotskian theory as *assistance*. Furthermore, the term *influence*, although connoting some lighter reins over the behavior, denotes exactly the same acts. The terms regulation, assistance, and influence are facets of meaning, but the three terms denote the same objective acts. These similarities will be elaborated in the chapter to follow, but for now the development of the theoretical argument may be followed if we understand that these three statements are identical in action referents:

> Stage I: where performance is *assisted* by more capable others.
> Stage I: where performance is *regulated* by more capable others.
> Stage I: where performance is *influenced* by more capable others.

This simple understanding will go far toward achieving a unified theory of influence and change.

In Vygotsky's discussions of the zone of proximal development, influence-assistance-regulation comes from more capable others. In his discussions of children, it is inevitable that perspectives of maturation and learning are mutually beclouding. From birth to, let us say, seventeen years of age, the young person needs assistance not only in developing specific repertoires, but in everything. Thus youth is perceived as one long and pervasive ZPD.

Accepting the strong version of the ZPD theory leads to a different perception. (The elderly, I can attest, seem to reverse and recapitulate the process of needing more and broader forms of assistance, an observation perhaps first dramatized by Sophocles.) However, in the more numerous and intervening middle years, it is quite clear that the individual life is a pastiche of ZPDs, opening and closing in the continuing drama of each individual history. Learning comes, learning goes; practice slacks; ambition rises; crises challenge; disaster strikes; help is needed. The telephone rings, the helping professional answers. There is no end to this dynamic. So in describing the natural history of the zone of proximal development in a unified theory of influence and change, a description of the process requires four stages.

Through this exposition of the zone of proximal development, we must not lose the holistic view of this unified theoretical perspective. Thus boxes like the next one will relate, in a general way, the stages of the ZPD to the three phases of Δαβ, that is, which phase is most characteristic of each stage of the ZPD (I, II, III, or IV).

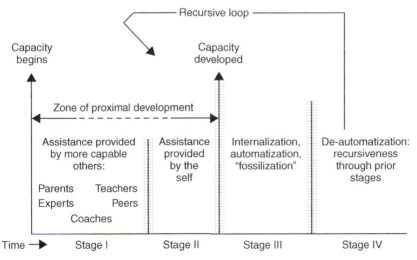

FIGURE 3.1. Progressions through the zone of proximal development and beyond from Tharp & Gallimore, 1989, p. 35.

Stage I. Where Performance Is Assisted by More Capable Others

Δαß	**Delta Phase**	organized for enhancing influence and change.

Before going on to a detailed examination of the zone of proximal development and its full implications for a unified theory, we must face the most radical extension of this Vygotskian insight, and we must not flinch. To my knowledge, Vygotsky did not assert the radical extension, but it is implicit in his structure of thought: Assistance-regulation-influence in the ZPD is more than a sufficient condition for development – it is *necessary.*

This means that all human behavior repertoires, all planes of consciousness, all higher order mentation, all language, all beliefs, all skills develop by means of social influence – or not at all. The empirical test of this assertion would require the "forbidden experiment" much discussed a century ago and approximated by studies of the "feral children" who came to some maturity without human association – the wolf children, not only of myth but of some fact and about whom there is some evidence. Such as that evidence is, it supports the strong (influence is necessary) version of the theory: Children raised without human influence are not recognizably human by their repertoires, and only barely by their appearance.

This issue of "sufficient" versus "necessary" is consequential for the practice and understanding of influence and change. If it is necessary to provide assistance in the zones of proximal development for which professional influencers are responsible, then we are obliged to provide it. That obligation carries with it a responsibility for understanding and using regulation, assistance, and influence in the most potent and effective ways.

However, a return to the explication of the zone of proximal development is in order. Some objections that arise naturally against the strong version of the theory may be mitigated by following the course of development of ZPDs themselves, and by a discussion of how assistance is effectuated.

During the earliest periods of the zone of proximal development, the person may have a very limited understanding of the situation, the structure of the task, or any real concept of the end state. At this level, assistors offer directions or modeling, and the learner's response is acquiescent or imitative. This is equally true for the beginning golfer, the child learning to read, and the recovering addict who has no real idea of what living a clean life would entail.

Only gradually does the learner come to understand the way the parts of an activity relate to each other and the whole, or to understand the meaning of the performance. In situations of informal or naïve influence, this understanding develops during the task performance through conversation between assistor(s) and learner – in simpler centuries, around the campfire or kitchen stove. When some conception of the overall performance has been acquired, the learner can be assisted by other means, such as questions, feedback, or explanations.

The developmental aspects of the ZPD itself can be seen clearly by considering the types of influence with which a zone of proximal development is opened. For example, a characteristic feature of Stage I is structuring tasks and/or situations.[1] (For a detailed description of this Means of Influence, see Chapter 4). Even before interaction between Subject and influencer begins, the influencer (counselor, coach, squad leader, teacher, parent) will have begun to structure anticipated situations: Choosing appropriate manipulanda, selecting appropriate tools, and preparing the settings are all important features of assisting and influencing performance. The assistor also provides a "grading" of tasks by structuring tasks into subgoals and sub-subgoals. In all likelihood, during Phase I, the Subject will not conceptualize the goal of the activity in the way that the influencer does. As interaction proceeds, different goals and subgoals emerge and change as the participants work together. The adult may shift to a subordinate or superordinate goal in response to ongoing assessment of the developing performance. As understanding develops, the learner's goals will shift. The goal structure is negotiated in the interaction itself. This is both the consequence of the interaction and the basis for its ongoing restructuring.

The capacity to prestructure and restructure during the developmental process is why a profound knowledge of the intended goal state (and the likely course of its development) is required of influence-and-change designers. Without such knowledge, goals and task structuring cannot be quickly adjusted. This fundamental aspect of interaction in the zone of proximal development will emerge repeatedly in our analysis. How much assistance is provided by the more capable other depends on the expertise of the influencer, not only in the processes of influence, but also in the task domain.

During a successful Stage I of the ZPD, there is a steady decline in expert regulation and assistance; reciprocally, there is an increase in the learner's proportion of responsibility. This is Bruner's fundamental *handover principle* – the learner who began as a spectator becomes a participant (Bruner, 1983, p.60). The developmental task of Stage I is to transit

---

[1] Rogoff (e.g., 1984) and Saxe (e.g., Saxe, Gearhart, & Guberman (1984) established definitive studies of these structuring processes.

from other-regulation to self-regulation. For example, by asking questions, and adopting other elements of the adult's assistance, children gradually take over the actual structuring of the task. By asking, "Which part do I do next?" or, "How do I decide?" the Subject begins to influence the level of help provided. The task of Stage I is achieved when the responsibility for tailoring the assistance, tailoring the transfer, and for the task performance itself has been effectively handed over to the learner.

Of course, this achievement is a gradual one, with progress occurring in fits and starts. The lines between each of the stages in the diagram of the ZPD are themselves represented as zones.

Domain Knowledge and Professional Expertise

Proposition (**§d**) in the requirements of a unified theory (see Appendix) states:

> *A universal theory must preserve the knowledge bases and effective explanations achieved by the various disciplines. This means that rising in the pyramid or matrix of concepts does not imply that subordinated concepts are superseded, but that the phenomena can be understood at a level more general and less conditional. Only such a structure can unify existing knowledge and draw varied scholars and practitioners into the enterprise of evolving a unified theory.*

Another reiteration is warranted in this context: *A "more capable other" can provide assistance; how much assistance – in quality and quantity – depends on the expertise of the influencer, not only in the processes of influence, but in the task domain itself.* Accepting the strong form of the social-influence principle of a unified theory does not threaten the various influencing professions or even weaken them. For example, I have decades of experience assisting clients and students as a professional psychological therapist and educator. However, I would be uncertain in designing influence plans for clients of occupational therapists, in criminal rehabilitation, in public health campaigns, and indeed for many client lists. I assume that each of these professions will find utility in the principles and dynamics discussed here, but the institutional contexts, behavioral repertoires, and social systems in which the professions and their clients are embedded require domain knowledge.

Process knowledge is also required – I mean the processes by which undesired repertoire was developed originally, and the processes by which it has been supplanted by influence programs. It seems to me altogether natural, and largely desirable, that many "influence and change professionals" were drawn to their domains by their own life stories, both the good and the sad chapters. Of course this knowledge can also be acquired by practice, internships, apprenticeships, and experience. However acquired, domain knowledge is indispensable.

Stage II: Where the Self Assists Performance

Δαß	continuing	**Delta Phase**	organized for enhancing influence and change.

In Stage II, Subject is still in the zone of proximal development. The fully developed behavior is still not present. Regulation/guidance/assistance is still needed. However, in Stage II, the influence comes not from others but from the self. The concept of self-assistance is fully consistent with the strong version of the theory. Recall that Vygotsky himself emphasized how social transactions become psychological functions, how the voice of the assistor goes underground and becomes thought. This is especially true in the developmental interactions in the ZPD. The voice of the influencer – structuring tasks, making suggestions, giving demonstrations – is internalized in a process: In the earliest step, the Subject continues to "hear the voice of the assistor" – a literal remembering of the statements or demonstrations provided by coach or counselor. In the second step, the voice of the self is used to remind, to instruct, to praise, to energize, and to give feedback. The developing learner talks to herself, structures situations, look for models – in short, functions as self-regulator of the last phases of change.

Self-directed speech and other acts of quasisocial individual behavior are not peculiar, not deviant, and not inappropriate. In fact, the phenomenon is universal, and the acquisition of the capacity for self-directed speech ontogenetically reflects a development of the most profound significance. According to Vygotsky, once a child begins to direct or guide behavior with his or her own speech, an important stage has been reached in the transition of a skill through the zone of proximal development. It constitutes the next stage in the passing of control or assistance from the adult to the child, from the expert to the apprentice. That which was guided by the other is now guided and directed by the self:

> [H]umans as it were preserve the "function of social interaction" even in their own individual behavior; they apply a social means of action to themselves.
>
> In this case their individual functioning in essence represents a unique form of internal collaboration with oneself. (Vygotsky, 1960, pp. 450–451, quoted in Wertsch & Stone, 1985, p. 173)

All the means of assistance are used in this self-collaboration. The self as source does not differ in means or differ in potential. The self as source is different, however, in the time when it is operative. Its use accompanies internalization in the mid-ranges of the ZPD.

Of course, self-instructions, self-questioning, and self-praise and punishment may be present even during the earlier stages of skill acquisition. Eventually self-assistance and assistance from the Agent will be brought into harmony, but before Agent and Subject have achieved an intersubjectivity of common values and understandings, the Subject is likely to perform old scripts, attempting residual and possibly competing skills. Thus, particularly in early stages of learning, self-talk and self-regulation may not be congruent with the Agent's goals; it may even be opposed. Whatever is going on in self-assistance must be considered and included in the orchestration of means and goals.

Vygotsky treated self-directed speech as both the manifestation and the mechanism of internalization. His practical work explored the social level as the independent variable, as it were, and the self-assisting level as the consequence or dependent variable. However, we know now that the acts of self-assistance themselves can be directly developed, then used not only "in collaboration with the self," but in collaboration with the Agent. There are now some four decades of research evidence and mature theory concerning self-influenced change. The self-conscious, systematic use of self-directed assistance strategies is one of the most vigorous movements in applied psychology.[2] Even so, self-directed change is rarely recognized as Stage II of the zone of proximal development. Those behavior-change professionals who do see self-direction as a stage following assistance by others are much advantaged. They will then ensure that the Subject, before discharge, has indeed acquired the requisite self-directing skills. Indeed, those repertoires become one vital goal of the plan for change. This point will be further illustrated in Chapter 9.

Stage III: Where the Performance Is Developed, Automatized, and Fossilized

Δαß	**Beta Phase**	characterized by behavioral and social equilibrium and stability

---

[2] For compilations of research, theory, and techniques for applications of self-assistance, see Watson & Tharp, 2006, 9th edition.

Changed behaviors do fully develop, capable of performance without external or conscious self-assistance. Once all evidence of self-regulation has vanished, the Subject has emerged from the zone of proximal development into the *independent* developmental stage for that task. In this stage, task execution is smooth and integrated. It is internalized, automatized. Assistance from an expert or from the self is no longer needed. Indeed, influence now is disruptive and irritating, and detrimental to the smooth integration of all task components; I need offer here only the example of the back-seat driver. *Automatized* is a stage beyond social control and beyond self-control. Performance here is no longer developing; it is already developed. Vygotsky described it as the "fruits" of development; but he also described it as "fossilized," emphasizing its fixity and distance from the social and mental forces of change.

Is automatized, fossilized behavior truly independent? Vygotsky developed these concepts to illuminate the child's increasing maturity and capacity. Once extended into all arenas of human development, the issue of independence is beclouded. Certainly there are domains of competence that appear incontrovertibly automatized. Consider again the expert automobile driver. This skill is best practiced automatically. But consider this thought experiment. Suppose a large number of roundabouts, common in Europe, were to be instantly installed in Chicago, each circle consisting of three lanes, so that moving from one to the other is required to exit at the desired street, thus requiring considerable forethought from drivers accustomed to simple turn-right, turn-left planning. Chaos erupts. The back-seat driver becomes indispensable – one person alone cannot possibly keep track of the necessary quick decisions. Marriage relationships shift. Drivers go on alert and shout aloud to themselves, self-assisting. Influence groups organize, political parties polarize, the No-Roundabout Platform sweeps into power, the young protest, and suddenly driving is not so automatic anymore.

The thought experiment results are clear: *Automatization is with respect to a stable environmental and social context.*

I bring this issue now as a caution that further complexity is to come. As we will see in Chapter 3, automaticity can be maintained only in a beta phase; the reciprocal of that statement is that a beta phase equilibrates so as to maximize automaticity. It is all about stability, the social equivalent of entropy. In Chapter 2, the dynamics by which these automaticities are practiced, reinforced, and perpetuated were discussed under the heading the Cycle of Social Sorting.

Stage IV: Where De-Automatization of Performance Leads to Recursion back through the Zone of Proximal Development

Δαβ	Alpha Phase	characterized by disequilibrium and instability

The lifelong learning of every individual is made up of these same regulated ZPD sequences – from other-assistance to self-assistance – recurring over and over again for the development of new capacities. For every individual at any point in time, there will be a mix of ZPDs – other-regulated, self-regulated, and automatized processes. The eighty-year-old man who has moved to the Arctic to learn an Inuit language is heavily other-regulated in that language-learning (and Inuit social) zone, although his other repertoires are largely automatized – he uses the Internet when he can, exercises every morning, and struggles to find a supplier of red wine. Humans have many ZPDs. The child who can now do many of the steps in finding a lost object might still be in the zone of proximal development for reading.

Yet this child is not obligated to rely only on internal mediation. He can also ask for help when stuck, for example, in the search for lost items. During periods of difficulty, children seek out controlling vocalizations by more competent others (Gal'perin, 1969). There are shifting and intimate relationship among control by self, control by others, and automaticity. Indeed, the enhancement, improvement, and maintenance of performance provide a recurrent cycle of self- to other-assistance. De-automatization occurs so regularly that it constitutes a Stage IV of normal developmental process. What one formerly could do, one can no longer do. This de-automatization may result even from slight environmental changes or individual stress, not to mention major upheavals or physical trauma. Toward the end of life, capacities fall into general decline. It is a law of life that all performance capacity eventually declines if one lives long enough, and if not, all capacity is abruptly terminated. Whatever the reason for de-automatization, if capacity is to be restored or some alternative developed, if the alpha phase is to return to the beta, the zone of proximal development process must become recursive.

The first line of retreat is to the immediately prior self-regulating phase. We have already discussed how children doing more difficult problems talk to themselves about it more. Competent adults recall talking themselves through some knotty intellectual problem or through the traffic patterns of a strange city. Making self-speech external is a form of recursion often effective in restoring competence. A further retreat, say, to remembering the voice of a therapist, may be required. "Hearing the voice of the teacher" has been shown to be one of the middle stages in the development of complex skills (Gallimore, Dalton, & Tharp, 1986). Intentional recursions – consciously reconjuring the voice of a tutor – are an effective self-control technique, a retreat to the strengths of Stage II.

However, no form of self-regulation may be adequate to restore capacity, and a further recursion – the restitution of other-regulation – is often required. The readiness of a teacher to repeat some earlier lesson is one mark of excellent teaching. The clients of psychotherapists are encouraged to call back, to reinstitute the influence of the professional when things begin to fall apart. In such instances, the process is to reproceed from assisted performance to self-regulation, to exit again from the zone of proximal development into a new automatic capacity.

4

The Means of Influence

INFLUENCE, ASSISTANCE, REGULATION

In an earlier section, I introduced the essential similarity – in psychological theory – among the terms *influence, assistance*, and *regulation*. In my gradual approach to a unifying perspective, the first step was to explore whether there is a set of means by which all human services may hope to change behavior and experience, regardless of profession or theoretical persuasion (Tharp, 1975; see also Tharp & Note, 1988). The term *means of influence*, I chose for its theoretical neutrality and common-language transparency. In 1989, I shifted the term to *means of assistance* to align those concepts with Vygotsky's elegant formulations of assistance in the zone of proximal development (Tharp & Gallimore, 1989; Tharp, 1993). Internationally, Vygotsky's heritors (Cultural-Historical Activity Theory, CHAT; or sociocultural theory) have magnetized the field of education but are little invoked in most other domains of human service delivery. So the clock has circled again to a time for theoretical neutrality and *means of influence*. The designations have varied to facilitate discourse; but the designata are the same: Modeling is modeling, and contingency management is itself.

A second reason for referring to the means of influence is even more compelling. Assistance is a benign term, appropriate to Vygotsky's concerns in his Pedagogical Institute and to my own work in education between 1971 and this writing. Now, however, my intention is to broaden the range of sociocultural concepts so as to explain not only the effective nurturance of primary socialization and education, but to encompass even the intentional influence for the development of evil. (Any unifying theory must be so burdened.) Influence is the more inclusive term,

38

the term stripped of values, the simple term describing how we get one another to change.[1]

"SCAFFOLDING"

In the earliest days of American use of Vygotskian concepts, acts of influence, regulation, and assistance were described as "scaffolding" (Wood, Bruner, & Ross, l976). Greenfield (l984) noted that the characteristics of the carpenter's scaffold are an apt analogy for the teacher's selective assistance to a learner. She adds that scaffolding is similar to the concept of behavior shaping except in one important way. Shaping simplifies the task by breaking it down into a series of steps to the goal. Scaffolding, however, does not involve simplifying the task; it holds task difficulty constant while simplifying the learner's role through the graduated assistance of the expert (Greenfield, l984).

For whatever reason, scaffolding has been an unusually durable metaphor. However appealing, it is time to take scaffolding down and discard it. The field has advanced to the point that more differentiated and precise concepts are available from social science. For example, scaffolding suggests that the principal variations in assisting actions are quantitative: How high is the scaffold? How many levels does it support? How long it is kept? Yet the acts of the change agent in influencing behavior are qualitatively different from one another. "Sometimes, the adult directs attention. At other times, the adult holds important information in memory. At still other times, the adult offers simple encouragement" (Griffin & Cole, l984, p. 47).

The various means of assisting performance are indeed qualitatively different. By referencing and employing the several different means of influencing performance, we have the opportunity to connect a unified theory of influence and change to a broad literature of scientific psychology.

To abandon metaphor in favor of scientific explanation inheres in the course of scientific theory building. What, then, are the means of influence that social science has established? Only a few have been codified: far fewer

---

[1] "Influence" in this discussion includes only change induced by means that are directly social, not the indirect effects of, for example, drug prescription, imprisonment, or conscription. Even these, however, can be seen as consequential for delta effects insofar as they destabilize or destroy beta psychosocial systems and thus prepare the ground for subsequent delta system influence effects. Conscription will not change a civilian into a soldier; but it will forcibly induce nonvolunteers to participate in the training activities, which probably will.

than naively might be supposed, and far fewer than implied by the vague metaphor scaffolding. By codified, I mean sufficiently studied, scientifically and theoretically, so that parameters and instances can offer guidance for use. Of course, there are also beguiling mysteries of influence and transformation: the casual remark, the piercing glance, the dream that diverts our habits and intentions. These remind us that much is left to search out. Yet these, being mysteries, are now unavailable for planning or understanding. If the sun of science continues to rise, so will the number of known means. To date I have found only eight that seem sufficiently codified, but what astonishes about the known means of influence is not how little we know, but rather how very much is fact – and how little these facts now affect professional human service delivery.

MEANS OF INFLUENCE: THE LIST

By considering the several means of assistance simultaneously, we can link large areas of knowledge into an articulated structure and provide clear guidance to the practice of influence: These are the means by which influence is achieved. This is the list; this is what we now know. Influence will work through these means or not at all.

All the means, of course, are observable in humans. Many of the means are also currently observable in species well below us in the evolutionary "tree." Below, the means are charted in terms of their observability in species, lower to higher. All means operate in human society, of course. Logically, the verbal means of influence (questioning, instructing, cognitive structuring) emerged only with the appearance of human language. Others of the means, however, are visible in subhuman species. These are more than curiosa. These animal behaviors, persisting into *Homo sapiens*, suggest an anchoring of the means of assistance in biological science and phylogenetically provided dispositions. However, in the absence of comparative genome studies or eventual brain-science investigations this can be no more than a strong hypothesis. It is a *strong* hypothesis, given, for example, the pan-species effects of contingent reward and punishment as an influence on behavior change. It is *only* an hypothesis, however: Vygotsky insisted early in the twentieth century that behaviors, observed across subjects to be the same may have had different developmental histories, and thus function differently. We know, for example, that certain patterns of social caretaking of the young appear similar in some primate species, although it is genetically determined in some species and culturally developed in others.

For example, consider *nudging/propping*, a means of assistance observable in small mammals (the Agent physically moving the Subject's body into a more appropriate position for the desired behavior). My argument within Delta Theory is *not* that because meerkats do it we can expect to find meerkats to share a nudging space on genomes with ballet masters and marital arts instructors. Rather, there is a different proposition: As both phylogenetic processes and cultural processes can and do produce the same means of influence across species and cultures, so these propositions of Delta Theory about means can be more persuasively argued as deep foundational structures in the edifice of a universal theory. Fitness to the environment makes capacities more survivable. Phylogenetically, selection operates through differential mating. Culturally, selection operates through differential social patterns proceeding across life spans – in many species, far past reproductive activity. In both systems, natural selection and cultural selection, and in both species, meerkats and humans, nudging/propping has persisted because it fits the tasks necessary to survive in the environment better than does not nudging.[2] As to the proportion of contribution between these two sources of selection, I remain agnostic.

Means of Assistance	Evident Period of Emergence
Task Structuring	
Propping/Nudging	pre-human
Modeling	
Contingency Management	
Instructing	
Questioning	with language
Cognitive Structuring	
Feeding-back (against a standard)	?

This list is open ended. It is vital that a universal theory adjust to emerging knowledge. I have used one criterion for inclusion: a thoroughly studied variable by which behavior is influenced and changed. "Thoroughly" includes analyses sufficient that a professional change Agent can go to the research to understand the complexities and find generative ideas for designs of intervention. These means of influence phenomena are so well published and understood that if influence is frustrated, the research literature will

[2] This conception illuminates the fluid and interdynamic relationships between trait survivability through mating and trait survivability through social processes. A cultural preference for a certain capacity, because its presence across life spans makes for greater survivability, then makes it a more valued characteristic to potential mates.

provide guidance: For *Modeling*, how to select models, design their performances, and react to them; for *Contingency Management*, how to reinforce or punish responses, under what circumstances, and how to link these responses to future events; and for *Feeding Back Against A Standard*, how to set a standard, collect pertinent data, devise a comparator, and send a signal back to the action point. The other means may have a smaller base of experimental data, but they are patently obvious in every arena of change, training, development, and influence, and have been studied sufficiently to give any Agent stimulation, guidance, and hypotheses.

In discussing the social origins of cognition, Vygotsky insisted on the primacy of linguistic means in the development of higher mental processes. The signs and symbols of speech are primary "tools" of humankind. Only when linguistic tools are integrated with the tools of physical action can the potential for full human cognitive development be reached. Indeed, he wrote that semiotics – the study of signs – is the only adequate method for investigating human consciousness. Writers in this tradition have continued to presume the primacy of interpersonal speech for the development of intra-psychological functioning, and language is featured almost exclusively in their detailed accounts of the internalization process.

Vygotsky correctly argued that much thinking, certainly in schooled societies, originates and is perpetuated in speech. This does not mean, however, that all means of assisting performance are linguistic. Thinking is representational, relying on the full range of icons available from all the sense modalities. A full account of development must also include an understanding of nonlinguistic means of assisting performance.

A necessary task of a unified theory of influence and change is to integrate these concepts with demonstrated relationships and functions central to behaviorist and cognitive studies of learning and self-control. Modeling, contingency management, and feedback: These are pervasive mechanisms for assisting learners through zones of proximal development. As we will see, learners use these same mechanisms during the emerging self-control of Phase II in the zone of proximal development. In the same way that speech carries signs into the "underground" of thought, these other means of assistance are also carried by representations and icons into the emerging plane of consciousness.

In industrialized, urban society, linguistic means of assistance do appear to be central. The predominance of social science evidence comes from formally educated societies, and thus from a narrow range of cultural interactions. Technological culture may seem to require verbal explanation before children can understand adult activities; but this is a cultural requirement, not a necessity for cognitive development (Nerlove & Snipper, 1981; Rogoff, 1982; Scribner & Cole, 1981). In nontechnological societies, many adult behaviors are learned and understood with only occasional verbal explanation. Such societies rely heavily on "observational" learning (influence through the means of Modeling); this is practical where adult behaviors and role performances are available for prolonged and careful scrutiny by learners – in cultures that are "within the direct reach of the sensory organs" of the learner (Fortes, 1938; Pettit, 1946), where learners are incorporated into the activity settings of the society.

Models and demonstrations may be internalized and represented by the learner as images for self-guidance. The image of the expert's hands on the loom is transformed into an intra-psychological standard for comparison and feedback as the learning weaver watches her own fingers fly (Tharp & Gallimore, 1988).

Task Structuring

Structuring the prescribed activities through which change is to be influenced is obviously indispensable to success but is so pervasive that it is "hidden in the open," and when considered at all, is thought of as "curriculum" or "lesson planning." However, it is also ubiquitous in nonformal settings. Rogoff (1984) discussed some of these issues in terms of structuring situations for children. Even before interacting with the child, a parent or teacher assists by an age grading of manipulanda: The choice of puzzles, the selecting of kindergarten tasks, the selection of appropriate tools and materials for an apprentice – these are all important features of assisting performance. Saxe, Gearhart, and Guberman (1984) discussed "grading" of tasks by structuring them into subgoals and sub-subgoals.

Task structuring is most obvious as a means of influence in instances of task *restructuring*. Athletic coaches rearrange practice sessions in response to levels of performance; orchestra conductors expand or shorten segments of rehearsal in response to performance quality; choreographers will lengthen, shorten, or resegment the length of dance sequences in response to rough patches in developing dancers. This means of influence is also a staple of behavior modification techniques for autistic or developmentally delayed subjects, the goal for which is often increasingly longer and longer chained sequences of repertoire.

Task structuring is also practiced by species well below *Homo sapiens* in evolutionary emergence. A recent study of teaching by meerkats in the wild (Thornton & McAuliffe, 2006) reveals that adult meerkats, as they assist the development of hunting skills in meerkat pups, restructure the teaching tasks as the pups' hunting behaviors proceed through a zone of proximal development. Some of their prey is dangerous (spiders, scorpions); in the earliest stages, adults (including parents or other adult group members) gradually introduce live prey to the pups. That is, they may first bring dead scorpions for the pups to eat; as the pups mature and develop orientation to the dead prey, the adults may bring live but disabled prey (if a scorpion, the adult may bite off the sting); then less disabled, and so on, as is appropriate to the developing level of the pups' prey-handling skill.[3]

As is so clearly illustrated in this study of nonhuman species influence, task structuring and restructuring is an integral means of assistance as Subjects progress through the zone of proximal development. This is a general proposition, applying also to *Homo sapiens*, regardless of the repertoire under influence.

This same study of meerkats influence provides descriptions of using another means of assistance, propping/nudging.

Propping/Nudging

This means of influence refers to the physical placing of a learner in position to perform the next approximation of the desired behavior. Propping/ nudging is frequently used also in behavior modification programs for developmentally delayed or physically handicapped subjects. In behavior modification literature, this form of assistance is called *propping*. In animal studies, the same means (moving the body of the learner more closely to the goal position) is generally called *nudging*, a term closer to common usage.

Adult meerkats use nudging in their prey-handling assistance. In the early stages of influencing hunting behavior, the pups may not orient to or attend to the prey. Adults then are seen to nudge the pups up to touch the prey or nudge the prey against the pup.

---

[3] Whether or not teaching is practiced by lower species has been a matter of negotiating an accepted definition of, and criteria for recognizing, teaching (Thornton, Raihani, & Radford, 2007). The Thornton & McAuliffe meerkats study (op. cit.) used a definition (proposed by Caro & Hauser, 1992) comprising three criteria: "(i) an individual, A, modifies its behavior only in the presence of a naive observer, B; (ii) A incurs some cost or derives no immediate benefit; and (iii) as a result of A's behavior, B acquires knowledge or skills more rapidly or efficiently than it would otherwise, or that it would not have learned at all" (Thornton & McAuliffe, op. cit, p. 227). From the perspective of the unified theory presented in this book, such problems disappear. Teaching is defined as providing responsive assistance (regulation, influence) within the zone of proximal development (Tharp & Gallimore, 1988).

Propping/nudging is not restricted to influencing "primitive" behaviors. In domains of high skill and art, propping is also a staple of trainers/ masters as Agents of influence. Martial arts instructors physically reposition Subjects' arms and body to better approximate classic stances. Ballet teachers and choreographers fine tune body positions of their dancers by physically molding postures. First approximations of body skills are often influenced through demonstration, using the means of modeling; fine tuning is influenced through propping/nudging in all domains of athletics and physical performance. Many nurses-in-training require their instructors to place their hands correctly on patient groin veins to better feel abnormalities of blood coursing. Similarly, in learning to count my pulse beats in wrist or neck, I asked the nurse to place my fingers correctly and assist me to correctly modulate their pressure. At the rollout of a new computer game at a convention recently, the game developer's staff put their hands over the hands of potential distributors, propping the finger moves of the new wave of joy-stickers.

As for teaching meerkats, so also for human teachers: Several means of influence are intertwined in any program of influence and change. We see multiple means employed across all goals. Task structuring, modeling, and propping/nudging are frequently coordinated means of influence/assistance.

Modeling

Modeling is the process of influencing a subject's behavior by offering a model for imitation. The developmental processes of interaction, from the point of view of the Agent, constitute modeling; from the point of view of the Subject, it is *observational learning*. Imitation of others is a fundamental tendency that begins a great distance below *Homo sapiens* in the phylogenetic scale. Chimpanzees and orangutans perform demonstration teaching (Miles, Mitchell, & Harper, 1996). The most dramatic instance in recent history may be the epidemic speed with which birds acquired, through imitation, the behavior of lifting cardboard caps from milk bottles on the stoops of Europe, necessitating an entirely new form of packaging.

In *Homo sapiens*, modeling is probably the principal mechanism by which new behaviors are initiated, at least until language maturity is reached. Language development itself is pulled along through imitation. One could make the case that a problem of maturity is resisting imitating others, so strong is the native proclivity.

Not all imitated models are intentionally offered, of course. The socialization of children and other new members into cultures is largely

accomplished by their imitation of mature members' culturally organized but unreflective acts. Most traditional and pretechnological cultures
teach their offspring largely through modeling rather than through verbal
emphasis (Scribner & Cole, 1973). These acts of modeling take place during activities created by the family's ecocultural niche – working the fields,
caring for domestic animals, collecting and preparing food, caring for children, weaving, and other such tasks. Children take part in these activities
through a process of *guided participation* (Rogoff, 1989), in which opportunities to learn through modeling are seamlessly woven into the fabric of
everyday life.

Likewise with anthropoid primates: "As to how socioecological knowledge is transmitted from generation to generation, young anthropoid primates acquire socioecological roles and scripts through repeated episodes
of *guided participation in activity sub-groups* with various of their conspe-
cifics" (Parker, 2004, p. 56, italics in original).

Modeling as influence was exhaustively studied in the second half of
the twentieth century (Bandura, 1977). Many parameters of the modeling-
imitating process are now known: Whether or not imitation of models will
occur is affected by the comparative age and sex of modeler and imitator;
the presence of reinforcement for the behavior; whether or not the model
is live or depicted; relationship factors among the actors; and many other
variables, all of which are complexly interactive. Imitation itself, as a gener-
alized repertoire, can be strengthened or weakened by reinforcement and
punishment (Staats, 1968).

The processes that underlie the modeling-imitation connection are far
more complicated than simple mimicry. They involve central processing
of the modeled behavior prior to performance. Modeled activities can be
transformed into images and verbal symbols that guide subsequent performances. Indeed, research has shown that active coding of modeled activities into either descriptions, labels, or vivid imagery increases learning and
retention of complex skills. Through watching others, then, a person can
form an idea of the components of a complex behavior and can begin to
visualize how the pieces could be assembled and sequenced in various other
settings. All of this can be achieved through central processing, without
having performed the action:

> The basic modeling process is the same regardless of whether behavior
> is conveyed through words, pictures, or live actions. Different forms of
> modeling, however, are not always equally effective. It is often difficult
> to convey through words the same amount of information continued in
> pictorial or live demonstrations. In addition, some forms of modeling

may be more powerful than others in commanding attention. Children – or adults, for that matter – rarely have to be compelled to watch television, whereas oral or written reports of the same activities would not hold their attention for long. Furthermore, the symbolic modes rely more heavily upon cognitive prerequisites for their effects. Observers whose conceptual and verbal skills are underdeveloped are likely to benefit more from behavioral demonstrations than from verbal modeling. (Bandura, 1977, p. 40)

Modeling is a powerful means of assisting performance, one that continues its effectiveness into adult years and into the highest reaches of behavioral complexity. Instructors of activities that are obviously psychomotor – from athletic coaches to musicians – seem to understand intuitively that modeling is indispensable to assisting performance. However, verbal-cognitive activity is also composed of acts and is in fact often imitated. Modeling is a highly effective means of establishing abstract or rule-governed behavior. On the basis of observationally derived rules, people learn, among other things, judgmental orientations, linguistic styles, conceptual schemes, information-processing strategies, cognitive operations, and standards of conduct (Bandura, 1971; Rosenthal & Zimmerman, 1977). General rules of thought and conduct can be induced through abstract modeling and observational learning (Bandura, 1977, p. 42).

The use of modeling to influence psychomotor performance is such a well-known technique that we need give no detailed examples here, such as from teachers of tennis to tractor driving to potting. Influencing cognitive performance through modeling is less obvious but is a frequent activity in both formal and informal settings for development. The coach who talks aloud about designing a defense against the strength of the opponent, the parent who questions herself aloud about the last place she saw her handbag, the surgeon who verbalizes about the condition of the patient to the medical students and explains why procedure one and not procedure two is preferred – these are all examples of modeling cognitive routines for problem solving. In these and other good instances of modeling, the "demonstration" is not taken out of context or isolated, but rather provides an interaction that will be the basis for the eventual internalization of the strategy of adducing evidence and reaching conclusions (Tharp & Gallimore, 1988).

The importance of observational learning is further increased by the phenomenon of *emotional contagion* (Hatfield, Cacioppo, & Rapson, 1994), that is, the tendency of emotions to spread among observing/participating group members. Many of the mechanisms underlying this contagion are well below consciousness; research is revealing the broad phenomena of behavioral imitation and synchronization, and many of these appear mediated by known brain functions. We will return to this topic in Chapter 12. Emotional contagion studies from social psychology may further illuminate the dynamics of shared activity increasing intersubjectivity and, indeed, influence and change generally. The means of influence of modeling/demonstration affects not only behavior's probability, but also how to feel about it and during it.

Contingency Management

Contingency management is the means of influence in which rewards and punishments are arranged to follow behavior, depending on whether the behavior is desired or not. It is composed of a set of techniques widely practiced for four decades (Bandura, 1969; Tharp & Wetzel, 1969); there is an inexhaustible library reporting research and practice. Briefly, all manner of rewards have been used in contingency management – the social reinforcements of praise and encouragement, material reinforcements of consumables, or privileges, tokens, and symbolic rewards. Ordinarily, professional change Agents avoid punishments whenever possible because of the negative emotional secondary effects of punishing. "Negative" consequences are more often confined to the loss of some positive opportunity ("time-out" or removal from a social situation) or to brief, firm reinstruction.

Although contingency management is a powerful means of influence, it cannot be used to originate new behaviors. This is an important point, one that distinguishes the relationship of contingency management from other means of influence. New behaviors are not originated by managing contingencies; developmental advances are originated by other means of assistance – propping, modeling, instructing, cognitive structuring, and questioning.

Instructing

The next three means of influence are specifically linguistic: instructing, questioning, and cognitive structuring. *Instructing* calls for specific action. *Questioning* calls for a response in language. *Cognitive structuring* provides a structure for organizing elements in relation to one another, thus influencing understanding.

Instructing is surely the most ubiquitous of all means of influence attempted in ordinary life. People are forever telling one another what to do, although compliance is less frequent. In programs of intentional influence, when Subject is committed to be influenced by Agent, instructing can be the most efficient means, provided the behavioral repertoire is present.

In noncoercive settings, instructions too authoritarian may provoke opposition. A harangue of instructions is avoided even by some stern coaches of athletics (Gallimore & Tharp, 2004; Tharp & Gallimore, 1976). In coercive institutions (even those whose coercive nature is voluntarily accepted by subjects, such as the military), instructing is the foundational form of influence, although not the only one. Feeding back is also central, as are task structuring, modeling, and contingency management. Corrective institutions vary in their means of influence, although instructing (ordering) is pervasive, as it is in malign settings, such as those of families that produce dangerous criminals.

However, instructing is a valuable means of influence in benign settings. In the transition from apprentice to self-regulated performer, the instructing voice of the Agent becomes the self-instructing voice of the Subject – that heard, regulating voice, that gradually internalized voice, which then becomes Subject's self-influencing "still, small" instructor (Tharp & Gallimore, 1989).

Questioning

It was Plato who set the standard of questioning as the *sine qua non* of teaching, as all ideas are discovered by the questioning-and-answering dialogue, as enacted by his own teacher, Socrates.[4] Since those first Socratic seminars, questioning has been the most characteristic means of assistance in formal academic learning. Of course, questioning is used in all assisting interactions, but neither in the bulk nor with the same social dynamic as in the formal instructional setting. School is a place where teachers lecture, ask questions, and assess answers. Few questions are used in responsive, in-flight discussion. By contrast, questioning is the form of assistance most characteristic of psychological treatments and counseling, from psychoanalytic to client centered.

To begin an analysis of questioning, we may compare and contrast the ways that questions assist and the ways that instructions assist. Ervin-Tripp (1976, 1977) considers both instructions and questions as subclasses of directives. For example, we may say to a child, "What flowers did you see yesterday?" or we may say, "Tell me what flowers you saw yesterday." These are functionally equivalent in assisting the child by requiring recall and categorization. At one level of analysis, the question contains the implicit

---

[4] Although Socrates as a pedagogue (as recorded and portrayed by Plato) talked entirely too much and dialogued too little, as judged by contemporary understanding of the means of influence (see, e.g., Dalton, 2007).

instruction, "Tell me (or think of) what flowers did you see?" According to Ervin-Tripp (op. cit.), whether this regulation is phrased explicitly or not is a matter of courtesy, or role-regulation, not of the process per se.

Let us examine this position by taking a hypothetical example. A sergeant is unlikely to say, "Will you march?" He is much more likely to instruct, "March!" Obedience is both presumed and reinforced in the instruction, whereas to phrase the communication as a question lacks those presumptions of role. Even though marching results from both, a question on the parade ground is socially and contextually inappropriate.

Certainly a part of the difference between questioning and instructing has to do with managing acquiescence. Courtesy and compliance aside, there are consequential distinctions between questions and instructions. If the speaker wants action but phrases the directive as a question, this is likely to produce a "misfire" (Ervin-Tripp, op. cit.). "Will you march?" and "March!" are not the same, in that the interrogative form, in linguistic logic, requests a reply in language. If the troops are asked "Will you march?" they might shout "Yes!" but stand still. The instructional form "March!" requests a reply in action.[5]

> In linguistic logic all questions require a linguistic reply; logically and socially, a question is a request to speak. Questions and instructions are not interchangeable. When instructions are translated into questions, there is a risk of changing the social and cognitive interaction; whereas questions can be translated into instructions by the trivial manipulation of adding the implicit "tell me." (Tharp & Gallimore, op.cit, p. 59)

Socrates can either ask "What is the good?" or he can give a lecture on the subject. If Socrates questions, he gains two great teaching advantages. First, the subjects are activated mentally and verbally, which provides practice. Second, by listening, Socrates can then assist and regulate the students' assembling of evidence and their use of logic. If he only lectures, he will never see into the subjects' minds.

Cognitive Structuring

The simplest synonym for this means of influence is *explaining*. Cognitive structuring assists by providing explanatory and belief structures, which organize and justify:

> As a preliminary definition, cognitive structuring refers to the provision of a structure for thinking and acting. It may be a structure for beliefs,

---

[5] Wertsch (1979) has also given examples of this kind of misfiring.

for mental operations, or for understanding. It is an organizing structure, which evaluates, groups and sequences perception, memory and
action. In science, it is theory; in religion, theology; in games, it is rules.
In everyday life, cognitive structures are like all of these, more or less formalized, more or less conscious. (Tharp & Gallimore, op. cit, p. [63])

Influencing one another by giving ideas and interpretations is a basic form
of maintaining psychosocial systems, from families to friendship groups. A
liberal mix of cognitive structuring, questioning, and instructions characterizes the influencing dialogue. The Agent may provide cognitive structures
as broad as worldviews, philosophies, ethical systems, scientific theories,
and religious theologies. Or they can be specific explanations: psychoanalytic interpretations or behaviorist explanations of the effects of intermit-
tent reinforcement. In any event, influence flows by suggesting new ways to
organize events and emotions.

Instructing calls for a specific action, *questioning* calls for a verbal
response, and *cognitive structuring* provides an organization of understanding. An artful mix perhaps is most effective; the goal is to influence behavior
through reorganization of understanding. Whether through the thought-
fulness induced by a question, a direct instruction to read or observe something, or the provision of an overarching worldview, the power of cognitive
structuring cannot be doubted: As in instances of religious conversion, the
acceptance of a cognitive structure can have revolutionary effects on human
behavior and experience.

Feeding back against a Standard

Feeding back information on performance is a powerful means of assistance, often sufficient to guide a Subject to substantial improvement on
the next try. In self-regulation, providing for feedback is the most effective
means of self-influence for virtually all behaviors for which self-regulation
has been studied (for a review, see Watson & Tharp, 2006).

Feedback is a concept derived from cybernetics, and its meaning derives
from other concepts of that system. Feedback implies the existence of a
closed loop in which information is fed to a system that features an adjustable standard and a comparator (a mechanism for comparing specific performance to that standard). Simply providing performance information
is insufficient; there will be no performance influence unless the information is compared to the set standard. In the self-regulation literature,
therefore, much is made of the necessity for setting standards (as goals and
subgoals), and for setting up specific procedures for regular comparison
of feedback information to that standard (Carver & Scheier, 1981; Tharp,

Gallimore, & Calkins, 1984; Watson & Tharp, 2006). In Stage II of the zone of proximal development, feeding back is a vital form of self-assistance. Self-recording of behavior, in terms of frequency, setting, and quality, provides data records that can be compared to a self-standard. This act of comparison is the final and activating step of influencing through feedback.

The previous chart, indicating the evolutionary emergence of the means of influence, offers only a question mark for feeding back. Perhaps it is language dependent; it could be thought of as having emerged only with the development of science. Certainly the settings of standards and comparators, as stipulated by cybernetic concepts, have made this means of influence self-consciously precise. On the other hand, many physical and mental activities have improved by observing performance against aspirations throughout human history. The classification itself is not important; I raise the issue to call attention to the interplay of deeply embedded processes with the emergence of newer scientific technology, a process sure to intensify as the human sciences mature.[6]

The various means of influence, because of cultural norms, are practiced comparatively more or less. In Chapter 6, we will see that Navajo use instructing and questioning seldom and warily; modeling is frequent and normative. Among Native Hawaiians, instructing and contingency management are most frequent. Other norms for means of influence are under continuous cultural development, as a recent contretemps over propping/nudging illustrates. In 2008, the Musicians' Union in Great Britain advised its members to desist from touching their students during lessons to avoid the potential for charges of abuse. "Any physical contact with pupils can be potentially subject to misinterpretation or even malicious allegations. The best advice for instrumental teachers is to avoid physical contact with their pupils altogether."

A union spokeswoman said: "A cello teacher should have a cello to show a pupil what to do. There should be no need to touch." Other members insisted that music teaching and learning would inevitably suffer. One stated: "It's bad for the child and bad for the teacher. Children need to have their fingers placed on a keyboard or a guitar to show them how to play" (Harrison, 2008, p.1).

---

[6] The technology of visual recording is transforming feeding back as a means of influence. When Agent provides verbal feedback to Subject – whether dancers, basketball players, teachers, or any other performers – subjects may misunderstand or disagree with Agent's description. Video replay is accepted instantaneously as valid and obviates the need for negative evaluation, thus improving relationships between, for example, choreographer and dancers during the installation of a new ballet (Lily Cai, personal communication, 2003).

None of these instabilities in the preferential use of the means of influence invalidates their individual potency. However, all human transactions occur in cultural context, and culture itself is an evolving construction, a topic to which we will return in depth in Chapter 6. Science itself is also evolving and open ended, thus so is the list of the means of influence.

5

The Organization of Activity

Psychosocial systems in their phases – alpha, beta, or delta – have been discussed from several perspectives. In Chapter 3, they were seen as functioning in cycles of psychosocial systems. In Chapter 2, psychosocial systems were related to social network theory, and in that instance the dynamic aspects of Delta Theory were offered as an explanation for data collected from a social network perspective. In both previous instances, I proposed that the appreciation of the dynamics of psychosocial systems can be aided by considering the circular flow of four processes: *propinquity* (the degree of access of members to one another); *joint activity* (doing things together and talking about them); *intersubjectivity*, (coming to experience, interpret, and value the world in like ways); and *affinity* (feelings of preference and enjoyment for the company of other members). In the circular dynamic, the greater the degree of one of the four processes, the greater the likelihood of an increase in the degree of the next, in the order just listed.

Each of these processes is the subject of intense study in social sciences and philosophy, and each plays its own part in influence and change. It must never be forgotten, however, that the engine of this dynamism is *joint activity*, and that indeed the core enterprise of intentional influence and change may best be understood as the *organization of activity within psychosocial units*. Certainly the proximal determinant of influence for change is proffered and accepted means of influence, but this does not occur in a vacuum; it occurs during and as a part of activity engaged in together by influencer and Subject. The proximal source of the influence may be the master organizer, the Agent, but typically it is not; rather, the most effective influence is often by other members of the psychosocial unit, through whose mediation Agent brings means of influence to bear on Subject. This conceptual tangle can be simplified in this example: *I will get James to help you*. It is a simple idea, but it may be a challenge to Agent's organizational ability to secure James's agreement as to time, place, and circumstance in which influence – the assisted performance within Subject's zone of proximal development – will bring forth the fruit of change. Even when there is only Agent and Subject, the smallest and simplest change-directed psychosocial unit (wherein Agent assists John), joint activities must be planned and organized. Choices made by Agent in the organization of activity are the most consequential for the outcome of intentional influence.

THE CONCEPT OF ACTIVITY SETTINGS

The primary unit of analysis in the organization of activity for behavior change is the *activity setting.* Activity settings are the contexts in which collaborative interaction and assisted performance occur – when influence occurs. The concept of activity settings does incorporate cognitive and motoric action itself (activity); but it also contains the external, environmental, and objective features of the occasion (settings). For example, learning centers in classrooms that allow peer assistance can be activity settings that have specific purposes, occasions, and participants. Activity settings have goals, values, collaborative activity, and a spatial locus. They contain cognitive as well external social components, and they have meaning – the meaning attached to the activity by the participants, which in turn determines the strategies employed and the manner in which participants interact (Tharp & Gallimore, 1988; O'Donnell, Tharp, & Wilson, 1993; for measurement of activity settings, see Rivera, Tharp, Youpa & Dalton et al., 1999).

In the natural world, activity settings arise from the pressures and resources of the larger social system of which the participants are a part – the habitats or ecocultural niches of human groups (Wiesner, 1984; Wiesner & Gallimore, 1985). The goal-directed action of activity settings show the invisible hand of ecocultural factors, although these factors may neither be acknowledged nor understood by participants. Likewise, activity settings and their goals are shaped by the institutional structures in which they occur. Appropriate activity settings for achieving behavior change are quite different in the army than in the psychotherapist's consulting room. The goals of activity settings are likewise contextually formed and of course differ between friendship groups and basketball practice.

The personnel who can achieve the goals of action are determined by goal and setting. Influence is not guaranteed by random assemblies of persons in places; it is only the goal-driven activity that makes the maximum contribution of each individual desirable to the entire group, thus motivating assistance for the less competent [as] for the good of all. The actual acts of influence in the service of the goal are distributed according to the personnel mix and are given shape by the goal itself.

An activity can be performed only when the time is congruent with the character of the operations and the nature of the personnel. The meaning of activities, and thus the motivations for them, is determined by the goal – but not entirely, because in the emergent intersubjectivities resulting from group performance, meaning continues to develop.

Thus the activity setting cannot be unpackaged without wrenching out its explanatory heart. Activity settings simultaneously incorporate cognitive and motoric action as well as the external, environmental, and objective features of the occasion. Maintaining a unit of analysis that incorporates simultaneously all these features – features that social science has heretofore separated – requires some discipline of thought. On the other hand, nothing could be more congruent with ordinary experienced life. When Agent designs activity settings for influence and change, it means organizing *who* is going to do *what, when, where,* and *why.*

These famous "five W's" of good journalistic writing can assist us here as well, as an outline for considering the interlocked dimensions of activity settings and as a heuristic for designing a complex plan of influence. At this point in the exposition, it is not necessary to examine each W theoretically; *what, when,* and *where* design issues are so case specific that they will be better explicated through the dioramas of Chapter 8 and the case examples of Section Two. The dimensions *who* and *why,* however, involve issues of theory and strategy that require consideration here at the level of the unified theory itself.

MOTIVE AND MEANING IN ACTIVITY SETTINGS

Activity settings consist of individuals engaged in goal-directed actions and operations within a framework of implicit cultural, institutional, and community assumptions and expectations. Therefore, *why* actors engage in the activity settings has substantial impact on the scripts that guide their behavior. At a given moment, the same tasks in two activity settings may seem equivalent at the objective descriptive level, but at the level of motives of participants may be entirely different and thus may evolve an entirely different developmental course. How people perform at a given observed moment provides an insufficient basis for inferences about cognitive activity or any other process. To be the same, tasks must be equivalent not only at the level of *what,* but also at the level of *why.*

Why an activity setting exists and functions must be examined in two facets: motivation and meaning. The goal of an activity setting usually provides its motivational energizing. If the goal is to design new software, the software itself – which may be important for the continued existence of the corporate work team – carries within it the motivation for the activity, at least for the more powerful authorities who sanction it and who make available the needed resources. This is not necessarily the motive for participation by every member of the activity setting; Some may join in escape from a disliked supervisor; others might join to gain new experience and an upgraded résumé; less powerful members, like children in family activities, may participate only under unwelcome orders; others may participate because they like the society of the peer group.

As an elementary example, consider a simple classroom lesson. The teacher's goal is to teach reading, and that motive energizes the teacher for the activity. However, for many students this goal provides no motive. Therefore, the more powerful member must provide supplementary motivation for students until they incorporate the values, meanings, and motives of the controlling member of the activity setting. (That is why assistance by contingency management is useful in working through the zone of proximal development until the motives of the larger institution – or Agent – have been internalized by the Subjects.) The most general point is this: Initial motivation is not always identical for all activity setting members, but activity settings tend to create motivational homogeneity for members through the processes of emergent intermental subjectivity (Tharp & Gallimore, 1988). This generality is crucial for the organization of any systematic effort for influence and change.

The second facet of the *why* of an activity setting is its *meaning*. How participants understand the activity, how they explain the activity to others and to themselves – these are crucial aspects that may determine the vigor of participation and indeed determine whether or not participation will continue. That is, the activity setting includes the organizational structures in the minds of the participants, and those cognitive structures are contextualized by cultural meanings of the activity setting. However, the organization and cognitive representation of motives within an individual and within the society need not be isomorphic. Portions of the same activity setting may be more motivating for one participant than another. Perhaps neither participant values that element as highly as other members of the activity setting or even the culture at large (Minick, 1985; Cole, 1985; Tharp & Gallimore, 1988). Thus those who initially participate in an activity setting may have wildly different motives for so doing; consider the involuntary participations described in the dioramas of Chapter 8. This divergence of motive is perhaps especially notable for settings that have the most profound implications for repertoire change.

Therefore, all change Agents, as they design activity settings, may well expect the meaning of prescribed activities to differ across participants. Agents must assess, and when necessary supplement motivation to energize participation in early stages of activity creation or modification. In the foregoing example of the reading lesson, the meaning of the activity setting in the minds of the teachers was *lesson*; but in the understanding of the young children, it was *story talk*. Over time, students come to understand the events the way their teachers do, because activity settings, through semiotically mediated interactions, converge, develop, and evolve a common understanding (Au & Jordan, 1981; Tharp & Gallimore, 1988).

As we will see in Chapter 9, this developmental course is normative for programs of intentional influence and change. A reading of the dioramas of Chapter 8 will reveal that evolved instances and institutions for influence and change are illuminated by the constancies of activity setting dynamics; one of these constants is the moving meaning of *activity*, the engine of influence and change.

6

Unifying the Study of Culture and Psychology: Philosophical and Scientific Issues

This exposition of Delta Theory has thus far approached the unification of the various contexts of influence and change by recourse to fundamental concepts and processes of biology, psychology, and sociology. A parallel task awaits the challenge of incorporating culture studies into the Delta theoretical structure.

To any unifying ambition, cultural differences bring the most daunting challenge. That awareness came to me through a career's work in striving to improve human services through specific cultural compatibilities – primarily in education, psycho/behavioral therapies, and applied developmental and community psychology[1]. Where the issue has been examined, cultural elements have been seen to condition the effectiveness of procedures in human influence and change. The working assumption of any universal theory must be that cultural contingency, which is potent and ever present, lays over a deeper unity of *Homo sapiens*. The theoretical and empirical challenge to the universalist is to find the concepts and dynamics by which cultural variation and species unity articulate.

That challenge cannot be met in sterile laboratories. The study of culture, historically and currently, is mired in political agendas both macro and micro. How could it be otherwise when culture divides people into groups that compete through explicit and implicit power struggles, justified by claims to the high grounds of values, control, resources, and pride. Unifiers and their critics agree at least on the seriousness of the issue. Beyond Delta Theory, or any other attempted unifying schema, the organizing and differentiating forces of culture constitute the greatest challenge to any possibility of a unified theory of the human sciences. Therefore, that challenge had

[1] An earlier version of this chapter appeared in the *Journal of Theoretical and Philosophical Psychology* (Tharp, 2007).

best be launched straightforwardly and immediately, because if it cannot be met, the unification enterprise cannot succeed.

Perhaps because of my personal intellectual journey, I believe rich and deep studies of many cultures are necessary to comprehend not only how cultures differ, but also how and at what levels they are the same. How can we know how all humans are alike except by knowing each other so well that underlying unities become apparent? So for understanding practicalities of influence and change, unified concepts will require continued intense studies of particular cultures.

Cultural psychology and psychological anthropology as specialized fields have moved toward maturation during the past half century. Some optimism seems justified for a future in which we will be wiser about cultural differences. Further, scientific general psychology may be maturing sufficiently that we can understand principles operative for all peoples. In my opinion, this stereoscopic view is required for understanding the relationships among the individual, the cultural, and the universal.

THE GAME AND THE CANDLE

What are the advantages of a potential unified theory that encompasses culture? Disadvantages may include social dangers. Past universalist views have been used by dominant cultures to denigrate others. Yet is this a greater disadvantage than the fractionating of particularism? A second danger is trivializing. It is obvious that cultural groups feel, behave, think, and organize in consequentially different patterns. Thus, it might be argued, a universalist view can only discuss trivial phenomena, such as reflexes, or make trivial arguments, such as "all cultural groups rely on language communication." If results are trivial, the game will not have been worth the candle.

We should feel compelled to pursue a theory that incorporates culture, social sciences, and biological and physical sciences. Empirically and logically, it makes no sense to ignore the enormous similarities among *Homo sapiens'* individuals and groups, particularly considering the startling overlap of genomes with subprimate species. If we are scientists, we must accept and coordinate with foundational, validated evidence and theories of other disciplines, particularly physics and biology. This is likely to be, for a time, more goal than achievement, but even a human sciences theory of everything is a mountain whose base can be scouted.

My own quest is more modest. I aspire for a common lexicon and concepts in which culture and a universal theory of influence and change can be meaningfully and usefully discussed. Is a unified perspective worth the attempt? Judgment awaits the doing. However, the doing requires a careful consideration of the disciplines, limits, and inevitabilities that a unified theory entails. I have accepted that a unified perspective must be philosophically realist and scientifically based, and thus in accord with the best available scientific theory and evidence. Certainly others can take other perspectives with different assumptions. My purpose is not to dispute or defend against other perspectives, but rather to explore the logical and theoretical issues that must be addressed by those of us who would have a unified science of human behavior and experience that includes psychologists and culturists in a common-language dialogue.

As a further demur, this chapter's purpose is limited to working on that common language. It is not my intention to encompass culture's many other domain borders. As one example, ecological shifts bring cultural shifts. There are no doubt lawful relations between structural elements of ecology and structural elements of cultures (Steward, 1972). That work is for other writers. I am content to establish the processes by which culture members influence and change one another in response to ecological shifts.

RELATIONSHIPS BETWEEN STUDIES OF CULTURE AND PSYCHOLOGY: A BRIEF RETROSPECT

The first steps in the enterprise of reconciling studies of culture and psychology were daunting. Even decades ago, the two social sciences of culture studies and psychological studies were separated by what seemed a chasm. But the bridging effort began.

Anthropological Perspectives

In anthropology [following White's (2007) brief history] we see the outlines of the earliest attempts at unification with psychology. The study of the continuities of life forms required a line dividing *Homo sapiens* from all taxonomically lower species. That demarcation asserted that only humans are capable of the cognitive processes necessary for creating and maintaining culture. (This position survives today, although disputed at definitional borders). A second stage involved the growth of typologies based on geographical area and – closely related – ecological similarities. Clark Wissler, whose generative work developed these typologies, was a pioneer in universalist theorizing, arguing that specific cultures must be considered as expressing their own *pattern* of universal traits. (We will return to that issue in the discussion of pattern to come). In the developmental history of universalist culture thought, Wissler was a distinguished social scientist and a pioneer universalist. We can learn both from his assumptions and reasoning and from the shortcomings of his theory, which, although no fault of his own, delayed further major unifying attempts for almost a century. His thought can be easily followed through his summarizing book, *Man and Culture* (Wissler, 1923), from which the following brief quotations are taken.

For Wissler (1923, pp. 49–56), culture is "neither more nor less than the aggregate thoughts and deeds of the tribe." A *culture trait* is "a unit in the tribal culture," but units occur in chains and aggregates, as *trait complexes*: for example, wild rice complex, headhunting complex, couvade complex, and so forth. Many cultures may contain the same trait complexes; these constitute a *culture type*. Of course, trait complexes are not identical across tribes within the type; any trait complex is a *variable* across cultures containing it (p. 53). A culture type is the "norm, or standard form of tribal culture readily distinguishable from others" (p. 55). Culture types are geographically localized in clusters. Across cultures within same type, the trait complexes vary, with the *cultural center* (ordinarily coterminal with the geographical center) tending to be more normative, and with less pure trait complexes at the more distant margins of the culture type (p. 56).

For this discussion, it is less important to attend to the content of Wissler's universalist assertions than to the level of conceptual integration he attempted. Wissler's universal assertions begin thus: A culture has a plan, or a pattern. "If we should liken trait-complexes to building materials, then the plan of the house to be built of them would correspond to the pattern of a culture" (p. 73). However, "the same general outline will fit all of them; thus we may say the facts of culture may be comprehended under nine heads" (p. 74–75), which he referred to as *culture complexes*. The universal culture complexes were the following: speech; material traits; art; mythology and scientific knowledge; religious practices; family and social systems; property; government; and war.

Wissler's universalism lies in his assertion that all cultures contain these same nine culture complexes. Wissler's empirical ethnographic work, from which he derived his typologies and concepts, was and is much respected. However, his conceptual work on the culture complexes has met little enthusiasm. For example, it was considered by Linton (1936) to be no more than an unsatisfactory guide for arranging descriptive material.

Wissler had high ambitions. He sought a universal theory of culture and realized that such a theory must be based ultimately on common human attributes. He introduced his work as emphasizing "culture and its biological background" (p. v.). He considered his work objective, realist, and behaviorist. He rejected "an interpretation of culture as acquired behavior to the exclusion of other kinds of behavior, for that is the crux of our problem. What we do now, is to assert that culture is the outcome of human behavior, and thus define its biological basis and origins" (p. 253). Thus the human is born fitted to participate in culture. At several points he considers Watson's conditioned responses as an instance of how traits are culturally conditioned through innate processes. Thus the conditionability (or "habit-forming ability") of the infant "is an important part of his equipment for culture" (p. 200).

After examining the scientific work available from psychology and sociology, Wissler concluded that the culture complex pattern is based on psychophysical functions and that these are inborn. After all, "It seems reasonable to suppose that what all men have in common is inherited" (p. 260). The universal culture complex thus must be "the functional pattern for inborn human behavior" (p. 279).

In addition to the logical problems in that reasoning, it is painful to read Wissler's attempt to extract from his contemporaneous psychology an adequate account of the units of psychophysical characteristics upon which he could build an adequate unifying theory. Searching, he turned over the stones of drives, reflexes, and conditioning, but the principal "psychophysical functions" that he took as inborn and the foundation of culture were grasping, vocalization, and reflection. "The universal pattern for culture is then largely determined by the number and kind of these inborn responses" (p. 267). The details of specific trait complexes are a matter of emphases and grouping of expressions of these inborn responses.

The social scientific knowledge that Wissler found useful was largely psychophysical, which he subsumed as biological. Theoretical and scientific psychology and sociology were not then adequate to support the unified structure that Wissler sought. Most contemporaries of Wissler treated his *universal cultural pattern* superficially and largely dismissively; it rarely receives serious attention today. However, Freed and Freed (1983) provide a clear and sympathetic overview of Wissler's work and his historical place in anthropology: "... 60 years after it was proposed, it still merits attention in any consideration of the relation of biology, psychology and culture" (p. 818).

Wissler deserves recognition for his early sketches of what a unified theory of human behavior and experience should be, which were well in advance of science's capacity to provide it. The feature of Wissler's work most central to my own argument is his theory's insistence on the incorporation of biological and psychological science, a position I accept as necessary for a valid unified theory encompassing the human behavior and experience of all cultures.

In the meantime, between Wissler and this writing, progress has been made in psychological thought and science.

Psychological Perspectives

Historically, psychologists typically assumed universalism of the regularities they observed; they did not even see culture as a challenge to universalism, much less a threat. Even today, in most psychologists' meetings, culture is the undiscussed elephant in the room. On the margins of psychology, this dominant assumption of universalism is certainly contested; culture offers serious challenges – logical, empirical, and theoretical – to conventional universalism. The relatively small specializations of cultural psychology, culture and personality, cross-cultural psychology, and the like continue to produce a respectable scientific and speculative literature.

For psychological research in cultural phenomena, a recent review by Cooper and Denner (1998) analyzed the field into seven theoretical perspectives. Some of these theoretical perspectives are little more than single ideas about dichotomies; others are extrapolations from more general social science theories to cultural phenomena. The authors state that bringing concepts of culture into psychological theories "is crucial to both social science and policy in multicultural societies, particularly democracies" (Cooper & Denner, op. cit., pp. 3–4). In the reviewed research, they find that all seven approaches are attempting to link culture and psychology; many are doing so in practical investigations; a few are attempting to enlarge psychological theory itself. They also state that actually bringing concepts of culture into psychological theories "is an abstract, disputed, and inherently irresolvable process" (Cooper & Denner, op. cit., pp. 3–4). Unresolved, certainly; but irresolvable?

Six years later, the field of psychology and culture was reviewed again in an examination of the mutual influences of psychological and cultural processes in the research fields of evolutionary processes, epistemic needs, interhuman agency, self-worth, and contextual activation of cultural paradigms (Lehman, Chiu, & Schaller, 2004). The authors conclude with a caution about the "essential tension that accompanies any investigation into the intersection of the study of culture (which typically assumes meaningful cross-cultural differences) and the study of psychology (which typically assumes fundamental human universals). It remains for future research in cultural psychology to confront this tension, and to find ways of resolving it" (p. 706).

Are there grounds for hope that the problem can be resolved? What are the requirements for a resolving approach?

FOUNDATIONAL CONSIDERATIONS, PHILOSOPHICAL AND SCIENTIFIC, FOR A UNIFIED PERSPECTIVE

To illuminate the possibility of a unified human science that incorporates cultural phenomena in their full complexity, certain philosophical and scientific issues must be confronted and clarified. For the unification agenda, the philosopher John Searle (1995) provides the ideal texts. His fundamental assumptions are that human behavior and mind are not mystical but rise in the physical, and so they ultimately and necessarily must be explained by physical concepts of elements and forces. This means that we should accept theoretical physics, because it continuously clarifies; and biologically we should accept evolution theory, as we fully expect brain science soon to further inform and limit our propositions. He puts the assumptions and challenge succinctly:

> Here, then, are the bare bones of our ontology: We live in a world made up entirely of physical particles in fields of force. Some of these are organized into systems. Some of these systems are living systems and some of these living systems have evolved consciousnesses. With consciousness comes intentionality, the capacity of the organism to represent objects and states of affairs in the world to itself. Now the question is, how can we account for the existence of social facts within that ontology?[2] (p. 7)

I associate his line of thought explicitly with my own, as I will rely heavily on Searle's reasoning in the discussion of crucial conceptual issues to be developed later. However, as for the possibility of continuity between the physical science's particles and fields of force and the social sciences' phenomena that we wish to explain, is there reason for optimism?

Social sciences are showing promise of a rapprochement with biology and post-Newtonian physics in such bridging discussions as with

---

[2] Searle uses *intentionality* "as a technical term meaning that feature of representations by which they are *about* something or *directed* at something. Beliefs and desires are intentional in this sense.... Intentionality, so defined, has no special connection with intending. Intending, for example, to go to the movies is just one kind of intentionality among others" (p.7).

complexity theory (Byrne, 1998). Synchrony theory likewise appears to be a vein worth mining (Strogatz, 2003). The "billiard-ball causation" of positivism has never been adequate to deal with human behavioral and experiential phenomena, but post-Newtonian physical science is itself dealing with phenomena of such complexity that potential relevance to psychological theory need no longer be disdained.

To accept that physical/biological science is the bedrock of human sciences has the logical consequence of being bound to one level of universalism through particles and forces, through evolution and genetics. This binding may be gladly accepted, in my view, because it actually frees us to elucidate how the conditionalities of diverse human lives account for such varied expressions of universal forces. Universal? Conditional? Which is which, and how can these relationships be articulated?

THE FOUR LEVELS OF HUMAN DEVELOPMENT

I have proposed a model for articulation between physical and behavioral sciences in the form of a simple diagram[3]:

The model is heavily indebted to Vygotsky (1978), who discussed developmental "domains." In the diagram here, they are presented as "levels," to which I have added clarifying details; more important is the modification of the level of which I call *ethnogenetic*.[4] This is necessary for the incorporation of cultural data and concepts not available in Vygotsky's time. Many other of his interpreters have addressed this same issue with variations (e.g., Engeström, 1987; Cole, 1998).

It is conventional in social science to presume causative influences both proximal and distal, both historical and contemporary. Of course we know that all human events are overdetermined – that is, they cannot be understood by any simple causal attribution. The phylogenetic and ontogenetic levels of explanation, for example, are not contradictory, but mutually enriching. The model suggests that we can most fully understand the forces acting on any one developmental event as operating through a "funnel" of four levels, in which each level is simultaneously potent, inter-influential,

---

[3] Adapted from Tharp, R. G. (1994). Intergroup differences among Native Americans in socialization and child cognition: An ethnogenetic analysis. In: P. Greenfield & R. Cocking, Eds. *Cross-cultural roots of minority child development* (pp. 87–105). Hillsdale, NJ: Lawrence Erlbaum.

[4] *Oxford English Dictionary: ethnogenesis*. L. Singer in *Social Research XXIX*.423: "I propose that this formative process be referred to as 'ethnogenesis,' meaning by this term the process whereby a people, that is an ethnic group, comes into existence."

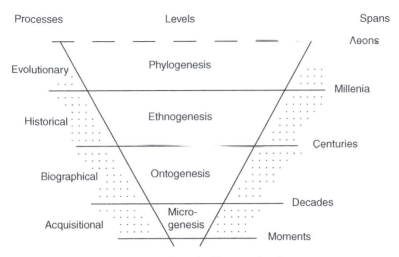

FIGURE 6.1. The funnel of human development.

and whose expression in any contemporaneous event is conditioned by the levels above it (Tharp, 1994).

At the top of the diagram is the *phylogenetic* level, operating through evolutionary processes, typically in spans of time between eons and millennia. (The link here to sciences of particles and force fields is evident through biochemistry.) The *ontogenetic* level comprises processes that we describe as biographical, and in time spans roughly between years and decades. The *microgenetic* level operates through acquisitional processes (teaching and learning) in time periods that vary from decades to moments.

Less frequently considered, however, is the level of development that operates in processes that we call historical, which vary in time periods between millennia and centuries.[5] In this funnel diagram (Figure 6.1), I have labeled that level *ethnogenetic*, designating by this term the process whereby a people (we may think of ethnic or other cultural groups) come into being and evolve the terms of their continuing existence.

Vygotsky's levels of developmental processes are vital to many living theorists, and many of his interpreters have offered representations of this fundamental idea. However, *ethnogenesis* as an explanatory level has been too frequently absent in major theoretical systems of Western psychology.

---

[5] Vygotsky (op. cit.) discussed this "developmental domain" as *historical*, but briefly and with less centrality.

This is in spite of the obvious: Conditions of human life, present in every significant transaction, flow from historical processes, processes that have matured for hundreds of years and that operate causatively in present time.

To consider the relationship of culture to any unifying theoretical approach, it is necessary to consider the interrelationship among these four levels. None of the four levels invalidates or even discounts the others. However, those levels above it condition the operation of each level. Consider the simple proposition that the probability of the reoccurrence of a behavior is increased by contingent positive reinforcement. In a four-level analysis, we would see that this relationship is phylogenetically prepared in evolution long before the emergence of *Homo sapiens*. However, the reinforcing value of a stimulus varies sharply across cultures (the ethnogenetic level), and indeed across individuals depending on variation in life histories (the ontogenetic level). At the microgenetic level, actual teaching and learning operations of elicitation and reward of desirable behaviors must – to produce development – proceed in accordance with specieswide genetically provided regularities, as those regularities are conditioned by culture and life history. Inuit behavior is not much reinforced by pork, and few Arabs think of whale meat as a treat; but even these probabilities can be surprised by unusual life histories. I use the Skinnerian example for simplicity (and as a nod to Wissler), but the same form of analysis is valid for more complex and consequential social repertoires and preferences, such as the courtesies and conventions of conversation, patterns of adult-child relationships, and indeed all developmental processes and conditions. Even the processes of phylogenesis, through assortative mating, are to some degree conditioned by cultures. My argument is that unifying propositions can be adduced that operate in each level, illuminating the interactive effects on development across all.

For example, assortative mating has direct consequences for species development at the phylogenetic level. But as we have seen in Chapter 2, assortative mating in *Homo sapiens* is strongly influenced by psychosocial systems' cyclic dynamics of propinquity, shared activity, intersubjectivity, and affinity. Certainly at the ethnogenetic level, the very process of development of ethnic identity[6] proceeds through shared activity and shared interpretations of meaning in multiple psychosocial systems with overlapping memberships. Ontogenetically, entire life histories can be told through

---

[6] Identity is also strongly conditioned by place (Kana'iaupuni & Malone, 2006) as would be expected, because a foundational feature of activity settings is their location, their "where."

chronicles of psychosocial system memberships and their developmental influences. And microgenetically, influence and change – the major concern of Delta Theory – operate directly through psychosocial system effects.

The practical value of that theoretical effort remains to be demonstrated, although I will offer some examples to illustrate the potential utility.

UNDERSTANDING THE CULTURAL THROUGH *BACKGROUND*

It is not possible to proceed further without confronting the basic questions: *What is* culture, and *how* is it to be understood? How may the logical, dynamic, and descriptive status of the concept of culture be clarified? On the surface, cultural differences appear to invalidate even the possibility of a unified theory of behavior change. Of course, the daunting variety of human existences must be understood. Patterns of consciousness, intentionality, and behavioral repertoires arise from many sources, such as temperament or unique ontological events and conditions. Cultural patterning, however, is of particular interest in any unifying approach because it affects not only the individual, but also the social systems on which behavior change depends. This leads inevitably to the intractable problem of *defining* culture, a task that has led to many proposals and universal exasperation.

Because we feel culture everywhere, many have treated it as the largest element among elements or as the strongest force among forces. Both approaches, in my view, are erroneous. I propose (with a nod toward Wissler) that culture is not a motive among motives, a performance among performances, or some preferences among preferences. Culture is the *pattern* into which elements and forces (those conceptualized by biological and psychological science) are arrayed. Such arrays are best likened to *fields*, not separate forces or elements. In that view, culture rightly should refer to *that field resulting from shared developmental history*. Rueda (2006) independently (and unusually for social scientists concerned with culture) has come to similar conclusions, at least with respect to research and conceptual operations. He concludes that the understanding of culture advances when it is seen in terms of basic psychological processes: cognition, motivation, learning, and so forth.[7] Yet Rueda's aim is broad. He concludes that

---

[7] Rueda illustrates this by interpreting the facilitations of cultural compatibility in behavior change in terms of "load," a concept of cognitive science. Cognitive load theory "integrates the origins of human cognition in evolutionary theory with the structures and functions of human cognitive architecture in order to provide effective instructional design principles" (Sweller, 2007).

culture is an appropriate consideration even in individual cases because it must operate through basic psychological processes.

So culture can be described as a shared psychological and social *pattern of function arising from shared history.* The idea of culture-as-pattern is not novel (viz., Wissler); indeed, it is implicit or explicit in most definitions or discussions of relativistic culture. But a pattern of what? I specifically subsume the patterning in the field that we call culture under the philosophical concept of *Background* as developed by Searle (1998; 1995; 1983), which he associates with previous work of Wittgenstein (1969), with roots and complements to David Hume and Friedrich Nietzsche, as well as the anthropologist Bourdieu's concept of *habitus* (e.g., 1977; Searle, 1995, p. 132). The logical advantages of this subsuming are enormous in that Searle has cleansed the concept of Background of any vicious circularity – a rare condition for most uses of culture in social sciences. Further, his rich explication of Background offers several clarifications of component relationships.

Culture and Background are not the same; I propose rather that culture is one of the pattern types by which Background may be understood. Before elaborating this distinction, let us note that Searle ordinarily capitalizes Background, indicating its status as a technical term.

Searle believes that Wittgenstein's later work (1969) elucidating the socialization/developmental process of mentation deals with the same phenomena that Searle calls Background. Wittgenstein writes:

> I did not get my picture of the world by satisfying myself of its correctness. No: it is the inherited background against which I distinguish between true and false. (§94, p. 15e)

> We do not learn the practice of making empirical judgments by learning rules: we are taught *judgments* and their connexion with other judgments. A totality of judgments is made plausible to us....When we first begin to believe anything, what we believe is not a single proposition, it is a whole system of propositions. (Light dawns gradually over the whole.) ...

> It is not a single axiom that strikes me as obvious, it is a system in which consequences and premises give one another mutual support (§140–142, p. 21e).

So *Background* arrives all at once, in a cloud of premises, consequences, propositions, and judgments, as a picture. Searle says:

> The Background, therefore, is not a set of things nor a set of mysterious relations between ourselves and things, rather it is simply a set of skills, stances, preintentional assumptions and presuppositions, practices, and habits. And all of these, as far as we know, are realized in human

brains and bodies. There is nothing whatever that is "transcendental" or "metaphysical" about the Background. (Searle, 1983, p. 154)

> We are ordinarily not conscious of Background. It is ordinarily unexamined, and many of its deep elements (psycho-physiological capacities) cannot be reached by understanding or intentionality. It is important to see that when we talk about the Background we are talking about a certain category of neurophysiologic causation. Those functional details not being available to us, we are forced to describe them at a much higher level, which is no more disreputable "than speaking of the ability to speak English without knowing the details of its neurophysiological realization." (Searle, 1995 pp. 129–130)

Background enables linguistic interpretation to take place, enables perceptual interpretation to take place, structures consciousness, creates dramatic categories (that is, sequences of events take on meaning and explanations – narrative shapes), and provides motivational dispositions, facilitates readiness for some things and not others, and creates dispositions to certain behaviors (Searle, 1995):

> Part of the Background is common to all cultures. For example, we all walk upright and eat by putting food in our mouths. Such universal phenomena I call the "deep Background," but many other Background presuppositions vary from culture to culture. For example, in my culture we eat pigs and cows but not worms and grasshoppers, and we eat at certain times of day and not others. On such matters cultures vary, and I call such features of the Background "local cultural practices." There is of course no sharp dividing line between deep Background and local cultural practices. (p. 109, 1998)

Indeed there is not a sharp division, because the levels of phylogenetic processes and ethnogenetic processes are mutually influential, resulting in the particulars of Searle's "local cultures, Wissler's "tribal cultures," ethnocultures of such interest to contemporary social science, and in my view, the micro-cultures resulting from an assortment of institutional shared developmental histories.

Subprimate Asides

Evidence is accumulating for similar analogous dynamics in the societies (perhaps "proto-cultures") of subprimate species. A deeper phylogenesis of functions central to Delta suggests robustness, just as the "old" brain underlies and often overrides the "new." That analogy is arguable on several grounds, of course, until resolved by further research. Nevertheless, the greater grounding of Delta Theory in evolution data, the tighter is Delta's grip on its own intellectual standard of adherence to biological science.

Grandin & Johnson (2006) write: "A dog is born knowing how to kill a groundhog, but he isn't born knowing that a groundhog is food. Strange as it may sound, a dog has to learn from other dogs that groundhogs are good to eat. Predators have to learn from other animals *whom* to direct their hardwired predatory behavior against" (p. 137). Further, dogs are emotionally wired to learn "prey" and "not prey," and they never get confused about the categories but, like humans, must learn which creatures (such as cats and toddlers) go in which classification.

Banded mongooses show stable preferences for alternative foraging techniques passed down generations through imitation of adults by pups during foraging. Multiple techniques exist simultaneously within the "groups" or "villages" of mongooses (Müller & Cant, 2010). These authors suggest this is strong evidence for *traditions* in wild mammals.

Even some birds transmit attitudes/values intergenerationally. Researchers wearing masks trapped and banded seven crows on the campus of the University of Washington. For several months thereafter, experimenters wearing those ("dangerous-to-crows") masks walked specified routes without approaching or addressing any crows. The crows, however, scolded people in the mask significantly more than they did before they were trapped, even when the mask was disguised with a hat or worn upside down. Other experimenters wore a similar but different mask, which provoked little crow reaction. The effect not only persisted, but also multiplied over two years. In an interview with the lead researcher, "Wearing the dangerous mask on one recent walk through campus, Dr. (John) Marzluff said, he was scolded by 47 of the 53 crows he encountered, many more than had experienced or witnessed the initial trapping. The researchers hypothesize that crows learn to recognize threatening humans from both parents and others in their flock." (Interview, Niiuhuis, 2008; research article, Marzluff et al., 2010.) Most recently, the television program *A Murder of Crows* (Remerowski, 2010), with the assistance of the Marzluff research group, has dramatized this crow repertoire, including parental teaching of these attitudes toward masks to young still in the nest.

Is this not a form of community protolinguistic semiotic process?

Background Resumed

Cultures appear to be self-perpetuating, which is to say that the pattern of Background replicates. In Searle's terms, most if not all deep Background replicates causatively through genetic inheritance. The preponderance of the cultural pattern of Background also seems to replicate from generation to generation of cohorts. This phenomenon has been well studied by socio-cultural researchers who find the causative links in cultural perpetuation in the processes of primary-through-formal socialization, that is, through patterned activity and semiotics among new and experienced culture members. Intersubjectivity both increases and is increased by shared semiotics, increasing affinities, increasing receptivity toward assistance, and influence during joint activity, which itself propels further interaction. These are the processes of primary socialization by which the young are brought into the societies of their families, communities, and cultures, and by which those entities are perpetuated (Cole, 1998). This is an example of the intellectual benefits of basing explanatory statements on universal elements. If we do not have the scientific explanatory concepts interpolated in these next-generational interactions, we are left with the logical absurdity of asserting that culture members socialize their young because of their culture – that is, the notion that culture causes culture.

Understanding the causative relations between culture and other concepts has been problematic. The culture pattern is the *product* of historical development (through social guidance, assistance, and influence), and so it has been seen as *effect;* and also it is the resultant pattern of activity that *produces* developmental social guidance, and so it also has been seen as *cause.* I prefer the concept of cultural pattern as a *field* in which elements and forces are in a continuous dynamism, so that cause and effect is an appropriate analysis only for isolated microphenomena. This allows us to better understand how cultural patterns spin in self-perpetuating place; but being permeable by changing context and circumstance, culture moves (with some wobble) on.

Anthropologically, we think of *culture* writ large as closely tied to ethnicity and other macrohistorical conditions, manifesting intersubjectivities broad in scale and incorporating a wide range of activities and psycho-social units which themselves share Background. Primary socialization is the context by which we theoretically and experientially attribute our own Backgrounds. However, in Delta Theory dynamics, intersubjectivities of psychosocial systems throughout the life span continue to build their own contributions (and even cancellations) of primary socialization Background. That fact is evident in common usage of the term culture, which is more and more applied to smaller societies of briefer history. Thus we speak of corporate cultures and cultures of classrooms or institutions. In the view presented here, this usage is appropriate and indeed facilitates the image of the condition of any individual's Background super-patterned by nested cultures, like graduated trays lying within one another, each conditioned by its stacked contexts. Thus can we explain individual differences within larger cultural patterns: Various nestings produce unique combinations. These are more than analogous to the individual multivocalities Bakhtin (1981) has elucidated as developed through language sharing within multiple genre-sharing communities. It is more than analogy, because multivocalities and multicultural identities both develop through symbolic mediation in shared activity and most often are simultaneously and fully interwoven.

Nested identities are a normative condition of complex societies; indeed, they often serve to relieve pressures, contributing to an overall social stability. When instability threatens, we resort to our prioritized identities: "First a Briton, second a conservative, and only third a sailor!" and other more consequential declarations illustrate that spilling the trays by some conflict is routinely corrected by righting the nests into good order.

Culture also identifies a collection of individuals of like Background pattern and like intentionality, and thus of similar activity repertoires and performances. An individual sharply displaced into a different culture will usually lose sustaining relationships and activities, and thus many suffer the anxieties of value conflicts of contending cultural identities. Indeed, in these days of great movements of peoples, cultural identity conflicts produce virtual epidemics of intrapersonal conflict.

To summarize this point: In a unified theory, universal scientific concepts must be discernable beneath culturally patterned phenomena at a level below the surface, as along a stream the surfaces of each pool will be patterned by the trees and breezes in which each lies. Yet below their varied, beguiling surfaces, all their waters are moved by temperature, volume, resistance, and all the other particles and forces comprising hydrology.

AN EMPIRICAL EXAMPLE

Let us consider again here, in the context of cultural phenomena, Vygotsky's concept of the zone of proximal development (see Chapter 3), which is the zone between what can be done alone and what can be done with assistance/influence of others. In Chapter 4, a list of universal means by which assistance/influence is offered to learners was explicated, a list that grows as psychological research advances. Several of these means will be discussed in the following empirical example, which focuses on differences across cultures in preferences as well as differential probabilities of use for the various means of influence and the contexts in which they are employed. These preferences develop within each culture's characteristic activity settings and daily routines, which are in the best available balance with their ecological and economic niches (Gallimore, Goldenberg, & Weisner, 1993). Cultures are perpetuated and evolved through primary socialization and other shared developmental processes (Cole, 1985, 1998). In this way, Background is patterned. For theory building, studies of how culture expresses basic psychological processes illuminate the basic scientific concepts themselves (for an excellent review, see Lehman, Chiu, & Schaller 2004).

Culture influences Background through the organization of activity settings (for a rich review of this issue, see Maynard 2005). In contemporary industrial and postindustrial society, instructing and cognitive structuring are more salient. Each culture's characteristic activity settings and daily routines are in the best available balance with their ecological and economic niches (Gallimore et al. 1999; Weisner, 1984). Knowledge of culture repertoires, values, and expectations are essential for designing or understanding influence for change. For theory building, studies of how cultures pattern basic psychological processes illuminate the basic science itself (for an excellent review, see Lehman, Chiu & Schaller 2004). Cole's (1985, 1998) explanations of how cultures are evolved and perpetuated can be seen as operating through the Delta phase. Our theory asserts that the Delta phases' conditions, processes, and variables are cross-culturally valid, but the Delta phase cannot function unless expressed in forms of activity and assistance that are valid in the program's social and cultural context (Gallimore & Goldenberg, 2001). Culture influences delta and beta conditions through the organization of activity settings. "What matters is the ecocultural factors that in turn influence the who, why, what and how of the activities in which children [and adults] spend their time" (Weisner & Gallimore, 1985).

As a practical example, consider the work with Native Hawaiians conducted by the Kamehameha Early Education Program (KEEP), a research and development effort to devise an educational system to improve literacy learning. (The story of that program has been well told in hundreds of publications; summary documents include Tharp & Gallimore, 1989; Tharp, Jordan, Speidel, Au, et al., 2007.) Raising those achievement levels required the design of an alternate pedagogy that afforded opportunities for teachers and students to employ elements of Hawaiian culture – primarily social and linguistic – in a variety of teaching and learning activities. This cultural compatibility between school and home culture was only enabled by a system of instruction far different from the traditional transnational model with which we began.

Assistance in student performance occurred in the culturally compatible teacher-student and student-student exchanges; following Vygotsky, we defined *teaching* as providing assistance in the zone of proximal development (Tharp & Gallimore, 1989). The means of assistance employed in that culturally compatible teaching were responsive to the pattern of the Native Hawaiian culture.

To better demonstrate the cultural conditionality of the means of influence in instruction, we took the same KEEP pedagogical system to another culture, the American Indian Navajo nation of the U.S. southwest. Chosen because of the many sharp differences in cultural style evident in published ethnographies of Hawaii and Navajo, we expected, found, and employed several sharply different sociolinguistic, cognitive, and social organizational variables to maximize student engagement, linguistic and cognitive processing, and the provision of teaching assistance. On surface appearance, the Hawaiian and Navajo classrooms' common pedagogical system made for their instant recognition as sister programs. The more subtle differences in the means of assistance were equally important (Vogt, Jordan, & Tharp, 1991; White et Al., 1989; Jordan, 1985; Tharp, 1994).

A few examples of the Hawaiian/Navajo examples may clarify: (1) Although the Instructional Conversation was a daily, central instructional setting in both, the sociolinguistic patterns engaging for Navajo children included longer speech turns and longer wait times between turns; for Hawaiian children, rapid overlapping speech turns and co-narration were characteristic. Both were "imported" from cultural conventions and courtesies of conversation. (2) Although small-group classroom organization was characteristic in both, effective assistance in peer interaction required smaller groups in Navajo than in Hawaiian society and same-sex grouping in the (gender-graded) Navajo society, whereas in the (age-graded) Hawaiian society, mixed-gender student groups produced more mutual assistance. (3) In both groups, cognitive processing during dialogue was frequent and deep. However, a more holistic cognitive style was employed in Navajo; American Indian cognition has been long and widely reported as holistic in style. Elaborations and analyses of these differences can be found in Vogt, Jordan, and Tharp (1992).

All teachers of Hawaiian and Navajo students practiced all means of assistance on our universal list to some degree, regardless of the teachers' own cultural memberships. However, the preferences and frequencies in the patterns of usage were sharply different in effectiveness across cultures. Hawaiian children were most responsive to *questioning, instructing, and contingency management (arranging consequences for behavior)*. Navajo students were far less responsive to these means, because in Navajo family and community life such forms of assistance are avoided as a matter of cultural values. For Navajo culture members, the most effective assistance is through the means of *modeling/demonstrating*, and through *cognitive structuring (providing explanations or concepts)*. These forms of assistance – especially modeling/demonstrating – are central to socialization practices across Native American culture and the peoples of the circumpolar North (Tharp, 2006; Darnell & Höem, 1996). These two patterns – Hawaiian and Navajo – are clearly related to widespread patterns of activity and values in the two cultures. Thus the effective conditions of the classroom took their potency from their culturally conditioned patterns of assistance and the valuation/emotional coloration of the assisting interactions.

During primary socialization, and indeed in all educative activity, more is learned than taught: attitudes, values, and interpretations of shared experiences. All effects are maximized if the implicit and explicit interactions are embedded in joint activity. Such "lessons" are not abstract; they are tied with total clarity to shared actions and activities. "Cultural preferences for varied means of influence" sounds dryly abstract. Yet in the joint practice of specific activity, it is far from abstract. For Navajo, instructing others is not a matter of low priority – it is *wrong*. By word and deed, young Navajo come to feel its visceral wrongness.

As a visual analogy, a display of universals (such as means of assistance) might be drawn as fields of lights on a dark sky. For different cultures, the same means would be drawn in different sizes, the illusion of proximity indicating probability, preferences, and effectiveness. However, few should be moon-white. They are all burning with values and emotion; in different cultures, the universals appear not only in different sizes but different colors.

We tend to think of emotions in primaries; perhaps anger, love, fear, revulsion, wonder, and/or others will prove to be universal primaries. Even so, as the three primary colors combine into infinite shadings, likewise are the numberless feelings with which Background phenomena are washed. From the same emotional palette, cultures brush on their characteristic shadings so that some same abstracted human monochromatic script would be virtually unrecognizable when projected in the colors of different cultures.

I have used figurative language here, aspiring toward greater clarity by representations across sensory modalities. This language should not obscure the fact that the representations are readily translatable into testable hypotheses and disciplined inquiry, which allows discomfirmability.

Shweder & Goldstein (1995) discuss how similar practices are infused with different value principles across cultures.

In our example of the Navajo people, the frequency and preference of observation/demonstration as a means of assistance is an expression of a deep structure of cultural values – so deep that it functions as a principle of Navajo interaction. This observational learning complex has neurological, sociological, psychological, familial, and ecological features (Vogt, Jordan, & Tharp, 1987). An example of this complex, so important in classroom education, is the principle of *competence before performance* (Cazden & John, 1971). Observation of competent performance continues until the learner is ready to perform. There is no expectation of trial and error, nor are teachers to call out learners to perform. The learner alone judges readiness – it is up to him or her. "Up to him or her" is the usual translation of *bílá*, which is the most fundamental Navajo value (Shepardson & Hammond, 1970). No one is to direct, instruct, exercise power over, or attempt to control anyone else, save in emergencies or dire straits. Learners observe models and perform when ready. Thus is the preference for one of the universal means of assistance laden with the value freight of centuries of developmental processes at the ethnogenetic level.

Nevertheless, when an educator (Navajo or otherwise) wishes to design an effective activity of modeling, choose the best model, or determine which level of expertise should be demonstrated, the voluminous literature on imitative learning provides useful and systematic knowledge. These universalistic psychological scientific principles must, of course, be expressed in culturally compatible forms, but the relationships among variables will hold, in the same way that the simple processes of respondent or classical conditioning operate uniformly across cultures.

Specialty-skill performances aside, humans share almost all performance capacities; it is emotional preferences that maintain cultural activities and practices. Even in the courtesies and conventions of conversation, all people *can* shorten or extend wait time. They *can* expand or abbreviate speech turns. We prefer to speak as we do because we find our culturally characteristic patterns to be pleasing in emotional aesthetics and thus in meaning. Values are perpetuated in every semiotically mediated joint human activity. In everything we humans teach – even the most technical – we simultaneously and inevitably teach how to feel about it.

In considering these variations, I see no threat to the possibility of a valid unified approach, so long as it recognizes that expressions of universals in the repertoires and values of human beings are culturally conditioned. The next task is to detail in theory and research the lawful relationships by which those expressions are developed phylogenetically, ethnogenetically, ontogenetically, and microgenetically.

These levels of genesis and their interactions provide an explanation of the cultural conditionality of the expressions of basic phylogenetic provisions. This perspective on a unified approach to culture and psychology fully incorporates Searle's basic realist and scientific assumptions and his logically elegant concept of Background. The development of various patterns of Background in different cultures can be explained through the processes of psychosocial systems in delta, beta, and alpha phases. The concepts and processes of Delta Theory presented in previous chapters are expressed in historically determined patterns of culture and Background. A unified, universalist Delta Theory is not weakened by cultural variation; on the contrary, it is strengthened by a tighter and stronger conceptual weave.

CULTURE AND ECOLOGY

It is settled science: Culture develops in adaptation to ecology. Culture arises through shared developmental history; the repertoires and values of a culture can be seen as person/environment adaptations common to the community. In the Arctic, ice and snow require certain repertoires from all.

Those adaptive processes are in principle orderly and knowable, but cultures' structural relationships to ecological variables are outside the domain of interest of Delta Theory. Interest for Delta arises in the interpersonal influences exerted in negotiating those adaptations. By and large, we have only speculation and good reasoning to analyze the survivability advantages of cultural variations in response to eco-conditions, just as we have only rationality to surmise the specific advantages of certain genetic evolutionary developments. We have no direct knowledge of the influence-and-change processes that might or might not have been part of the selection process among possible eco-survival alternatives.[8]

At this writing, an opportunity exists to directly observe influence-and-change processes in a culture adapting to a dramatically changing ecology. Greenland is melting.

After five hundred years, Greenland has been decolonized from Denmark, the last European colony to be let go. Though Greenland is the world's largest island, it has the smallest national population.

---

[8] Both cultural and genetic evolutionary analyses too often explain the way things are with Panglossian simplicity. But when complex human agency is involved, can it be doubted that much might have been different, but for influence and change?

Greenlandic political leadership has been signally aware of their new nation's limitations and potentials as well as the challenges of building new repertoires and values. The leadership is well educated, multilingual, and world-aware, and they realize that global warming is coming to them perhaps as quickly and drastically as any other populated land mass. Greenlandic students of today will as adults face the challenge of a drastic reorganization of work and society and consequent cultural evolution. It is the new schools that must prepare their citizens to meet this challenge. Thus in the gradual decolonization process, the leadership chose Education as their first Ministry to control.[9]

To change their educational system from Danish centered, they are grounding educational reform on Greenlandic values, potentials, and possibilities. The Education Ministry has organized a national dialogue (in districts, municipalities, and schools) about Greenlandic values. Are they, and should they be, traditional Inuit? Only? Or somehow also Scandinavian? Who is a real Greenlander, when after five hundred years few Greenlanders do not have some Danish blood, language, and common history? What capacities will today's children need to meet the challenges of rapid ecological change, as climate makes more land arable, fish stock species change and shrink, and the development of oil and minerals becomes feasible? The venues for these discussions are the local schools, districts, and municipalities. A major topic of the discussions is which values and actions should be part of the school reform.

Greenland's national professional development program for teachers has been designed on Delta Theory principles (Olsen & Tharp, 2011 in press). The reform is labeled *Effective Pedagogy*; one of its basic principles is that students from the earliest weeks of formal education begin to participate in activities beneficial for developing the valued capacities. A brief example may suffice. To date, there appears to be a developing consensus that certain traditional Inuit values will translate well into the future. For example, the preferred *size* of traditional Greenlandic work groups depends on the task. Whaling activity varies from "one small man in the world's smallest boat hunting the world's largest mammal" to total community involvement in the butchering and distribution of whale meat. Thus work-group size can vary between one and hundreds. *Leadership* likewise is task dependent: During specific tasks, the most skilled leads. Thus far, the discussions appear

---

[9] The author has consulted with the Greenland Education Ministry for ten years. There are probably other geographies in which similar discussions are under way.

to endorse this Inuit cultural system as continuing to be highly adaptive to a changing ecology.

This example focuses on traditional cultural values that should be *strengthened* by schools. Greenlandic planners also see new values and repertoires as necessary additions. Among them are language competencies: Reformed school graduates will be trilingual, adding both English and Greenlandic to the traditional Danish language. Beginning in preschools, an intense focus is under way on language development itself. In the future these linguistic reforms will involve student and faculty exchange programs with other nations in addition to Denmark. A third addition will be increasing student's enjoyment and aspirations in science and mathematics, thus aiding in the discovery and fostering youth of talent.

What is the Effective Pedagogy Reform's response to this apparent consensus? From the first grade, children are set to develop those skills by enacting them in multiple activity settings. Whole-class cohesion is built by daily discussions of how students are or are not working together in terms of classroom values that they have helped negotiate. The majority of the time, students work together in smaller activity settings organized to allow for varied leadership, which is not formally assigned but emergent depending on task-specific competence in assisting others. Every day, each child has a small group instructional conversation, during which the teacher assists each child at the forward edge of their emerging competence.[10]

In attempting this change from the lecture method of instruction, Effective Pedagogy confronts the *culture of school*, a transnational culture deeply institutionalized politically and economically (Tharp & Dalton, 2007; Jordan & Tharp, 1979). So, of course, Effective Pedagogy reform is contested. Shifts in culture involve shifts in power and privilege. Greenland's national dialogue is public and often confusing. Yet it offers a window for considering how cultures of old and cultures of the future work out their adaptations to ecology.

We can see in Greenland how influence and change is orchestrated and how it evolves. As they are confronted by implacable ecology, we can tune our observations to their debates and compromises. This may allow us a new appreciation of ethnogenesis and to imagine the efforts of influence and the passionate debates of old among such groups as the hunter-gatherer

---

[10] Details of Greenland's school reform can be found in Wyatt, 2009; and Wyatt & Lyberth, in press. Native Hawaiian versions of Effective Pedagogy can be found in Tharp & Gallimore, 1989; Navajo versions in Vogt, Jordan, & Tharp, 1991; and a Zuni version, in Dalton & Youpa, 1998.

proto-Navajo and the voyaging Polynesians on the beaches of their new islands of Hawaii. Shall we stay and be here? How then shall we divide the land and divide ourselves? It becomes almost possible to imagine the scripts, although in the history of ethnogenesis, dynamic conversations and compromises of influence and change have left few inscriptions.

Yet much else is left: Cultural repertoires and values persist long after early ethnogenesis. In part, cultural-pattern survival continues with its own momentum through the dynamics of psychosocial systems and networks, although "original cause" conditions have altered. Yet many cultural patterns continue to be maintained, less by terrain and weather and more by the socioecology of human cultural and physical constructions of villages, barrios, reservations, and economic systems.

In Chapter 11 we will consider how influence and change are permeated by culture; and we will see how influence programs that ignore the robustness of cultural repertoires and values will fail.

SECTION TWO

THE PRACTICE OF INFLUENCE AND CHANGE

7

Influencing and Change: Delta Theory of Practice

INTRODUCTION

We move now from a concentration on Delta's foundational theoretical concepts to an exposition of Delta's theory of practice. This may be likened to a shift from "science" to "engineering"; that is to say, the scientific aspect of Delta Theory, which is founded on general features of *Homo sapiens* regardless of persons and settings, now shifts to the *practice* aspect, which treats the variation of persons and settings as it affects the delivery of efficacious influence. Everyone who has purposed changes in others knows that every instance requires actions particularized to the situation. Every engineer who has designed a bridge did so by applying the principles of physical science to the infinitely variable local conditions of soil and stream.

THE SPREAD OF OBESITY

Consider the study "The spread of obesity in a large social network over 32 years" (Christakis & Fowler, 2007). Analyzed with the concepts and mathematics of social network theory, the results created a stir not only in health and social science circles, but also in the popular press. Social distance (degrees of separation) plays a stronger role than geographical distance in the spread of behaviors or norms of obesity. For example, no effect was observed on ego if an immediate neighbor became obese. But if an ego stated that an alter was a friend, ego's chances of becoming obese increased by 57 percent if the alter became obese. Between mutual friends, ego's risk of induced obesity increased by 171 percent; however, if only the alter and not the ego declared friendship, there was no statistical relationship. Among pairs of adult siblings, one sibling's chance of becoming obese increased by 40 percent if the other sibling became obese, but the effect is gender specific: Among brothers, an ego was 44 percent more likely to follow obesity; among sisters, an ego's chance of following a sibling into obesity increased by 67 percent. Husbands and wives affect each other similarly in following the spouse into obesity (husband egos 44 percent, wives, 37 percent). The authors are persuaded that the mediating factor is a change in norms, not a direct imitative phenomenon such as diet change.

That increased obesity can be an adventitious result of relationships within social networks struck journalists as a "man bites dog" story, presumably because popular understanding severely underestimates psychosocial units' dynamic tendency to bring members into a normative uniformity of behavior and values. Of course, parents know too well the effects on their children of undesirable friends. Less obvious, apparently, is that fat friends make even adults fatter. Psychological science has several process concepts through which such effects may be explained: identification, imitation, and the like. For our purposes, the obesity study reveals the ramifying effects of intersubjectivity extending to image valuation, normative adjustment, and thus self-evaluation, even though these elements were never any part of the attentions or intentions of the system members, nor were they intentionally influencing the behavior of others.

That is yet another enactment of the adage, "More is learned than is taught;" teachers teach their values – willy-nilly, inadvertently – as much as they teach formal content. This is likewise true of each assistor/influencer; during joint activity, these influences are mutual. Many such effects are inevitably inadvertent and adventitious and, in most cases, unremarked and indeed unnoticed, like white background noise under the strong signals of the system's routines and preoccupations.

Christakis and Fowler (op. cit.) suggest that network phenomena might be exploited to spread positive health behaviors. "Smoking- and alcohol-cessation programs and weight-loss interventions that provide peer support – that is, that modify the person's social network – are more successful than those that do not. People are connected, and so their health is connected" (p. 378). We will return to this issue in detail in the following chapter, but here Christakis and Fowler are quite correct: Once obesity becomes problematic for Subjects, many seek organized activity settings directly focused on weight loss. Agents and Agencies, such as fitness centers or weight-loss groups or businesses, offer purpose-built activity settings of fellow weight losers, dieters, and exercisers. We see in this instance, as in most cases of problem development and correction, corrective influence also involves psychosocial systems whose activities will reverse – in fact, often mirror – the etiology. As in a mirror, the right becomes the left: The valued body image of overweight friends is supplanted by that of new friends losing weight. The new system is focused on slimness; the preexisting one was unconcerned with weight. The success of the new system is measured in pounds and in sustainability. But in this new system, other adventitious and inadvertent effects will certainly be present, as in any psychosocial system, and new slimmer friends may interest Subject in Buddhist texts or the shorter hairstyles of the other women – or not. The point of concern here is that both the preexisting and the purpose-built psychosocial systems operate by the same system dynamics. The differences lie in purpose, intention, and activity. Delta systems of formal and/or intended programs of influence and change subordinate adventitious effects to goals. Most often, a mature beta psychosocial system does not have any goal beyond its own continuation; its dynamic is toward homeostasis and stability.

Hammond's (2010) updated review continues to link social network influence to obesity. He stresses the need for establishing a mechanism by which network connections might affect individual behaviors related to obesity. This call is answered formally by Delta Theory in Chapter 12.

INTENDED INFLUENCE, INTENDED CHANGE, SUBJECT TO

Having noted inadvertent and adventitious effects of influence, it should also be clear that the general propositions and concerns of Delta Theory are for intentional influence, for intended change. This requires noting a crucial condition for an Agent to successfully effect intentional change in a Subject; that is, intended change can be expected to occur only when the persons being changed are *subject to* the Agent. The Oxford English Dictionary defines *subject to* as "under the control of … subordinate to." This condition may be voluntary or forced, partial or complete, initially granted or gradually yielded. It is present between child and parent, student and teacher, prisoner and jailer, leader and group. *Subject to* is also a condition of the mind or will. Whereas influence may begin before a psychological yielding, strong resistance to imposed influence is difficult to overcome. But to what degree should Subject be *subject to* Agent? For inclusion within our domain, the sufficient level of *subject to* is when the Subject *engages the activities* organized by the change Agent. From the famous Stanley Milgram (1974) experiments, we know that even mindless self-subjection to apparent authority can produce quick obedience and engagement in dictated activities. Even when violently forced, engagement in Agent's designed activities meets these minimum conditions. This issue will be discussed in the context of malign cases of influence and change (Chapter 8).

Most of these subjections in professional work and in benign human complexity are voluntary and often only lightly considered. That is, if I am moved to court a woman or develop a friend, I happily choose them, blithely unaware or unconcerned that a delta has been opened – unaware that I am no longer fully in control and that I have surrendered myself into a state of *subject-to*, into influence, and into inevitable change. Likewise in choosing a counselor, coach, or teacher: In these cases, we choose cautiously, after vetting and concluding that the change will be contained; in the former, we may offer ourselves up broadly and joyfully, welcoming the exhilaration of the unknown.

In well-functioning social systems, including delta phases, participants are subject to influence by one another. I am subject to influence by my wife, and simultaneously and reciprocally she to me. In delta-phase dialogues, and indeed in formal consulting/teaching situations, the change Agent *should* be influenced by the client in negotiating activities, forms of assistance, and the like. Good practice in many domains from professional development study groups, to Alcoholics Anonymous – all involve systematically developing mutually assisting units. However, in professional practices, the clients – even if at some remove – are subject to the system of influence devised by the change Agent.

Of course *subject to* is a matter of degree. Engagement itself has the surface appearance of a variable but in fact may operate discontinuously, as "quanta," consistent with the widely reported phenomena of stages of acceptance of influence, which advance from tentative to conversion to automaticity. For our immediate purpose, we can say that the proposed universal theory comes into force when the subject (willingly or not) engages in the prescribed activity. However, our concerns extend to understanding how and why change – after the withdrawal of the original change Agents – persists into a stabilized repertoire (or fails to do so).

Successful programs, thanks to the Agent, organizer, or institution, involve Subjects in activities designed to build a new psychosocial system, building intersubjectivity/affinity/propinquity, dialoguing together, and becoming a social network. Successful business plans necessarily achieve their goals through organizations of psychosocial systems, because that is the way the world works. All enterprises of influence and change, including every professional and/or intentional endeavor of influence and change, achieve their goals through organized psychosocial systems: public health; government; occupational therapy; special education; psychotherapy; residential treatment centers; self-help organizations; advertising; lobbying; and rehabilitation. Successful enterprise is typically attributed (as in dog bites man) to cleverness, effort, or good execution of disciplinary knowledge of administration, business principles, social science, and so forth. Although true, these attributions obscure the underlying unity of influence and change principles.

In summary, Subject must indeed be *subject to* the Agent sufficiently to induce engagement in the prescribed shared activity. Otherwise the Delta dynamics cannot operate as described in the Cycle of Social Sorting. The condition of *subject to* may be coerced, seduced, or persuaded, and achieved at close range or en masse by politicians, leaders, and preachers. The attitude of Subject may be resentful or enthusiastic. In any of these situations, Delta process can operate. Without engaging in Agent's prescribed *activity*, however, change is precluded. In the following chapter, this range of Agent-Subject attitudes will be seen in extreme forms of coercion producing successful change programs involving the creation of dangerous criminals, the conversion of captives, and the seduction of underage girls into prostitution.

Of course, the minimum conditions of *subject to* and *activity engagement* do not guarantee change. The practice of Delta is both science and art.

8

A Natural History Museum of Influence
and Change: Dioramas

INTRODUCTION

We turn now to analyses of actualities of influence and change. Ironically, rather than in professional successes, the basic dynamics of influence are best illuminated in dioramas of natural enterprise, that is, in the evolved ways we have influenced one another, whether for good or for ill, whether successful or not.

Therefore, prior to considering professionally organized change operations, I begin with an analysis of reliably successful, phylogenetically or historically evolved "natural" behavior change systems whose stories are known – and one huge, dramatic failure. Each of these intentional programs of change will be discussed in terms of Delta Theory's concepts: psychosocial systems and their phases, development through the zone of proximal of development, and the means and sources of influence.

In this chapter, "A Natural History Museum of Influence and Change: Dioramas," the instances are *natural*, that is, not influenced by theory or professional conventions. Events are *historical*, that is, recorded. To continue the metaphor, they are *dioramas* insofar as I have made these displays seem alive. Included are major undertakings of influence – benevolent and malevolent, inadvertent and unintended, successful and incompetent – each of them on the historical record. It is a fair challenge to Delta Theory, asking it to plausibly and usefully explain a wide range of significant operations of influence and change across historical time, as well as in the present.

ABORIGINAL AMERICANS VS. THE UNITED
STATES OF AMERICA

For notable examples of influence attempts gone right and gone wrong we can turn to no more dramatic contrasts than those involving Aboriginal

Americans versus the expanding United States of America. Wretched failures of U.S. social policy toward Native Americans has plagued us since the first European colonists encountered the resident "Indians." Influence and change, as practiced by Native Americans themselves, has meanwhile achieved some startling successes.

U.S. public policy toward the Indians fluctuated but always failed, even at efforts of extermination. At times, the United States wanted to educate Native Americans for their benefit. It never succeeded. The merciless attempt to use public education to destroy Native culture also failed. Every attempt at influence and change of Native American populations by Euro-American institutions has been impotent. This includes the infamous boarding schools of the early twentieth century, into which Indian youth were forced. The boarding schools did wreak intentional havoc on Indian native languages by forbidding their use and inadvertently deeply wounded the cultural continuity of parenting skills, but the boarding schools' academic successes were slight, and their purpose of destroying Indian identity failed utterly.

Our theoretical opportunity is to examine the successful instances of influence and change achieved by Native Americans themselves in the same domains that U.S. attempts failed and continue to fail. Two such successes are richly documented from the seventeenth through the nineteenth centuries.

Education and the Cherokee Syllabary

Sequoia, a Cherokee Indian in the nineteenth-century United States, accomplished one of the great individual intellectual feats in recorded history. He invented a complete orthography[1] for an oral language, and within a blink of history's time his people became literate (Foreman, 1938; Montheit, 1984; [Walker, 1969; 1984; Walker & Sarbaugh, 1993]). Perhaps because of my minor quantum of Cherokee blood, I want to praise the great Sequoia,[2] but that is not the purpose here. One of the world's signal triumphs of a whole people was the Cherokee achievement of a virtually immediate universal literacy. How was such a feat of influence and change brought about? How did the schools accomplish such a heroic feat of education?

---

[1] The Cherokee syllabary is a form of writing in which eighty-five "letters" each stand for a whole syllable (except for the letter "s").

[2] Recent archeological discoveries reveal fascinating details of Sequoia's early development of his orthographic characters (Powell, 2009).

They did not. Schools had nothing to do with it. How did the Cherokee leadership, their families, and communities organize their literacy learning? Cherokees learned literacy in activity at the fireside and the roadside. In the 1820s, thousands of illiterate Cherokees were teaching each other wherever families were – in their cabins and on the trails. Families taught each other and learned together. Reliable stories exist for hundreds of children and adults who learned to read and write in several days or weeks. Ninety per-cent of Cherokees became literate within ten years of Sequoia's invention, and schools had no part in it. The Cherokee Syllabary was

> never taught in schools. The people have learned it from one another; and that too without books, or paper, or any of the common facilities for writing or teaching. They cut the letters, or drew them with a piece of coal, or with paint. Bark, trees, fences, the walls of houses, &c., answered the purpose of slates.
>
> That the mass of a people, without schools or books, should by mutual assistance, without extraneous impulse or aid, acquire the art of reading, and that in a character wholly original, is, I believe, a phenomenon unex-ampled in modern times. (Foreman, op. cit, p. 29)

Cherokee literacy was achieved with dramatic suddenness through delta-phase psychosocial systems. Existing delta-phase systems of families were employed, but also ad hoc systems developed even by strangers who united in activity settings to assist one another to learn to read and write their Cherokee language. The semiotic processes of learning word representations together in learning-groups of overlapping membership created an inter-subjectivity and interpersonal communicative capacity that contributed to an overall Cherokee tribal cultural identity that was maintained through the activities and valuation of reading and writing their own language.

Traditional American schools, in which the delta phase is assumed to exist, have insufficient joint activity, dialogue, and provision of assistance. To this day, they fail to produce competitive reading proficiency in Native American children.

Of particular interest in this diorama is the rapidity and enthusiasm with which the Cherokee embraced the goal of literacy and threw themselves into activities *subject to* the expanding number of Agents of change. Sequoia's own influence and change campaign began by finding a way to convince tribal leaders that reading and writing were real and of value. The break-through event was an arranged participatory demonstration to the leaders. Sequoia asked the leaders to make a statement to him, which he would then transmit to his daughter by means of an inscription. Representative leaders then carried the inscriptions by representative leaders to his daughter (his first pupil in Cherokee literacy). She was many yards distant, unable to see or hear Sequoia. When she read the inscription to the leaders, using the same words the leaders had dictated to her father, the entire audience was stunned, the demonstration was undeniable, and the enthusiasm for learning this literacy became an avalanche.

Like other persuasion events (including advertising), Sequoia attempted to bring people into a *subject-to* relationship in which they would engage in prescribed activities. Persuasion is often designed to disrupt beta-phase psychosocial systems into alpha, in the hope that changes may eventuate. Persuasion and advertising often attempt to create aspirations toward new identity and membership in more desirable – that is, glamorous, successful, or powerful – psychosocial systems. In the Cherokee literacy instance, the effort was so successful because Sequoia enlisted his first audience into a shared activity setting through which his subjects began to share with him a belief and values intersubjectivity.

Both among the Cherokee and Native Hawaiians in the nineteenth century, literacy was very quickly and widely perceived as extremely desirable as an economical and accurate means to create historical records, particularly of lineage, thus easing the rigorous demands of the memorization required by oral histories. Rapid and widespread literacy was the result. Broadsides and native language newspapers were widely read. Once the native languages were suppressed in public education and the use of native language forbidden in boarding and private schools, native populations' literate proportion shrank. Reading and writing were no longer seen as instruments of achieving cultural goals.

Retention and Conversion of Captives

For four hundred years, New World schooling failed, and continues to fail, to "educate" Indians. During that same period, Indians succeeded in socializing not only themselves, but also their white captives. They did it by establishing an integrated system of delta-phase psychosocial systems. We have records of the processes they employed. Here is a testimonial from Benjamin Franklin, a major figure of the Enlightenment. He was statesman, scientist, inventor, and writer – and also was an early behaviorist who kept a self-assessment record of his progress toward personal goals. Thus we must take his observations seriously, as in his 1753 letter to Peter Colinson:

> When an Indian child has been brought up among us, taught our language, and habituated to our Customs, yet if he goes to see his

relations and make one Indian Ramble with them, there is no perswading him ever to return. [But] when white persons of either sex have been taken prisoners young by the Indians, and lived a while among them, tho' ransomed by their Friends, and treated with all imaginable tenderness to prevail with them to stay among the English, yet in a Short time they become disgusted with our manner of life, and the care and pains that are necessary to support it, and take the first good Opportunity of escaping again into the Woods, from whence there is no reclaiming them.[3]

Not all captives were gently influenced to change their behavior to the Indian pattern; some were held as slaves and coerced. Many were captured to replace lost tribal members and were drawn into the socialization nexus of the captor tribe.[4] The Indians changed captives into "white Indians." They were more successful with children than adults, but there are reported successes at all ages. Data come from the many personal narratives of former captives (e.g., Derounian-Stodola, 1998; Drimmer, 1961; Zesch, op. cit.).

The activity settings into which the captives were incorporated were designed to increase intersubjectivity – that is, to come to understand and value the world in the Indian way. Thus every specific activity setting included development of the captives' use of the captors' language. These joint activities were broad and thorough, drawing the captives into the routines of Indian life. Each joint activity of captive and captors included a thorough teaching of language, communication through ceremonial and other forms of visual symbolism, and a full discussion of values in the context of activity. Whether captives were learning the skills of bow and arrow, tracking, tanning, or doing laundry, their performance was fully assisted by modeling (ample opportunity for observational learning) followed by performance feedback and, almost invariably in the successful instances, loving support and dialogue with a provided/adopted mother or lover. This interlocked set of activities and the facilitating psychosocial systems created a broad Delta condition.

Even if instituted after an initial period of coercion and slavery, with few exceptions, this system achieved a permanent alteration of the captive's behaviors, values, and identity.

---

[3] (Benjamin Franklin to Peter Colinson, May 9, 1753, in Leonard W. Labaree et al., eds., *The Papers of Benjamin Franklin*. (New Haven, 1959), 4:481–482; quoted in Axtell 1981, p. 172.

[4] This was particularly true during the Comanche wars with German settlers in nineteenth-century Texas (Zesch, 2004)

MALIGN-PURPOSED INFLUENCE

Human depravity and human transcendence work through the same processes. The difference lies in the goals of influence. Delta Theory must also encompass the malign to meet the requirements of unification and universalism. The dynamics of malign influence must be recognized and accounted for in order to defend ourselves against it and to take care of those we socialize, both as individuals and society.

A unified theory requires common explanations for influence and change across settings and purposes, including not only benign change efforts, but also those of malign intention. The following examples are four settings of malignity and, moreover, evil.

Recruitment and Socialization of Underage Prostitutes

Interstate crime syndicates systematically recruit underage females into prostitution, then socialize, organize, and control them.[5] The process is heartless, deceitful, exploitative, and corrupting. On a moral level, robbing these young girls of their youth and potential is irredeemably reprehensible. As a system of influence and change, it is a masterpiece of design. The system can be sketched quickly in Delta terms. Underage young female Subjects are covertly assessed for their needs and susceptibility. They are then gradually seduced into a new delta-phase psychosocial unit, first by a male pimp, then into the larger psychosocial system of other recruits. The girls' ties to the prerecruitment psychosocial systems of friends and family are weakened and finally ruthlessly severed by pimps moving the young prostitutes to work in a distant city. Their participation in psychosocial systems are then and thereafter exclusively in the prostitution ring. Attempts to find other friendships or activities are prevented by force. During this progress of socialization by the Agent/pimp and later also maintained by their psychosocial system of sister prostitutes, their attitudes and beliefs undergo such radical transformation that even when they are older and the crime syndicate is finished with them, most are reluctant and/or incapable of leaving "the game." This system of influence and change is standardized and enforced by the bosses of the pimps.

The details of the influence reveal a systematic exercise of the dynamics of psychosocial influence systems. In the assessment phase, pimps observe

---

[5] This section is based on the work of Natalie Crespo (1997, 2007); Crespo & Dowrick, 2007.

the girls, in settings such as shopping centers, looking for likely Subjects exhibiting vulnerabilities: poverty, homelessness, low self-esteem, greed, or feelings of being unaccepted or unloved. These vulnerabilities are made more likely by the usual risk factors: an impaired or dysfunctional family psychosocial unit, a lack of positive role models, or a lack of prosocial activities in existing psychosocial systems. These conditions describe unstable alpha-phase systems. Once the Subject is "marked," the new criminal delta psychosocial system begins. This new system is masterfully designed.

Propinquity. The pimps go where the girls are: schools or their perimeters, malls, or other places where early adolescent girls congregate. This allows the pimp to initiate joint activity.

Joint Activity. The pimp makes a date with his intended Subject. They go where she likes to go and do what she likes to do, except at a more expensive and glamorous level. They date again. They talk. He romances her. She believes he loves her. He has learned what she wants: money, affection, or understanding. He gives it to her.

Intersubjectivity. She believes he thinks and feels as she does. Through his influence, she comes more and more to understand events and value activity settings as he intends.

Affinity. She is drawn more and more to his company. Other relationships are weakened. She really only wants to be with him.

Propinquity is increased, and the game whirls on.

The zone of proximal development. Agent induces the Subject into sex for money in gradual steps. The pimp first asks the girl to have sex with his friend, just this once – he needs her to do this favor for his friend. Next she will be asked to sell a sexual encounter for money, because he really needs cash now. The process is repeated again and again. Her gradual acceptance that sex for money is a reasonable activity is also strengthened by praise from her pimp, who "loves" her. As other young prostitutes from the pimp's string are introduced to each other, and they begin joint activities (though each believes that the same pimp is her boyfriend), they come to reinforce each other's views of their world and their places in it. A stable beta phase psychosocial system is in place, and continues (absent the introduction of some opposing force).

Means of Influence. Within the psychosocial influence system, a range of means is employed. Contingency management during the seduction stage is positive; during the later stable stages, violations of instruction are severely punished. Verbal means of influence are rich: clear instructions, questioning, and feedback against the pimp's standards. But the dominant means of influence is the contingent withholding and awarding of the pimp's attention and "affection."

Soon each is in Stage II of the zone of proximal development, in which they influence themselves, giving themselves instructions, praise and scolds in the internalized voice of the pimp. Soon the stage of automaticity is reached, in which they no longer talk to themselves, they merely act. Their psychosocial system, pimp and girls, has then entered the stable beta phase.

Programs to rescue or influence prostitutes away from their system generally attempt to reverse the processes of induction.

The Creation of Dangerous Violent Criminals

The criminologist Lonnie Athens designates *dangerous violent criminals* as those who commit heinous violent crimes. His theory and research describes the social-influence processes that produce them. This work has two levels of pertinence to Delta Theory.

First, Athens's inquiries employ the method of universals. His data are life-history interviews of incarcerated dangerous violent criminals, all conducted in conditions of maximum security yet daunting in difficulty and often dangerous to Athens himself. From these interviews, he extracted patterns from the inmates' gradual development of their violence and criminality. He has posited four stages in that development: *brutalization, belligerency, violent performances,* and *virulency,* which describe the developmental processes through which violence is taught and learned, that is, the process by which ordinary men and women, boys and girls, are turned into murderers. Athens further notes that "stages" is the correct concept, because each subject progresses through the four experiences in that order; and his theory asserts that no one becomes a dangerous violent criminal unless all four stages are completed. The fully developed dangerous violent criminal is, by definition, one who will (without hesitation) kill anyone who (however mildly) provokes him or her.

The original book describing the evidence and articulating the theory is Athens's *The Creation of Dangerous Violent Criminals* (1992).[6] The Pulitzer Prize–winning Richard Rhodes[7] has provided for general audiences a masterly account of Athens's work, *Why They Kill: The Discoveries of a Maverick Criminologist* (1999). "Maverick" is apt; Athens's work and method has been

---

[6] Subsequent elaborations and additional evidence may be found in Athens, 1997; and Athens & Ulmer, 2003.

[7] Rhodes (1986).

criticized,[8] but his descriptions are far more detailed and dynamic than the typical sociological assertions about what leads to criminal behavior. There have been, to my knowledge, no published exceptions to Athens's propositions since their publication.[9] By rule of the universalist methodology (there being no identified "white crow"), his theory continues to stand.

Second, the influence on youth to change them into dangerous violent criminals should yield to a Delta Theory analysis. That is, the developmental trajectory should consist of activity settings orchestrated or enacted by Agents who influence subjects to develop repertoires of aggression and violence. Does Delta Theory illuminate this tragic course? If so, what added value might this unified theory bring to Athens's domain-specific one? I discuss his theory in depth because it is detailed, extensive, and fully articulated, and thus appropriate for considering the relationship between a unified Delta theoretical account and a thorough specific-domain theoretical account. Before discussing this relationship further, let us consider his theory itself.

Significant members of the young yet-to-be criminals' psychosocial units (members of immediate families or equivalents) systematically and (eventually) intentionally influence their young charges to develop belligerency so that others fear them; influence them to perform violence often enough to maintain that fear; and influence them to use violence as intimidation, retaliation, or merely because they can. Regardless of whether the Agents in the delta-phase psychosocial systems consciously intend to make murderers, they develop in their Subjects a readiness for potentially lethal violent performance that makes criminal outcomes almost inevitable.

Brutalization. In the first stage of influence, Agents themselves brutalize these child and adolescent Subjects and teach them to brutalize others. Brutalization has three elements: violent subjugation, personal horrification, and violent coaching. *Violent subjugation* may be either coercion or retaliation; in both settings, Agents use violent battery until the subject experiences terror, panic, and hopelessness. Once the battery finally ceases,

---

[8] For example, Joyce Carol Oates (1999) complained of Athens's interviews from memory and deciphering of quickly taken notes, unassisted by tape recording. She also found his subjects' stories to smack of rehearsal and self-glorification. Soon thereafter, other methods have been applied in violentization studies: questionnaires using items drawn from Athens's criminals interviews (Rhodes, Allen, Nowinski, & Cillessen (2003); and post hoc violentization analyses of lengthy analyses of large numbers of violent incarcerated youth (Jarjoura & Triplett, 2003).

[9] More recently, Athens has published a new case study, coauthored with the Subject (Athens & Starr, 2003). Their account fully accords with his theory.

these feelings are succeeded by torments of humiliation and fantasies of retaliatory, even murderous, vengeance. *Personal horrification* occurs when the Subject witnesses an Agent violently subjugating another member of the psychosocial unit; the Subject experiences rage against the perpetrator, which quickly turns to self-loathing for the inability or unwillingness to intervene. In *violent coaching*, the intentionality of brutalization is explicit. Agents (most often more senior family members) use every means of influence to teach the subjects that it is good and right to use violence against an antagonist. Subjects are forced to use violence against antagonists or face violence by the coach against themselves. Violence is then praised and further encouraged.

Belligerency. In the stage of belligerency, the Subject's problem crystallizes consciously. Here I quote Athens (1992) posing the typical self-questions and answers by the Subject:

> "What can I do to stop undergoing any further violent subjugation and personal horrification at the hands of other people?" ... The real solution that finally dawns upon the subject is to begin taking violent action himself against other people who unduly provoke him. ... The belligerency stage ends with the subject firmly resolving to resort to violence in his future relations with people ... the subject has now reached the plateau of his development where he is ready and willing to injure badly or even kill someone, should the proper circumstances arise. (pp. 59–60).

Violent Performances. The belligerent Subject now awaits only provocation sufficient to trigger a violent and potentially lethal performance. That provocation will certainly include a threat of violence or subjection of the Subject or someone in Subject's intimate psychosocial unit. In imagining the prospect, he or she is haunted by whether the courage can be found to actually perform violently. When the provocation comes, and Subject attacks the antagonist, the immediate consequences have profound effects on Subject's further development toward dangerous criminality. A victory over the antagonist will make similar attacks more probable, but even a defeat can produce a resolution that next time Subject will be even more violent – as violent as is required to win. Every victory by violence increases the likelihood of further violence. "Nothing expands a person's determination to be violent more than the repeated successful performance of violent action" (Athens, 1992, p. 71).

Virulency. The final stage of the development of dangerous violent criminals is termed *virulency* by Athens. Subject has now prevailed decisively over an antagonist whom he has seriously wounded by physical violence.

Athens points out that no matter whether Subject takes satisfaction in the victory, that victory will have no lasting impact unless the full significance is impressed upon on the Subject's mind by other people. Members of Subject's primary (and sometimes also secondary) psychosocial units become aware of the violent victory, and their opinions of it shape the Subject's own opinion of his performance. The Subject finds him or herself suddenly viewed very differently by psychosocial group members. Depending on the severity of the injuries to the antagonist, family and friends may now see the Subject as courageous, but also perhaps as "out of control," a "violent crazy man," or "insane." People take precautions, as though Subject is genuinely dangerous. "The subject has now reached the critical point in his violence progression where he has experienced violent notoriety and the social trepidation which it brings ... the subject must now decide whether to embrace or reject this personal achievement" (Athens, op. cit, p.74).

Subject embracing violent action sets in motion the final steps of virulency and completes the development of the dangerous violent criminal. Feelings of invincibility flood the consciousness of Subject, who then resolves to be even more violent, in the future to grievously wound or kill antagonists that stand in the way. Thus, psychosocial relationships and systems begin to change. Avoided by old friends and some family, Subject may become for a time a social outcast. New malevolent groups who value a violent repute welcome Subject, who has now completed the four stages and become a dangerous violent criminal.

The processes Athens describes are clearly consistent with Delta Theory. The four stages of brutalization, belligerency, violent performances, and virulency settle comfortably onto a diagram of the zone of proximal development. All means of influence are applied by Agents to Subject with a diabolical intuitive sensitivity to developmental progress toward the independent, automatic performance of criminal violence. Every means of influence is used by Agents in the basic familial psychosocial delta-phase unit to develop the repertoires and valuations of violence. Subject is not allowed to escape, is violently made subject to and forced to perform Agent's instructions, and is taught to believe that he or she can escape violent attacks in the future only by being more violent than encountered antagonists.

When Subject's own violence exceeds his or her psychosocial unit's tolerance, the psychosocial unit rifts into alpha phase. Subject departs that unit and drifts into other psychosocial units, drawn by propinquity and comfortable intersubjectivity into a group with whom he can engage in joint activity that includes and endorses violence. At that point in his progress through the zone of proximal development, Subject has reached Stage III, automaticity, and is ready to kill.

Military Training

Athens and Rhodes both emphasize that these universal processes are highly similar to those employed by trainers of police and armies, except that the final stage of virulency is ordinarily prohibited. Influence toward potential violentization is of course necessary in the training of ordinary soldiers. Delta Theory would predict a strong similarity in the activity settings and means of influence practiced by Agents influencing young dangerous criminals and new soldiers. Delta would also predict a major difference: Soldiers must also be socialized to restrain their violence to appropriate settings and appropriate authority. Sanborn's (2003) essay explores a comparison between the violentization of criminals and the violentization of soldiers. The parallels appear to support a correspondence in the influence activities of the two groups up to a point, but the military does not want to produce the explosive nondisciplined violence that characterizes the development of dangerous violent criminals, and so stops short of influence activities that would develop unrestrained violence. Sanborn's analysis explores this comparison across several armies, using Athens's categorical stages of development. His conclusions map exactly onto the Delta Theory hypothesis of that difference.

Reichstag Death Squadrons

Nazi Germany turned mobs of soldiers into *SS-Einsatzgruppen* death squads. Richard Rhodes (2002) has also told this story authoritatively through exhaustive research into the training and discipline of the Nazi death squads and an original analysis using the theory of Lonnie Athens (Rhodes, 1999, op. cit.). Rhodes demonstrates how virulency was finally developed in the SS-Einsatzgruppen death squads, leading to their mindless rampages of sadistic slaughter.

Why tell this story, even the reading of which can produce horrification? Rhodes answers in the preface that it must be placed on the human record. For those who can stomach it, the reading of Rhodes's analysis of Einsatzgruppen methods reveals like nothing else the apparently limitless potential for evil of malign psychosocial systems' capacity to develop malign repertoires and values. The involvement of soldiers in the joint activity of slaughter, the development of common discourse about their activities, the developing of intersubjectivity among them – these are a horrific example of the Delta influence-and-change processes.

How could such a thing happen? Using Lonnie Athens's theory of violentization of dangerous criminals (see earlier), Rhodes analyzes the violent criminalization of the Nazi war of extermination. He discusses this violentization at three levels: (1) the shared experiences of masses of Germans of early violentization in family and school; (2) the specific biographical analysis of the early violentization of the dangerous criminals Adolph Hitler and Heinrich Himmler; and (3) the recruitment and training of the German military – particularly the SS-Einsatzgruppen, the squads labeled the "Masters of Death."

During the early twentieth century, parental discipline in Germany was commonly violent. In German schools, for far longer than in other European pedagogies, severe corporal punishment persisted and was, according to many autobiographies, enforced by frequently sadistic teachers, producing widespread student suicides (Rhodes, 2002, p. 73).

This zeitgeist produced a generation of German citizens brutalized and to varying degrees violentized in childhood; thus the citizenry – both angry and vengeful during the post-defeat "humiliations" after World War I – was sympathetically responsive to the increasingly murderous policies of its leaders.

Rhodes uniquely assembles early biographical details of the childhood and early lives of both Hitler and Himmler. They read like case histories of Athens's dangerous criminals, each brutalized by their primary psychosocial units of family and school, and each brought to the stage of brutalization. Neither appears to have developed into successful violent performance, but both participated vicariously as messenger or desk officer. Yet both were violentized sufficiently to make them eager and deeply gratified by ordering others to kill.

Many of those so ordered were ready and willing to accept days of the grossest murdering. Laid over the cultural norm of the brutalization in childhood, military recruits were subjected to training uncommonly severe and sadistic. As discussed previously, militaries must constrain their members to *defensive* violence, as military training itself, particularly in the Wehrmacht, contained the early stages of violentization. As the death squads continued to kill after days of slaughter, the SS-Einsatzgruppen could constrain their troops from random reactive murder only by using ever more brutal methods of punishment and restraint. Thus, even though it seems in reading this chronicle that brutality could not possibly further escalate, it did.

The early psychosocialization into violence and the condoned and ordered murdering accomplished by shared activity and vicious justifications were a perfect witches brew of malign influence and horrific change. All those thousands of mass murderers were once children.

Universalism: Disciplinary and Cross-Disciplinary

There remains to be considered the relationship of Athens's universal theory, developed for explaining a crucial phenomenon in criminology, and Delta Theory, which attempts to encompass (but not supplant) Athens's in a larger-universe view. The cross-value of the two universal theories may differ. Athens and Rhodes have provided clear, extreme instances of systematic and successful malign influence operations, thus strengthening Delta's claimed universalism. Thus their work is invaluable to mine.

Does Delta make any contribution to a well-realized disciplinary theory such as that of Athens and Rhodes? Their theory is organic to the phenomena it describes in method, subjects, and events, and therein lays its strength for understanding and prevention. If Delta Theory has value, it is not to replace disciplinary theories that are organic to their phenomena but to assist them. Whether Delta's general analysis has utility for policy or practice of criminology is for criminologists to judge. However, that Athens's theory is found to be congruent with Delta's general, universal theory of influence and change certainly adds another level of credibility to violentization formulations. Ulmer (2003) has suggested the benefits of attaching specific disciplinary theories such as Athens's to more general theoretical structures in social science.

We may now return to consideration of benign influence and change.

CULTURE-BASED DELTAS

Ho'o'ponopono

Ho'o'ponopono is a traditional (and currently practiced) activity setting of Native Hawaiians that is rooted in historical Polynesian culture. Ho'o'ponopono is the Hawaiian process of setting things right and bringing the person's life back into its proper balance with the gods (or God), nature, and the community. In our theoretical language, the purpose of the activity is to restore the harmony of beta to an alpha phase by the creation of shared activity for an ad hoc psychosocial system. A large number of participants may be present in the meeting(s), typically the members of the extended family or *'ohana* (the group that shares resources and responsibilities). An elder leads the event. Prayers, invocations of Hawaiian values, ceremonial elements, and other symbols are salient. Emotions are expressed freely. Each person speaks until some felt consensus on a solution emerges. The solution is not like a "treatment plan." Neither is it a cathartic session only.

The resolution results in restoration or development of interpersonal relationships that will naturally involve alterations in behavior and/or attitude, as enacted in particular activities of daily routines (Mokuau, 2007, 1990).[10]

Ho'oponopono is an activity setting that evolved in the eco-niche of island life, a closed economy in which the exchange of goods (e.g., fish for starches) was vital to mutual survival. Departures and in-migration were minimal. Efficient dispute resolution and the restoration of harmony and productivity required the influence and change of the many people involved in the close and inescapable weave of relationships. The social organization of Hawaii society has survived modern radical shifts in commerce and transportation, and so has *Ho'oponopono*.

Ho'oponopono is neither group psychotherapy nor family therapy, which are activity settings that arose within a quite different ecocultural niche. In contemporary mental health and community development settings in Hawaii, the prescription of *ho'oponopono* is increasing. Hawaiian activists are working to reestablish a center of *pu'uhonua* (traditional place of refuge) for nonviolent offenders as an alternative to incarceration. The fundamental activity of the center would be *ho'oponopono* (McNarie, 2005).

This influence activity comports easily with Delta Theory: When a beta condition has deteriorated to alpha, there is available a delta-based activity setting that has evolved to restore the beta condition. The activity setting is commensurate with social roles and behaviors in Hawaiian society, as are the means of influence/assistance employed in the activity.

This is an illustration of fitting influence and change to the repertoires and activity structures of the subjects' culture (Gallimore & Goldenberg, 2001). Not every problem finds such a ready-at-hand culturally based activity setting. For example, the redesign of classrooms for effectiveness in teaching early literacy to Native Hawaiian children required the careful construction of school-based instructional activities that met Hawaiian social, linguistic, and behavioral strengths and preferences but did not occur in the daily routines of many Hawaiian homes and communities (Tharp & Gallimore, op. cit.).

Navajo "Sings"

In conceiving the task of corrective social influence to be the strengthening or restoration of alpha-phase psychosocial systems to beta phases of stability and solidarity, there can be no more direct and formalized means

---

[10] A similar process is known as *ijoga* in Samoa (Barnes, 2007).

than the healing "sings" of the Native American Navajo. In the treatment of almost any symptom of distress, the restoration of social harmony is an immediate imperative.

Navajo religion consists of a rich complex of oral tales of creation and the after-eras down to our own period of the Earth-Surface people. The celebration of the religion consists of the recitation of the tales – "bardic" in Western terms – in two settings: informal storytelling by elders and the formulaic recitations of the healing ritual tales, almost entirely in the "sings" or "ways" organized ad hoc for healing and performed by medicine men. The healing rituals are public and many ceremonies and myths have been translated and published.

The most serious disturbances – sickness, social conflict, and spiritual malaise – require one of their many formal ceremonies. Medicine-men practitioners specialize in one or more sings or ways, each appropriate for certain syndromes or causes of disharmony. The sings are expressed through recitation of creation myths and value-laden stories, an activity setting including primarily the medicine man and the Subject. This semiprivate activity is embedded in elaborate interclan social events that bring together members of the Subject's two clans (those of Subject's two parents):

> Curing rites, often referred to as "sings," reenact the creation of the world through myth, song, prayer, and drama, and place the patient in this recreated world, closely identifying him with the good and power of various deities. These deities are, in the words of Kluckhohn, "charged with positive spiritual electricity" (1949: 370). Ritual identification with them neutralizes the contaminating effect of dangerous things or evil deeds and restores one to the good and harmony of *hózhó*. ... The primary purpose of Navajo ritual is to maintain or restore *hózhó* (Witherspoon, p. 25–35).

There are many kinds of sings; a medicine man may know one or several. During my years of working with the Navajo, I met a mother whose son had recently been sent away to a residential treatment facility after being convicted of grand larceny. For his first home visit, she planned a Lightening Way, an Evil Way, and for good measure, a prayer meeting at the church. She had every intention of enrolling herself in parenting classes, but first she intended to organize a Beauty Way for the family's Earth Bundle.

The *Enemy Way* now is the most general all-purpose healing ceremony. The Enemy Way corrects imbalances in a person or group due to contact with non-Navajo, particularly whites. It was developed for those returning from a foreign war (thus *Nidaa'*, Enemy Way). It is also called

"Squaw Dance," but Navajo find that derogatory. The ceremony requires almost a week.

In a Delta Theory analysis, it makes perfect sense that a Navajo, drawn into new activity and developing intersubjectivity with an alien psychosocial system, may be expected to develop ideas and actions considered not Navajo. The Enemy Way constitutes an intense and extensive reminder and draws Subject into a complex activity schedule among Navajo people and values.

> There is a meeting night to start the ceremony. Most of the relatives and friends of the patients will come to the meeting night. It is usually on a Monday. The visitors and relatives will come into the hogan and make donations. Because the hogan is small and not everyone will fit, there will be some people standing outside. The people will talk about the ceremonial process ... a number of horseback riders join the patient carrying the staff (to the chosen medicine man). The rest of the people that don't have horses will follow the riders in their vehicles. This is a spectacular sight to see on the Navajo Reservation roads in the summer: a convoy of trucks and cars decorated with colorful yarn. The horseback riders will arrive at the hogan of the medicine man to receive the decorated staff. The main patient gets off his horse and comes into the hogan (to) hand the staff over ... (the) medicine man will sing a receiving song. Following this, the traditional food is served to all people that came. (Dennison, 2005)

The public portion of the ceremonies includes social dancing in the final evening, the culmination of seven days of singing by the medicine man, the sand painting, the horse-and-ribbon ceremonies, feasting and singing around the bonfire, and the Saturday-afternoon clan feast. Of course, the social dancing is also a social function and an opportunity for meeting and courtship, but these dances are organized as a follow-up activity to the healing sings.

Most of those at the event will never see the small enclosure where the sacred reconciliations are being held, never see the sand painting in front of the singer, the colored grains he poured onto the earth floor to form an icon of the narrative being chanted. It is essential that the prayer-tales be recited, but that is the medicine man's task, not the duty of the other attendees, who are occupied with social events – arrival ceremonies with the horses, feasts, or dancing. Healing is assisted by all these activities: through the chants, the sand paintings, the medicine man, the gathered solidarity of both clans, and the restoration of social and cosmic harmony – the smallest and the largest systems restored to a satisfying, stabilizing beta.

A NOTABLE HISTORICAL FAILURE: AMERICAN
SCHOOL DESEGREGATION

Gordon Allport's *contact theory* provided much of the theoretical rationale for the early work on improving race relations after the 1954 *Brown v. Board of Education* decision. For reduction of prejudice, Allport himself prescribed four conditions for the contact situation: (1) The members of the two groups hold equal status within the contact situation regardless of the actual distribution of power in the wider social context; (2) they would need to cooperate (3) in an effort to achieve a shared goal; and (4) the contact would be supported by local authorities, customs, and/or norms (Allport, 1954).

It is unfortunate that social science had not yet fully perceived the conditions that create "equal status" and the "perception of common interests and humanity." By pouring diverse students into the same schools, desegregation enforced propinquity between races, but this propinquity resulted in little joint productive activity with accompanying dialogue, and therefore little intersubjectivity and little perception of common interests and humanity. No matter how sanctioned or by whom, propinquity will not produce the harmonies of intersubjectivity. That requires working together. As it was, the typical result has been de facto resegregation of ethnic groups within schools' lunchrooms, auditoriums, classrooms, playgrounds, and psychosocial systems.

Enforced desegregation plans have virtually never provided for school- and classroom-based joint productive activity among diverse students. Within schools, activity groups have been determined by preexisting affinity-based, stable beta-phase psychosocial systems (cliques and ethnic groups, for example) and by "ability" grouping and tracking. The ill effects have been on academic learning and unimproved social integration.

This need not have been so. Since *Brown v. Board of Education*, several instructional reform movements have found that joint activity among cross-ethnic groups has felicitous effects on both academic achievement and interethnic friendship. A review of this body of work may be found in Tharp, Estrada, Dalton, and Yamauchi (2000); interested readers are directed also to Cohen (1994a, b); Cohen and Lotan (1995); Cohen, Lotan, and Leechor (1989); Epstein (1983b; 1989); and Estrada (1997, 2005).

For example, Slavin's seminal work in the *cooperative learning* literature (see Slavin 1985; 1995; 1996; Stevens and Slavin, 1995), although he does not use the concepts, clearly demonstrates that patterns of instructional activity that provide for increased propinquity, joint productive activity, and shared communication among diverse peers can affect student-friendship-selection criteria. Learning activities that involve meaningful, sustained, cross-race activity among students has a positive effect on the development of such relationships. Similar effects can be seen in the work of Cohen (1994a, b) and Cohen and Lotan (1995), especially in the Effective Pedagogy research and development movement, which is directly based on Delta Theory concepts (Tharp et al., 2000, op. cit.; Tharp & Dalton 2007).

In fact, these, in addition to other shared-activity programs, established a persuasive case that education based on cross-ethnic psychosocial systems can indeed improve academic excellence and social harmony. None of these programs, however, has yet been accepted into mainstream educational policy.

On a theoretical level, Slavin has linked the good effects of cooperative learning to contact theory, arguing that a number of Allport's conditions for reducing prejudice are met. However, Allport's theory is fatally flawed by its lack of understanding of psychosocial-system dynamics, especially the key role of activity plus semiotic exchanges in the origination of intersubjectivity and affinity.

PRIMARY SOCIALIZATION

As my final example, I address the most important criterion for a universal theory: It must explain universal natural processes of primary socialization. These examples are from human societies, although it should be observed that nonhuman primate socialization is also well explained by use of many of Delta Theory's concepts, such as repeated participation in activity groups and the zone of proximal development with guidance/social influence.[11]

Although largely naïve with respect to theory, evolved primary socialization across all cultures operates far more reliably than professional efforts.

Among the Nso

What is of interest in Delta Theory terms is not the per se differences among cultures, but rather the psychosocial means by which societies socialize and acculturate their new and young members. Nsamenang and Lamb (1994) have provided unusually specific accounts of these activity settings and semiotic processes among the Nso, a people of the Bamenda Grassfields of

---

[11] For an overview of such studies, see Parker, 2004.

Northwest Cameroon. The Nso values and norms are of collectivism, social intelligence, and progressive (stage-wise) social competence. For these (and other) West Africans, the infant is a "project-in-progress" (Nsamenang, 1992a) – in Delta terms, the infant is launched toward successive overlapping zones of proximal development during which the Nso provide assistance/ influence in a complex and orderly system. The growing child is incorporated into more complex activities and roles, not according to chronological age, but according to advancing social competence. In each of these roles and activities, the child is to be deferent to superiors and elders, including older siblings. All this is organized to foster shared responsibility within family and community. Nso child activity is primarily in peer psychosocial systems. Adults may organize activities, but their influence flows primarily through older siblings who also participate in the activity settings.

"Child care giving generally involves multiage, multi-gender groups with charges ranging in age from 20 months to 6 or 7 years under the supervision and guidance of one or two children (usually girls) ages 8 to 10 years (Nsamenang, 1992b). Although children spend a considerable amount of time in child-to-child interactions and engage in creative activities by themselves, they are still constrained by adult norms" (Nsamenang & Lamb, p. 143) through the older-sibling Mediators of the adult-Agent influence.

During activities, semiotic processes of sign and symbolic language, including terse proverbs and more elaborate cautionary folk tales, serve to create intersubjectivity and create felt identity as a member of the collective, with first responsibility to others. Agents and Mediators influence through modeling, instructing, and explaining both performance and values. Children are expected to observe and imitate and then to rehearse in their own child peer groups (surveilled and mentored by older siblings) in which they play at roles for which they have not yet the social competence to earn assignment. Thus, in this complex of psychosocial systems and activity settings, socialization is a shared responsibility among members of the social network and culture.

Sibling caretaking and the triadic pattern of influence delivery among adult Agents, older-sibling Mediators, and young-children Subjects are by no means unique to the Nso. Nsamenang and Lamb (op. cit) themselves liken much of the Nso system of socialization to that of Hawaiians/ Polynesians. Readers can pursue these similarities by reviewing the discussion of Hawaiian cultural practices of means of influence in Chapter 6, more generally in Tharp et al. (1994), and definitively in Gallimore, Boggs, and Jordan (1974).

"But I Am Your Mother ..."

"Mainstream" socialization in the traditional cultures of Europe and America is typically described as individualist rather than collectivist as among the Nso and Hawaiians. Nevertheless, Euro-American socialization also works through psychosocial systems and joint activity settings with language. Because that form of socialization will be so familiar to most European and American readers, it may suffice here to offer a small case study illustrating the operation of the Delta Theory processes. Note the joint activity, the dialogue, the teaching of values in the context of a meaningful shared activity, the emotional-value-laden influence – all present in a tiny activity typical of those by which we make our children truly ours. This is the way all family socialization operates: influencing and developing behavior, attitude, and values by doing things together and talking about it. Most parents in these cultures are mostly consistent with their general culture, but they also want their children to share their idiosyncratic values, as does the mother in this study. Even though she is bemused by her own contradictions, they are hers, and she wants them to become her daughter's:

FOR A FIVE-YEAR-OLD

A snail is climbing up the window-sill
into your room, after a night of rain.
You call me in to see, and I explain
that it would be unkind to leave it there:
it might crawl to the floor; we must take care
that no one squashes it. You understand,
and carry it outside, with careful hand,
to eat a daffodil.

I see, then, that a kind of faith prevails:
your gentleness is moulded still by words
from me, who have trapped mice and shot wild birds,
from me, who drowned your kittens, who betrayed
your closest relatives, and who purveyed
the harshest kind of truth to many another.
But that is how things are: I am your mother,
And we are kind to snails.

The writer is the distinguished Scottish poet
Fleur Adcock, from her *Poems 1960–2000*
(Bloodaxe Books, 2000).

9

Who Influences? The Triadic Model
of Influence and Change

As we considered in the preceding chapter, the meaning of activity settings may well be different for each participant. This insight brings us abruptly to the most crucial of activity setting elements: *Who* are the appropriate sources of influence? That is, who are the appropriate participants in intentionally designed activity settings for influence and change? Because so many elements in Delta Theory are congruent with unreflective actions of natural life so called common sense – it is almost reflexive for humans in action to pose the question, "Who can I get to influence John?" This is the basic form of the question that Agents address to themselves as they ponder plans for influence.

Agents' answers to that self-posed question may be grouped into three structural types. The first is: "I myself am the person most able directly to influence John." The second answer is: "Those most able directly to influence John are James, Y, and Z. My task as Agent is to indirectly influence John by directly influencing James and/or Y and/or Z." The third structural type answer is: "Present relationships are insufficient to influence John favorably. The entire vectored field of influence in which he operates must be adjusted by my indirect influence." I label these three structure types of psychosocial organization *dyadic, triadic,* and *field vectored.*

ORGANIZING FOR INFLUENCE AND CHANGE: DYADIC DELTAS

The traditional answer to the question of "Who?" by psychologists as professional practitioners of influence and change has been "Me!" Understandably, the most seductive answer type is dyadic, in which Agent directly influences Subject during activity settings that include those two, and most often only those two, as illustrated in Figure 9.1. Dyadic intervention is simple in conception, flattering to Agent's sense of expertise, and by far the model easiest

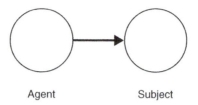

Agent   Subject

FIGURE 9.1. Agent influences Subject directly.

to control. However, influence in the zone of proximal developments requires the assistor to be in close touch with the learner's relationship to the task in the context of joint activity. Opportunities for this knowledge – that is, conditions in which the Agent can be sufficiently aware of the Subject's actual in-flight performing – are seldom available in consulting rooms of professional practice. In classic psychoanalytic or psychotherapeutic practice, analogue relationship activities of conversation take the place of observation of problematic behavior in situ. Assuming that relational repertoires are deeply ingrained, the psychoanalyst assumes that transference of problematic repertoires will occur in the analyst-patient relationship, where it is subject to direct influence by the Agent and from whence it will generalize back into the lived world of the Subject's psychosocial units. For this complex dynamic, there has been more hope than evidence. In similar forms of consulting-room practice – of counseling, coaching, tutoring, and the like – the same structural problem exists: How can activity settings containing only Agent and Subject be used to provide responsive assistance/influence for repertoires to be practiced in psychosocial units *not* containing the Agent?

Professional practice has slowly evolved into expanding the numbers of participants in the office – to couples, families, teams – and in parallel, agential professional practice has expanded the "office" into locations of the natural world, such as homes, workplaces, gymnasiums, and fields, while maintaining the dyadic model. Teachers, supervisors, managers, and trainers, among many others, rely on direct person-to-person influence, Agent to Subject.

All Agents, whether embedded in workplaces or schools or operating independently, will find themselves limited in quantity and content of activity settings that can operate as delta-phase units. And Agents, like members of hosting institutions, are limited by time and costs in the quantity and quality of influence/assistance they can directly offer. When a sports psychologist acts as Agent with the college baseball team, his Subjects being those athletes seeking or assigned his services, he must budget his own time and activities within the strict schedules created by coaches for other purposes. At the other extreme, how many clients can afford or could tolerate a personal psychotherapist for hours each day? Excessive participation of Agent in the activities of clients is sure to cause psychosocial disruption. Therefore it should not be assumed that the quality and quantity of influence/assistance can be provided best by Agents themselves in a dyadic model. To the contrary, if there is a probable best model, it is triadic, and to this model we now turn.

ORGANIZING FOR INFLUENCE AND CHANGE: A TRIADIC MODEL OF ASSISTANCE

The second structure type answer is: "Those most able directly to influence John are James, Y, and Z. My task as Agent is to indirectly influence John by directly influencing James and/or Y and/or Z." Thus Agent's influence is to be delivered indirectly to Subject through one or more Mediators. In all indirect designs, there are three actors: Agent – Mediator – Subject. Thus the Agent influences James and/or Y and/or Z, who in turn influence Subject John, and it is through these Mediators that Agent has effects on John. Of course, the principles and processes through which Agent and Mediators work are drawn from the same universal set of operations, but they may not be the same tools. For example, a professor often influences the induction of a new graduate student into desired laboratory skills and attitudes by working through an advanced-student Mediator. Thus professor influences new-student John by influencing advanced-student James to design appropriate activity settings for John and to influence him by demonstrations, explanations, and joint activity.

TRIADIC DELTAS

In a triadic model of influence and change, the functions are not primarily directing and assessing, but rather providing influence/assistance: The first responsibility of A is to influence/assist B, whereas the first responsibility of B is to influence/assist C. This triad of A – B – C, as illustrated in Figure 9.2, may be embedded in a much longer chain of responsibility, which may extend to x positions. In the final triad, Subject is in position C, whereas the first individual in the chain of x positions, the first A, is Agent. Placing a three-position template over any three successive positions reveals the crucial elements of the model. That is, a triadic template can be fitted to any three consecutive positions. This minimal triad is sufficient to illuminate the structural issues of the model.

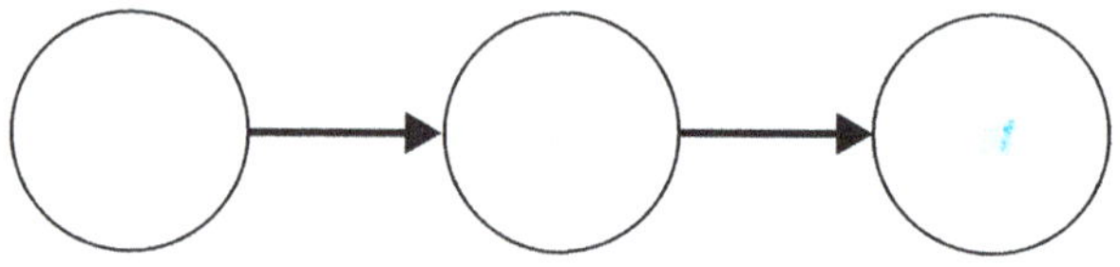

The basic triadic model

A   B   C

Agent   Mediator   Subject

FIGURE 9.2. Agent influences Subject indirectly through Mediator.

What is it that A is to assist B to do? In a school, presumably, the ultimate concern of the superintendent is the pupils, but the superintendent
is separated from them by many levels; the superintendent's direct interaction goes no lower on the organization chart than to the principals – or
to positions even further separated from students. Each position in the
organization is restricted in its contacts to those directly above and below
it in the supervisory line. Therefore, for any triad, *the role of A is to influence B.* Assist B to do what? *To effectively influence/assist C,* and so forth
down the chain for the ultimate benefit of the Subject. Of course, there
may be more than one Mediator in the B position. In the triadic model,
Agent's first focus is on influencing the Mediator(s) that lie between
Agent and Subject in the influence chain; that is, to influence Mediator to
influence Subject.

FIELD-VECTORED DELTAS

The third structural type of psychosocial organization is *field vectored.* An
Agent may concentrate design on modification and/or coordination of
psychosocial systems negatively or insufficiently influencing Subject's goal
development, working entirely through multiple mediators whose psychosocial systems' actions will affect one another.

In 1998, an organization called Save the Children Singapore (SCS)
determined to correct the plight of children of women prisoners and drug
inmates. These children were most often living in poverty, their bond with
mother severed, seldom if ever visiting her. They were subject to multiple
foster placements and suffered a constant fear of separation with an attachment figure, as well as depression, guilt, and grief. Although at least ten social
service agencies had responsibilities for prisoners' children, none had any
interaction with the women's prison or drug rehabilitation center relative

to the children's welfare. The small staff of SCS served as Agent, seeking to influence and change multiple Subjects (the staffs of the ten service agencies and the appropriate staff of the prison and rehabilitation center). This force field of influence was complexly vectored and first set in motion by individual contacts with SCS and authorities from each of the relevant agencies and institutions. A specific program was designed by this group of institutional representatives to facilitate child-mother visitations, including additional activities to strengthen the mothers' voices in their children's welfare. This steering committee quickly developed into its own psychosocial system, providing coordination and mutual support. The members then became Agents within their own agencies, influencing staff Subjects to adopt new procedures and assumptions. At the next level, those staff members were Agent to the foster-parents and others influencing the children.

This entire program was fully operational within two years. Not every initiative so ambitious succeeds at all. SCS credits the success of this field of complex influence to beginning shared activity immediately. The steering committee undertook research by interview, survey, and questionnaire to define the scope of the problem; moved quickly to involve prison and center personnel in program design; and continued to meet and discuss their own agencies' activity in the coordinated program. Their joint activity increased their intersubjectivity and their mutual respect, which made continued coming-together a professional pleasure. Each instituted shared activities within their own agencies and between the agencies and the prison and center. A report of this program's creation and operations can be found in Goh (n.d.).

SELF AS SOURCE OF INFLUENCE IN PRACTICE

A fully successful influence plan requires consideration of the durability of Subject's developed goals after the withdrawal of Agent. This requires that Stage II ZPD self-assisting repertoires be developed to a high level of reliability. In the practice of influence and change, this goal is perhaps the most neglected. In Stage II of the ZPD, individual development lies between the need for social assistance and full automaticity and so is invisible. Psychotherapies and other practices of direct Agent assistance are particularly prone to mistaking Stage II for independence.[1] However, the skills of

---

[1] Cognitive behavior therapies are far more likely to include Stage II repertoires in their influence plans. The behaviors of self-recording of events, self-instructing, and so forth are natural extensions of their specific-behaviors influence approach.

self-assistance comprise the final repertoire of any changing behavior; this repertoire too must be assisted as necessary as the final process of behavior change. Of course, these self-assisting behaviors may then be employed during Stage IV – de-automatization and recursion. Thus the development of self-influencing skills may be seen both as "final treatment" and "inoculation" against subsequent regression.

Self-assisting processes are the same as those provided by more capable others. That is, the identical means of influence are practiced; the zone of proximal development is respected; and psychosocial units are sought and entered to strengthen the probabilities of social support of the emerging repertoires. This is not the place to elaborate specific techniques of self-regulation, which is a mature field of research and development studied for four decades and with readily available handbooks of technique and examples (see, e.g., Tharp & Watson, 2006). Suffice it to say that the processes of self-directions, self-modeling, and self-provided feedback are the most potent self-enacted means of assistance.

What does warrant examination in this context are the ways in which the self-assistor takes on the role of self-Agent as well as self-Subject. That is, the Stage II subject must often take on the tasks of the Agent by arranging for continual social assistance. If there were one diagnostic test for adequacy of Subject's preparation for a successful Stage II, it would be thus: Does Subject have the capacity to find and use assistance when needed?

A few examples (drawn from Watson & Tharp, op. cit.) may clarify the issues of programming the social environment. Pre-commitment means arranging in advance for helpful antecedents to occur. This arrangement can be made when some problem situation is anticipated, especially for those moments of maximum difficulty. Ainslee (1992) points out that pre-commitment refers to any way of arranging in advance for conditions making it more likely that Subject will choose to act in Subject's long-range best interests. This may include posting schedules, setting alarm clocks, and the like. Such tactics also include arranging that others provide cues or reminders. (This may be seen as a triadic model of self-assistance, in which Subject influences Mediator to influence Subject.)

In terms of modeling, Subjects may join psychosocial groups (clubs, classes, etc.) in which experts or like-minded others congregate, to strengthen resolve and to learn further niceties of desired repertoires. In terms of self-influence through contingency management, the subject may arrange that reinforcers not be delivered by the self, but rather are contingently dispensed by Mediators (family, friends, others). Reinforcing effects have been shown to be stronger when mediators are involved in programs of dieting (Israel & Saccone, 1979), smoking cessation (Cohen & Lichtenstein, 1990), and many others.

Creating or joining a psychosocial system that is supportive of Subject's goals is, as theory would predict, an effective tactic for self-influence. Exercisers who have a regular aerobics partner are more likely to stick with their programs long enough to experience real health benefits (Lawson & Rhodes, 1981). Such support groups can be crucial, especially when Mediators in natural relationships are difficult to find. For long-term benefits, plans that involve regular, continuing psychosocial systems have greatest potency (as examples, see Fisher, Lowe, Levenkron, & Newman, 1982; Heinzelman & Bagley, 1970).

INFLUENCE, POWER, AND ORGANIZATIONAL STRUCTURE

Activity settings for change embedded in preexisting, "natural" psychosocial systems have advantages of authenticity and validity, but few natural psychosocial systems are Delta phased. In fact, it is difficult to find stable psychosocial units other than the family in which the purpose is development and change through influence and assistance. Although educational institutions are formally delta purposed, in functioning they are beta seeking, homeostatically functioning, and inefficient in offering direct, responsive, individualized influence and assistance; they therefore seldom operate as effective delta-phased systems.

All organizations have their own purposes and seek primarily their own homeostatic perpetuation. Of course, workplace and all performance-demanding settings may from time to time offer "professional development," "training," or "workshops." Most organizations respond in some way to the task of incorporating and orienting new members. Regulation of new members begins immediately through such systems as orientation and training programs. The acquisition, enhancement, and maintenance of specific individual competencies are the conditions for the survival of the institutions: Mail must be delivered and products manufactured and distributed. Many successful organizations also have settings for enhancement and maintenance of appropriate institutional behaviors: hence workshops, consultants, or retreats. These few and limited settings are organized to influence through "teaching," and so are viewed by managers as different in purpose from other systems for insuring good performance, such as inspections, merit reviews, or performance incentives. All these systems and activities – from orientation programs to salesmen's incentives – involve means of assistance: modeling, contingencies, feedback, instructions, questions, and cognitive structuring. Institutions may apply them self-consciously during "training," but the means of influence such as contingencies and feedback, applied during routine inspections or reviews-and-incentive programs, are considered to be motivational and regulatory. Performance is assessed and differentially rewarded, but little provision of assistance is offered. Employees or recruits can be dismissed. Most institutions carefully weigh the costs of influencing and developing members' repertoires against the likelihood of recruiting better replacements. Nevertheless, workplace interpersonal transactions and shared activities do affect performance and inevitably create patterns of meanings, values, and cognitive structures that perpetuate the culture of the institution (Tharp & Gallimore, 1988).

In the administrative system common to most organizations, individual A directs and *assesses* B, who directs and *assesses* C, and so on, whereas few organizations have similar layered provisions of influence for development and performance improvement. Our initial work in this model was conducted in schools, which might be supposed to be committed delta organizations, purposed for continual provision of influence and change. This is not the case, and schools, like other organizations, direct and assess at every level, from superintendent to classroom teacher. We argued that this structure prevented the professionalization of teaching and, indeed, was organically related to the paucity of teaching interactions in classrooms. We then detailed an alternative organizational structure based on a theory of schooling as assisted performance and the concepts already introduced in this book. Readers interested particularly in educational institutions can find a detailed exposition of the dyadic and triadic models of assistance in the original source (Tharp & Gallimore, 1988).

The triadic model elaborates and enriches the supervisory model but does not replace it. Organizational supervisors must continue to direct and assess, but they may also provide the necessary influence and assistance to provide desirable organizational behavior change. However, in most organizations, the role of assessor is incommensurate with the role of assistor when held by the same person. Supervisees are reluctant to subject themselves to the supervisor if they suspect that highest priority is given to the exercise of power. Therefore, the triadic formula is that the supervisor *provides influence/assistance, but does not necessarily, and usually does not deliver it personally.* Thus the assisting supervisor influences B most often by arranging for influencing resources wherever within or outside the organization they can best be found: Thus workshops, consultants, peer models, discussion groups, and experts of needed competencies.

Influence and change in members of an institution is effected only partially through formal lines of responsibility. Workers often have more influence on one another than does their supervisor. Individuals altogether outside the institution often provide interactions with profound developmental consequences, even for workplace skills. Institutions are bombarded with influences that change members at every point of the formal regulatory chain.

Effective influence does not require authority; indeed, influence is often more effective in the absence of power imbalances. Yet even authorities can assist performance only through the exercise of modeling, contingency managing, feeding back, instructing, questioning, and cognitive structuring. Authority can certainly affect other conditions upon which change depends: the mobilization of attention, the setting of standards, the making available of rewards to use in managing contingencies, and especially the use of authority to create the activity settings in which assistance can really occur. Rather than teaching dependence on authority, it is more nearly the opposite: Indeed, influence is the process upon which authority depends to achieve its aims.

For example, the person in position A may arrange opportunities to bring particular others into contact with B, even though A does not, cannot, or should not wish to provide the specific content of such influence on B. The effective administration of an institution requires many such arrangements. Indeed, A's ultimate impact on C often relies not only on A's good assistance to B, but also on A's accurate knowledge of B's psychosocial system. That knowledge can allow A to creatively alter the system by establishing activity settings that make others' influence on B congruent with A's goals for C.

When emphasizing the actions and responsibilities of A, who influences B for the benefit of C, we must be realistic about the nature of the supervisory chain of command. Very often, A is not as expert as is B in the matter at hand. Yet one need not be more expert in order to provide assistance/influence. In designing activity settings, A may use supervisory authority to arrange activity settings in which joint productive activity will produce the assistance that will increase B's competence. Authority is often indispensable in the creation of new activity settings, and in providing the time, place, and resources necessary for their operation.

A complete analysis of the use of psychosocial system as mediator in a triadic model (see Figure 9.3) requires analyzing Agent's options: (1) choosing one or more of Subject's existing psychosocial systems to influence, or (2) extricating Subject from existing systems and substituting another. These variations, with examples, are the subject of the next chapter.

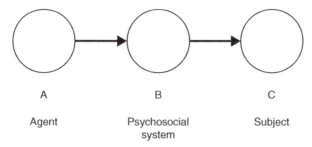

FIGURE 9.3. A psychosocial system as Mediator.

ACTIVITY SETTINGS: NOT ONLY WHO, BUT WHAT THEY DO

Here we must return briefly to Chapter 5's discussion of the activity setting. As the descriptive characteristics of the activity setting, I listed who, what, when, where, and why as design features, but asked to defer until now the discussion of the who (the persons therein) and the what (what they do – the activity itself).

All influence program design begins with Agent considering Subject in his or her vectored field of influence. Who are the sources of influence? Through what psychosocial systems do they operate? Are there psychosocial systems amenable to influence by Agent or Agent's mediators? Or must new mediating members be introduced? Or must Subject be placed into new or alternative systems?

This is the art of influence; it is so natural, it has been practiced intuitively for millennia. Science and the social "engineering" of professional influence have entered the field only yesterday in millennial time. It is a quick sketch of history, but one can see in sociology during the last century the emergence of studies of marriage, of the family, and of networks, as well as the development of the corresponding three "therapies" of marriage, family, and networks. Having studied order and disorder in those domains, researcher/professionals derived strategies for correcting dysfunctional patterns.[2] We psychologists and psychiatrists, meanwhile, noting the interplay of thoughts, feelings, and acts, devised practices of Agent on Subject (based on our science and philosophies). At the most fundamental level, all these approaches have been flawed by a bifurcated approach

---

[2] I myself once did so (Tharp & Otis, 1966).

to the individual and the group, whereas their indivisible unity demands a psychosocial approach to influence and change.

Thus bringing the appropriate people into joint activity is the core of the practice of influence. However, bringing them merely into joint presence is futile if not counterproductive (see the discussion of the failures of school integration in Chapter 8). Thus the efficacy of family therapy, marriage therapy, and network therapy depend on the activity settings of the influence program. Social-science-based contrived assemblages will fail to influence unless there is an employment of knowledge of the workings of psychosocial systems, whether provided by intuition or theory.

This point can be elaborated through the example of *network therapy*. A voluminous literature has been amassed describing an extensive practice of network therapy driven by its practitioners' recognition of the influences exerted by networks in everyday life and a repudiation of the one-to-one conventions of professional practice. In historical analysis, this may well have been a necessary developmental phase. In Delta Theory terms, we would expect bringing together large numbers of individuals, even fifty or more, related to Subject by one, two, or three degrees of separation, to produce a challenge for organizing potent psychosocial-system-based activity settings.

Nevertheless, although efficacy studies of network therapy are rare, the literature of its practice includes many reports of satisfying influence and satisfied Subjects. Of particular interest in this exposition is the endorsement of network-therapy-based programs in Native American communities by distinguished Native American social scientist Teresa LaFromboise and her associates[3] (see, e.g., Red Horse, 1982, 1977).

In Delta Theory terms, these programs find in Native American communities collectivist identities, values, and repertoires that well prepare participants for mobilizing the influence of psychosocial units within and through the larger community-cultural context. We have already considered Navajo sings and Hawaiian *Hoòponopono* as examples of formalized activity-setting complexes organic to the psychosocial structure of their respective cultures. For more individualized societies, however, assembling fifty or more participants offers a considerable challenge to those who hope to organize activity settings, beginning with the first meeting itself.

The possibility of successful influence and change rests on joint activity settings. Unhappy husbands and wives may or may not find useful influence

[3] See, e.g., LaFromboise & BigFoot (1988); LaFromboise, Trimble, & Mohatt (1990).

in marriage therapy; likewise, entire families may or may not be the appropriate participants in crucial activity settings. The outcome of influence rests not solely on the roster of participants, but on the activity settings themselves and their resultant intersubjectivities and affinities. Outcome depends not only on *who* is there, but *what* they do.

10

Basic Tactics and Strategy in Designing Influence

Professional and client domains that have published cases, theory, or research using process concepts of Delta Theory include the following: families managing child disability (Gallimore et al., 1999); literacy development (Goldenberg, Gallimore, & Reese, 2005); psychotherapy (Miltenburg & Singer, 1999; Tharp, 1999); counseling (Portes, 1999); community development (Roberts, 2005; O'Donnell & Tharp, 1990, 1982; O'Donnell et al., 2001, 1993); organizational development (Engeström & Middleton, 1996); delinquency and juvenile justice (O'Donnell, 2003); mentoring (Gallimore, John-Steiner, & Tharp, 1992); self-directed behavior change (Watson & Tharp, 2006); and enhancing parent-school leadership (Bolívar & Chrispeels, 2011.)

Education has been the enterprise most extensively explored using Delta Theory concepts. The research evidence is favorable for their effectiveness in advancing academic engagement and achievement (for reviews of that research, see Tharp & Dalton, 2007; Tharp et. al, 2004, 2000; Tharp & Gallimore, 1988). When a delta condition is stabilized – even at the classroom level or lower – a continuing pattern of successful influence and change flows continuously through curricular and value goals as they advance. However, in transnational schools of the common tradition, the delta phase psychosocial system is the rare exception, principally because of insufficient responsive influence, there being a paucity of joint activity in schools' academics; therefore, there are few opportunities for the development of delta-phased psychosocial systems. Instead, schools are typically organized by an uninterrupted reliance on existent affinities. At least in this respect, transnational schools are much more alike than different.[1]

---

[1] I am arguing the narrow case only: Transnationally, the delta condition is rare. Whether schools transnationally are more alike than different is disputed vigorously, even more so now that the TIMSS video survey of teaching has provided actual evidence over which the debate can be held (see, e.g., Givvin, Hiebert, Jacobs, Hollingsworth et al., 2005;

Although schools for youth have the widest and deepest institutional mandate for influence and change, their typical operational condition – as opposed to their formal responsibilities – is, if at all, only marginally delta; it is best characterized as beta – a condition maintaining relative stability of social class and social organizational functioning. Of course, this is not by intention, but rather through institutionalized habits and ignorance of contemporary developmental theory. I have described this fully elsewhere (Tharp & Dalton, 2007; Tharp et al., 2000): In transnational schools of the common tradition, activity settings allowing a rich quantity and quality of responsive influence; assistance and regulation are appallingly rare; and the same psychosocial systems, as established by neighborhood, culture, and network, continue uninterrupted for years.[2]

The example of education cautions us to beware accepting as evidence of actual functioning any institutional protestations of dedication to human development.

The use of Delta among the influence-and-change professions varies broadly. Among practices, occupational therapy strikes me as closely aligned with the structural requirements of the delta condition. That is, well-practiced occupational therapy works through productive, frequently joint, activity and uses those events as occasions for dialogue and for providing assistance both in general productive skills (attention; organization) and in more general applications to the context of a Subject's larger goals. Much the same can be said for the practices of rehabilitation. As forms of intervention, family-based and home-based treatment strategies influence primary delta-phased situations and so deal with systems of maximum potential potency.

PRINCIPLES AND PROTOCOLS FOR DESIGNING INFLUENCE AND CHANGE

The basic task of the Agent is the organization of appropriate activity settings, that is, specifying who, what, when, where, and why (product or

Heibert, Gallimore, Garnier, Givin et al., 2003; LeTendre et al., 2001; Stigler & Heibert, 1999, 1998.

[2] A 2004 report from the Organisation for Economic Co-operation and Development (OECD) has urged European education systems to better challenge school children, provide stronger leaders for teachers, and place greater emphasis on education rather than administration. "It is our clear impression that neither teachers nor school administrators are entirely clear about where they're going with education," said British professor and lead researcher Peter Mortimer, speaking with the Danish newspaper *Politik*. Educational direction in the United States is equally unclear.

outcome). Activity settings have a goal, the development of appropriate repertoires (behaviors, values) for Subject(s), but Agent must also consider the longer-term potential of those activity settings for evolving into a supportive psychosocial system. Activity settings may be found, utilized as is or revised, or created de novo. That choice requires an inventory and analysis of pertinent existing activity settings, which will always be found embedded in alpha/beta/delta psychosocial systems. Therefore, the diagnostic protocol is for the discovery and understanding of the psychosocial systems in terms of their strength, durability, and flexibility and the dynamics of their activity settings.

Units of Analysis

There are three levels of analysis, and thus a basic unit for each:

1. At the level of Subject(s), the unit of analysis is specific goal repertoires and values, under development through the ZPD
2. At the level of activity, the unit of analysis is the activity settings through which assistance will be provided in the ZPD.
3. At the level of system(s), the unit of analysis is the psychosocial system(s) in which activities are afforded and sustained.

At every level, the unit of analysis is necessarily psychosocial. I prefer that this term not be hyphenated. For many social scientists that requires elaboration. We traditionally separate the psychological from the social, the one referring to the individual, the other to the interpersonal. In Delta Theory, following the fundamental Vygotskian positions, human development is based on the rolling processes of the *social becoming psychological becoming social*. At any point in these cycles of *culture creating personality creating culture*, we can stop motion to measure, describe, and contemplate individual identities; likewise, we may measure, describe, contemplate social systems. However, when we restore focus on the dynamic processes, we see again the roiling unities of psyche and society: interacting, mutually causative, subject to every conceivable positive or negative charge, volatile, interruptible, puzzling – but lawful. And congruent at least metaphorically with Newton's First Law of Motion, beta-phase psychosocial systems too, once set in motion, will continue until some opposing force intervenes. Thus do psychosocial systems also roll on.

Psychosocial systems may be of many sizes. Subjects are usually involved simultaneously in several. Some are purpose-built: graduate seminars, Tai Chi classes for elders, book clubs. Others are more than purpose-specific. Vygotsky first wrote about young children as existing in a general ZPD, with assistance required for all repertoires. Correspondingly, delta psychosocial systems may be general-purposed and sustained. The paradigmatic example is the family, the institution which maintains a systematic but necessarily flexible dedication to supporting, assisting, and influencing its members through long periods of changing developmental goals and circumstance. Other obvious sustained institutional systems include schools, churches, and mosques that attempt to teach and otherwise influence participants without regard to passing time or developmental stages.

By contrast, delta systems of professional practice are typically planned for economically brief time periods, during which provision is made for making the goal behaviors sustainable.

Theoretically, the units of analysis are nested or overlapping. Traditionally, the unit of analysis has been the two person psychosocial system: Teacher and student, player and coach, therapist and client, doctor and patient, teenager and counselor. In my lifetime I have witnessed, in theory and practice, an expanding scope of Agents' activity. Now, the good life coach is more likely to include plans for influencing the entire family system and perhaps even a peer group. For that coach, the unit of analysis might include all individuals/groups who have roles in the influence system. Regardless of tactics, the challenge to the program designer is thus: How to influence those family, peer, or other psychosocial units that will continue to exert influence over the Subject – over *all* his or her repertoires. Existing or emerging psychosocial units are paramount in outcomes focus. The units will continue to seek equilibrium, to reincorporate from deviance, to settle into the beta phase – bringing Subject with them.

Design Protocol

Agent's overall challenge is to design a strategy providing influence for the changing Subject while developing a sustaining psychosocial beta system that can maintain those changes. Thus the task is to provide simultaneous assistance for development of goals and continuing psychosocial units. Actually there are three developmental tasks:

1. Develop goal behaviors to a high level of reliability
2. Develop Stage II ZPD self-assisting repertoires to a high level of reliability
3. Develop a sustaining psychosocial system

This is the overall delta system of change. It must be planned, coordinated, and initially energized by the Agent. An essential criterion for this system is survivability after Agent withdrawal.

BASIC TACTICS OF INFLUENCE AND CHANGE

No matter how much or how little Subjects are motivated for change, all Subjects of all Agents continue to live in other psychosocial systems that variously impede or assist their development goals. The influence between Agent and Subject will be exercised in psychosocial units and their activity settings, as is all social influence. From the point of view of the positions of Agent and Subject in their various potential psychosocial systems, I see five basic tactics for influence-and-change plans.

Tactic 1: Agent influences Subject directly
Tactic 2: Agent influences Mediator to influence Subject
Tactic 3: Agent influences Subject's psychosocial system(s)
Tactic 4: Agent curtails Subject's participation in competing psychosocial systems
Tactic 5: Agent creates or enlists additional psychosocial systems, (delta or beta phase) congruent with Agent's goals.

Of course in the strategy for an individual program of influence, these tactics may be combined, and usually are.

Understanding the dynamics of the flows of influence is certainly necessary to Agents. In Chapter 9's discussion of the sources of influence in zones of proximal development, simple flow diagrams sufficed. In choosing intervention tactics and strategy, however, even more important is understanding the psychosocial systems and activity settings that are the contexts and engines by which change is effected. Thus for this chapter, a different type of diagram is clearer. These Venn representations provide clear reminders of the psychosocial dynamics: Their ovals invoke the psychosocial systems' repetitive self-perpetuating dynamics of propinquity-activity-intersubjectivity-affinity-propinquity. In the following diagrams, only Agent (A), Subject(s) (S), and Mediator(s) (M) are indicated. However, it should be understood that all members of all represented psychosocial systems are also implicated. Through these overlapping representations, both psychosocial systems and their joint activity "engines" are represented; the shaded fields of overlap represent where joint activity is necessary.

The first diagram represents the presupposed paradigmatic professional practice in which Agent influences Subject as client, patient, student, and

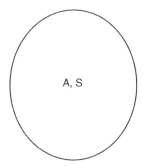

FIGURE 10.1. Agent influences only Subject with little or no shared activity.

so forth by a series of Agent-Subject conversations but little or no shared activity: Agent does not attempt to influence directly Subject's existing or potential psychosocial systems, but only Subject as an individual. When considering this tactic in terms of psychosocial systems and activity settings, Figure 10.1 provides representation.

As a matter of fact, such practices almost never exist, even in professional-client relationships. The vast majority of Agents eventually work toward changing Subjects' psychosocial systems by influencing Subjects to alter their patterns of interactions, activity, and communication with family members, friends, colleagues, and so forth, thus using Subject as a Mediator to influence fellow psychosocial-system members.

This "encapsulation" diagram also inaccurately and deceptively misrepresents the social reality in which this Agent-Subject interaction exists. Even in the most restricted two-party activity schedules, both Agent and Subject continue to be influenced by their own separate psychosocial systems: Agent by colleagues and professional associations, Subject by every member of his or her primary and secondary psychosocial systems; each of these influences is material to the shared activities and goals of Agent and Subject. If change is to be effectuated, Agent and Subject will constitute themselves as an additional psychosocial system, but that depends on the quality of their joint activity and consequent intersubjectivity.

Thus it behooves us to reexamine these "traditional" tactics in the light provided by Delta Theory.

Tactic 1: Agent Influences Subject Directly

Tactic 1 alone is generally presumed to be the paradigmatic professional psychosocial system. Advancements in the use of developmental psychological theory have recently been made in the field of psychotherapy, expanding the potential potency for influence and change and furthering the possibility of a unified theory (Miltenburg & Singer, 1999; Tharp, 1999, 1991; Ryle, 1995; Portes, 1999). However, at the present time, professional practice lags behind theory development.

As practiced by personal coaches, long-term interrogators, tutors, psychoanalysts, physicians, psychotherapists/behavior therapists, and their patients/clients, typical Agent-Subject activity settings are predominantly office bound. Economy of time contributes to this pattern, but it has been enshrined as theoretically necessary by psychoanalysis and other therapies, which deliberately restrict Agent and Subject to closeted contact. For some situations, a closeted Tactic 1 may be appropriate or even necessary because of an impermeability of Subject's other psychosocial systems, or because of practical restrictions on more complex strategies. However, Tactic 1 precludes the possibilities of more potent forms of influence available in other activity settings.

Traditional psychotherapy handicaps itself by insulation from broader shared activity and by its reluctance for authentic dialogic problem solving and assistance. As compared with the "talking cures," cognitive behavior therapy is focused firmly on providing assistance in the client's ZPD, but even most behavior therapists restrict their activity with clients to the consulting room. Tactic 1 plans need not be so restricted. In a theoretically excellent form of phobia treatment, cognitive behavior therapists may work in the professional office through the stage of desensitization (teaching relaxation, then gradually exposing the client to imagined feared situations) but then actually accompany patients on their (post-desensitization) approaches to feared open spaces or heights, providing assistance as needed to maintain relaxation, and then gradually fading the therapist's participation (Emmelkamp, 1990). This delta system strengthens goal behavior by providing assistance embedded in more complex joint activities, in authentic contexts as appropriate in the client's zone of proximal development.

However, authenticity of setting is not all. Home-based programs for child treatment would appear to be advantaged over office settings. A longitudinal investigation of a home visiting program for child treatment found that home visitors who emphasized their social support role and placed little emphasis on changing parenting behavior were not effective (Hebbeler & Gerlach-Downie, 2002). The more crucial feature is the parent-child activity itself.

The most restricted environments (Diagram 1, Agent and Subject in an isolated, closed system) are unlikely to be the most effective design.

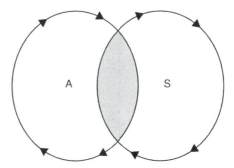

FIGURE 10.2. Agent directly influences Subject in their shared psychosocial system.

In Tactic 1, Agent directly influences Subject within their two-person delta system as both also continue to be influenced by other members of their respective psychosocial systems, as shown in Figure 10.2. *Subjects are also in other psychosocial systems that affect the goal behaviors.* Tactic 1 Subjects are in the overlapped portion of the Venn diagram of the Agent-Subject delta, as well as in psychosocial systems of marriage, family, friends, churches, enterprises, professions, and the like. Not all, but some will have a clear interest in the consequences of Agent's influence and may be opponents or proponents of Agent's work. Furthermore, an overlapped system may be in any of the phases – delta (such as family of an adolescent Subject); alpha (such as a deteriorating marriage); or beta (a stable crowd, clique, "posse," etc.). When Agent begins work, many preexisting systems have participated in the creation and/or maintenance of the behavior to be changed, and thus will be antagonistic to Agent's goal, or, on the contrary, may be potential allies in Agent's design. Agent's prudent presumption is that all these psychosocial systems are pertinent, pending inquiry. A cataloging inquiry about each system, focused on the influence being exerted, will suggest the appropriate tactic(s) and strategy.

In Tactic 1, Agent operates exclusively with the Agent-Subject system while recognizing the other systems that Subject is subject to, and assists Subject to resist, withdraw from, or more effectively manage those systems. Better management of Subject's relationships within systems may be the primary goal of the Agent-Subject delta. Such goals might include withdrawal from a destructive peer system, more effective negotiating strategies within the family, or renegotiating patterns of decision making with a significant other. The significant distinction of Tactic 1 is that the influencing activity settings contain only Agent and Subject. The object of the influencing activities may be improvement in social capacities and decision making.

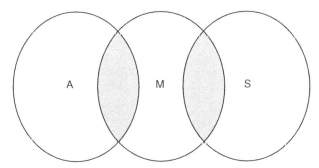

FIGURE 10.3. Through activity settings involving Agent and Mediator(s), the Mediator is influenced to use activity settings with Subject to influence Subject toward change.

Or Tactic 1 Agents may work exclusively and privately on simple, clear goals such as perfecting the fundamental movements of Tae Kwon Do, dance, or any individual sport. Of course, the primary examples of Tactic 1 are those of primary socialization between the caretaker-Agent and the child-Subject. Tactic 1 examples discussed in Chapter 8 include the influence operations of Fleur Adcock's Scottish mother and child and the Nso people of northwest Cameroon. As a malign example, we have discussed at length the familial influence on youth in the creation of dangerous criminals.

Tactic 2: Agent Influences Subject through Mediator(s)

As shown in Figure 10.3, Agent may plan to influence Subject through the use of a Mediator, as has been discussed often in preceding chapters. This is the instance when Agent influences Mediator John to influence Subject Mary.

Tactic 3: Agent's Influence Is Directed to Subject's Psychosocial System

In Tactic 3 (Figure 10.4), Agent participates in activities with members of Subject's psychosocial systems, influencing that system to assist and influence Subject.

Examples from professional practices include family therapy, couple counseling, and various home-based treatments in which Agent assists Subject through direct influence on Subject's psychosocial units that are crucial to Subject's developmental goals. In such practice, Agent's principal activity settings will involve all or most of Subject's psychosocial unit

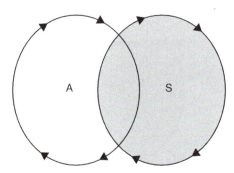

FIGURE 10.4. Agent influences by participation in Subject's existing psychosocial system(s).

with which Agent is an active participant, either in the consulting office, the family's home, or other available spaces, as illustrated in Figure 10.4. In such instances, the entire unit's functioning may be the target of Agent's influence, and in many instances may be considered the Subject itself. Many Agents' contracts for influence are explicitly focused on the marriage or family, not their individual members.

In such cases – when the psychosocial delta system itself is Subject – it must also be remembered that the system consists of individual subjects. Tactic 3 may well begin as a dyadic Agent-to-Subject delta but quickly morph into a plan that distributes Agent's influence among members of the psychosocial group, some of whom begin to function as mediators of Agent's influence on Subject. An example is home-based treatment plans, in which mother and older sister might be principal caretakers of the Subject child. Thus they become mediators of Agent's influence. Even so, it can be expected that mother and sister will require differentiated forms of influence (e.g., perhaps *instructing* for one, *modeling* for the other) to change their behavior toward the Subject child.

In more absolute uses of Tactic 3, Subject's entire psychosocial network, including many of its constituent psychosocial systems, may be assembled for influence activity. Two examples have been discussed earlier, in some detail: the Navajo *Enemyway* "sing," and the Hawaiian *ho'o'ponopono*. (See Chapter 8).

A widespread use of Tactic 3 is the marketing strategy of *product parties*. A variety of companies market their wares by salesmen's direct contact with potential customers at a social event hosted in a home. The hostess of the party invites her guests (perhaps including more than one psychosocial system), and food, drink, or games may precede or accompany the

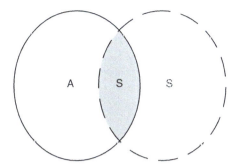

FIGURE 10.5. Agent influences Subject by preventing Subject's psychosocial interactions in existing competing psychosocial systems.

Agent-salesman demonstrating the products. (This gender distribution is typical although not necessary.) The hostess is both assistant-Agent and Mediator; her endorsement of the products constitutes modeling of favorable attitudes that spread like contagion within the psychosocial system. This business plan has been popularly called the Tupperware party (Frenzen & Davis, 1990), after one of the more active companies, but product parties market more than kitchenware: clothing, erotic items, pet products, tools, gourmet cooking items, shoes, and even craft kits for mothers and children. Reports of annual sales early in this decade reach $6 billion.

Tactic 4: Agent Curtails Subject's Participation in Competing Psychosocial Systems

Agents may weaken Subject's ties to psychosocial systems whose influence is contrary to Agent-Subject goals, or they may extricate Subject from them while enabling entry into more goal-congruent systems, as illustrated in Figure 10.5. We have already discussed case examples of this strategy: for example, the recruitment and retention of underage prostitutes and the capture and conversion of the "White Indians" in Chapter 8. This tactic is used frequently by cults and by those who extract cult members; it is also used benignly by many parents who extricate their adolescents from circles of bad companions.

Tactic 5: Agent Creates or Enlists Additional or Alternate Psychosocial Systems for Subject

Tactics 4 and 5 are frequently used in combination, so that as Subject withdraws from an undesired psychosocial system, a new system opportunity is provided or encouraged by Agent.

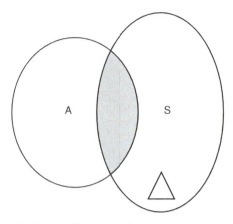

FIGURE 10.6. Agent influences Subject into new activity groups.

In this tactic, as illustrated in Figure 10.6, Agent prescribes that Subject join new activity groups. Most often, as the diagram suggests, this new activity will have a delta function vis-à-vis Subject. Specific "treatment" programs are delta in purpose, such as twelve-step programs, weight-loss groups, survivor groups, and so forth. Agents often also organize purpose-built groups, such as professors facilitating graduate school study groups in the expectation that they will mature into psychosocial systems. Such groups either are, or hopefully will become, beta phase themselves, with committed membership and strong intersubjectivity. Such psychosocial systems operate in delta phase toward new participants, by drawing them into changed activities, interpretations, and values.

In the foregoing diagram, Agents (such as parents, advisors, counselors, or friends), even after Subject is active in the new system, maintain some activity directly with the Subject. In a successful influence-and-change program, Agent's strategy is for an eventual withdrawal from this specific influence process as the beta-phased new psychosocial system takes over the maintenance of achieved change.

Examples of this tactic discussed elsewhere in this book include military training; the failure of school desegregators to provide shared activity in new settings; and inclusion into existing systems by the Indian captors (see Chapter 8). Other examples are the KEEP classrooms of Native Hawaiians and Navajo, and the Delta Classrooms to be discussed later in the chapter. For malign purpose, providing new psychosocial systems for recruits (while drawing them away from their existing systems) is central to the strategy of pimps converting young prostitutes. The same tactic is employed in turn by such rescue Agents as Save Our Sisters organizations.

A Strategy Involving Tactics 1, 2, and 3

The strategy of an overall program of influence integrating three tactics may be well illustrated by athletic-team coaching. In this instance, the Agent coach exercises influence for behavior change of the team to maximize its competitive prowess. The team's comprising individuals must improve and develop, but always in the context of the team's competitive success.

For many years, we studied the basketball coaching of John Wooden, nonpareil Coach of the Century[3] at the University of California, Los Angeles (Tharp & Gallimore, 1976; Gallimore & Tharp, 2004; Nater & Gallimore, 2005). Coach Wooden was distinguished by his system, which constituted an integration of values, activities, disciplines, and schedules. In Delta terms, Wooden systematically employed a strategy consisting of three tactics. Mediators (his assistant coaches) carried out much of his influence (Tactic 2). Of course, the psychosocial system of the team was his overriding Subject, and all coaching by himself as Agent or by his Mediator assistants was directed toward team-performance goals (Tactic 3). However, within that context, there were individual performance-improvement goals. These were highly differentiated and delivered primarily by Wooden himself (Tactic 1). Additionally, the means of influence exercised by Coach Wooden differed sharply across individuals. The means of feedback against a standard and modeling/demonstration were used for all players, but Coach Wooden reserved his positive contingency management for those who got little playing time in real games and whose value to the team lay in being determined opponents to the stars in practice. The five to eight players whose names all of Los Angeles knew needed no praise or encouragement from the coach, Wooden believed; fame and future provided incentive enough. But for the indispensable substitutes and practice squad, the coach provided a rich atmosphere of appreciation and personalized interaction. Thus was the psychosocial delta unit of *team* strengthened and perpetuated, but individual contributions to the team were maximized by responsive assistance in each member's zone of proximal development.

---

[3] ESPN's television program *Who's Number 1?* ranked John Wooden as the greatest coach of all time in any sport.

A Strategy Involving Tactics 1, 4, and 5

Agent simultaneously prepares an alternate delta system to accept Subject and extricates Subject from existing competing beta system(s).

Example: Pimps use direct romancing of Subject adolescent girls, gradually monopolizing their time and activities so as to weaken their ties and activities with school friends and families, then rupture the girls' affiliation with potentially competing psychosocial systems by moving them to another city and isolating them; they then introduce them to what will become their purpose-built new psychosocial system, the society of sister prostitutes (See Chapter 8). SOS (Save Our Sisters organizations) mirrors some of this strategy by extricating prostitutes and offering alternate influence systems.

A Strategy Involving All Five Tactics: The Delta Classroom

Perhaps the most thorough application of Delta Theory concepts thus far has been the design of the teaching method, pedagogical system, and social organization of school classrooms, which I will call here the Delta Classroom[4]. The work began in response to the wide achievement gap between mainstream, middle-class students and those of cultural and/or linguistic diversity. The phenomenon has been present in the schools of most nations, both in classrooms with diverse populations and in monocultural classrooms of minority communities. In diverse classrooms, social sorting reflects the social networks and social classes of the catchment residential areas, so that children arrive at school with psychosocial systems already intact. These groups, cliques, or crowds often last from kindergarten to graduation, with wide disparities in school adjustment and academic achievement. Preparation for academic work, particularly through language development, is much higher for professional and middle-class families than in working-class/public-assistance families (Hart & Risley, 1995). Thus is intergenerational transmission of social class perpetuated.

---

[4] The model has been under development by our group for some forty years, and in various stages of development has been known by our organizational umbrellas: KEEP (Kamehameha Early Education Program) (Tharp & Gallimore, 1998); CREDE (Center for Research in Education, Diversity & Excellence) (Tharp, Estrada, Dalton, & Yamauchi, 1999); Five Standards for Effective Teaching (Dalton, 2007); or currently in Denmark and Greenland, as Effective Pedagogy (Wyatt, 2007). The development of Delta Theory has sharpened our understanding of the dynamics of influence and change as well as the practice of Delta Classrooms.

The Delta Classroom takes as its first task the building of the entire classroom student group into a single psychosocial system by organizing rotating joint activity of all with all, which creates a broad intersubjectivity and felt affinities. As this system grows stronger, the relative strength of the cliques and crowds lessens. In the Delta Classroom, broadly shared activities, friendships, and mutual assistance become widespread.

The Delta Classroom's Agent-teacher begins the work of creating a class-wide psychosocial system by leading discussions that first create and then every day thereafter maintain shared classroom values: serious engagement with schoolwork, mutual respect, and mutual assistance. In "briefing" and "debriefing" daily sessions, the group's performance of the day is explained and then assessed, and improvements are considered. These group shared activities book end the class session. The original work of full discussion and creation of the shared values may take more than one day; but the maintenance sessions of briefing and debriefing are typically between five and ten minutes. During these activities, the teacher as Agent works through a variety of the means of influence; the Subject is the psychosocial system of the class itself.

However, the preponderance of instructional time is given to a variety of small-group joint activities, each with its own instructional goal, and through which students rotate. The rotations ensure that every student works with every other student. The activity centers may be writing centers, science observation centers, reading centers, computer stations, art or drama centers, performance rehearsal centers, or any of the limitless activities that forward instructional goals. The students themselves manage the activities on their own recognizance, as established in the classroom agreement on values. These values legitimate and encourage mutual assistance, reaching of consensus, and full discussions. Agent-teacher predominately works in the activity called the Instructional Conversation. There texts, research data, or shared experiences are discussed, with Agent-teacher influencing and assisting more complex understanding. During this dialogue, students speak as often as does the teacher, allowing Agent to influence/assist with authentic responsiveness to each student's zone of proximal development.

Tactic 1 is much in evidence during the Instructional Conversation, as the individual students are *directly* assisted by quite differentiated means, depending on the needs of the individuals, but in the context of a flowing, shared conversation. Tactic 2 is perhaps the most prevalent: Each student serves as a Mediator of the teacher's influence for each other student in their shared activities. Agent-teacher *influences the psychosocial system* of all students, that is, their shared whole-class system (Tactic 3). Agent-teacher *curtails the influence* of the cliques (Tactic 4) by systematically assigning every student to equal participation with all other students. This is quite different from ordinary classrooms, which allow groups to form according to their existing affinities, which, in effect, means that most students in the same classroom never know or influence each other. Tactic 5 results in the *creation of the psychosocial system* of the entire student group.

The Delta Classroom system maximizes the amount of assistance/ influence from both teacher and fellow students, and maximizes its differentiated responsiveness to each individual's zone of proximal development. Compared to the traditional classroom model of lecture followed by individual assignment and individual assessment, this increase in acts of responsive influence/assessment per unit time is in a probable ratio of 50:1. The reported effects (on academics, attitudes, affinities, and sociometrics) of the Delta Classroom as compared with traditional classrooms are as predicted by Delta Theory. For a review of the empirical evidence, see Tharp & Dalton, 2007.

11

Cultural Patterns in the Practice of Influence

In several places in this book, examples drawn from specific cultures contribute to the conclusion that natural influence and change is inseparable from culture. Indeed, the separation of the two only occurs in the *practice* of influence by professionals under the sway of conventions, traditions, and disciplinary specific theories, which are largely derived from experience with Subjects of limited cultural variation. In the history of the professional practice of influence, too many have assumed that their routine professional activity settings and means of influence are of equivalent effect across all Subjects.

In this chapter, there is room only for a sketch of the two major issues in understanding influence and change in the context of cultural patterning. First are the naturally evolved formal activities of influence practiced by indigenous peoples; and second, the professionally evolved activities of influence practiced with accommodations to specific culture(s).

INDIGENOUS FORMAL ACTIVITIES OF INFLUENCE

In general, *indigenous cultures understand healing as a quest for balance and restoration of harmony among the aspects of the person – such as body, mind, and spirit – and between the person and the sustaining community* (Poonwassie & Charter, 2005). These writers draw examples from native peoples of North America (consistent with my own observations in Navajo, Zuni, and Native Hawaiian communities), and although cautioning that care must be taken to observe local variations, they explain that healing activities are largely ceremonial and communal. Attendance and level of participation is voluntary; sacrifice on the spiritual or physical level is customary; the purpose is the healing development of the individual, but also and simultaneously, the purpose is the healing development of the community (Poonwassie & Charter, op. cit.).

In Delta Theory terms, the generic strategy of these aboriginal ceremonies is the development or restoration of stable and harmonious beta conditions in Subject's psychosocial systems – directly and immediately. Healing ceremonies are appropriate for virtually any manifestation of disruptive, unhappy, or out-of-balance behavior or experience. The entire alpha-phased psychosocial unit will become more harmonious as intersubjectivity is restored through the joint activities of ceremony and other joint-activity opportunities created by conflict reduction, and thus affinities are created or strengthened. Two examples have been discussed in Chapter 8: *hoʻoponopono* and Navajo sings. Delta Theory suggests that this is a desirable and correct primary intervention strategy for Subjects to whom the ceremonies are culturally meaningful. Whether sings, talking circles, sun dances, pipe ceremonies, sweats, potlatches, or other traditional healing activities of Subject's culture, these activities rouse the delta-phased psychosocial systems that are ready at hand, influencing Subject's behaviors of action and thought through well-developed activity settings employing culturally compatible means of assistance. Reasoning within Delta Theory, I would suggest that traditional practices for the restoration of harmony be considered the default first step of influence programs, even for Agents operating within the influence professions. Should that not be appropriate due to social conflict, intrapsychic conflict, or bicultural conflict, then the first step of an intervention might be achieving resolution of those conflicts, thus allowing traditional remedial activities to take place.

Many counselors and psychotherapists serving aboriginal clients advocate integrating traditional healing into their practices (e.g., Moodley & West, 2005). The need for ceremonial activities in urban settings is growing as more aboriginal people migrate into cities. Hart (1997) reviewed projects for reduction of family violence that were originated and operated by aboriginal people, several of which were in large Canadian cities. The projects were characterized by the crucial elements present in traditional ceremonies of healing (discussed in Poonwassie & Charter, op. cit.).

Among professional therapists that serve aboriginal clients, attitudes toward traditional healing activities appear more positive each decade. For example, many aboriginal people for many years used the sweat lodge as preparation for counseling or medical procedures. Now sweat lodges are in prominent use in conjunction with psychotherapy and can be found increasingly in hospitals, outpatient centers, retreat centers, and prisons.

Smith (2005) reports that the sweat lodge is increasingly viewed as an effective treatment modality in its own right; he argues that such a status should be formalized.

In Delta Theory terms, the effective influence interventions for aboriginal and psychotherapeutic activities both operate through the same psychosocial-system processes. The relationship to each other within an overall plan for influence would vary across Subjects, as Subjects vary in ethnic identity, cultural Backgrounds, and their ability to access supportive psychosocial systems. Understanding these issues undoubtedly requires that culture-based social, psychological, and value systems be taken into account by Agent and Subject, if necessary through the assistance of other knowledgeable culture members.

PROFESSIONAL ACTIVITIES OF INFLUENCE PRACTICED WITH CULTURAL ACCOMMODATIONS

In this globalized and migratory world, few professional change Agents work exclusively with Subjects of their own cultural membership. In urban settings particularly, members of each influencing profession faces the question of designing efficacious activity settings for a cultural variety of Subjects. In Delta Theory, what is the relationship between universal principles and cultural conditionality?

Rather than briefly review a broad sample of types of culturally accommodated programs, the issues can be seen with greater clarity by examining a single domain accommodated to many cultures. The domain of juvenile delinquency (the patterns of influence that develop it and the patterns of influence that can correct it) is particularly well suited to this discussion, for two reasons.

The first is theoretical. The decades-long work of Clifford O'Donnell has produced a clear and powerful theoretical hypothesis: *Delinquency develops through activity with similar peers, in settings lacking adult supervision* (O'Donnell, 1998, 2000, 2003). Furthermore, many of the same concepts that appear in Delta Theory inform O'Donnell's analyses (O'Donnell & Tharp, 1990). Because, like Lonnie Athens's theory of violentization (cf. Chapter 8), O'Donnell's theory of juvenile delinquency concerns a specific domain of influence and change, it offers another instance for assessing the values added of a general theory such as Delta.

Second, for a discussion of cultural issues in practice, this example is particularly appropriate because O'Donnell and his students have consistently incorporated culture in their analyses, thus offering an unusual and explicit set of analyses exploring issues of cultural difference and universality.[1]

For example, Acosta (2003) studied four cultural groups of delinquents in Honolulu: Caucasian, East Asian, South Asian, and Polynesian. Questions about peer attachment, peer influence, social interaction, cultural activities, and cultural identification were used. Some minor differences could be detected across cultural groups, but similarities were more striking than differences. All groups acted with, felt intersubjectivity with, and were influenced more by their peers than any adults, as predicted by the O'Donnell hypothesis and Delta Theory. Arrest rates are correlated with group differences in unsupervised partying and concert attendance. Acosta reports that these activities are often the basis for the formation of peer groups. Her general conclusion is that cultural variables, as commonly understood, are less predictive of delinquency than are features of an emerging universal *youth* culture, with a putative "Western" value for adolescent independence toward which other cultural groups are rapidly moving. This "independence" is correlated with, if not determinative of, unsupervised group adolescent activities, which are associated with arrest rates.

Two issues arise in this analysis. First, is it a value of Western culture that adolescents be independent? That adolescents should gradually be weaned toward the independence of adulthood? Or, as seems more likely in both an O'Donnell and a Delta analysis, is the valuation of independence by adolescents a by-product of adult-absent psychosocial systems?

Much delinquency can be seen as a youthful lack of self-control over behaviors more modulated, but often normative, in the adult-home culture. This relationship of delinquent activity to patterns observably normative in the host culture is complex, but not mysterious. I recall that idea dawning on us – in Las Vegas, after a long night with my hosts in a delinquency-prevention consultation visit. The most frequent early delinquency offense for Las Vegas youth was curfew violations – in a city inexhaustible in its determination to keep adults up and gambling all night (Tharp & Wetzel, 1969). Most delinquent and delinquency-supportive activities are rooted in patterns discernable in community-supported adult-activity settings.

Cultural patterns shape symptoms not only in delinquency, but also in psychological and psychosomatic disorders. Some childhood disorders are of particular frequency in certain cultural groups, due either to characteristic social problems or psychosocial structures. Weisz, Suwanlert, Chaiyasit, and Walter (1987) consider psychosocial differences by contrasting Thailand,

---

[1] This discussion adapted from Tharp (2003).

a Buddhist nation that discourages children's aggression and encourages inhibition, peacefulness, politeness, and deference, with the United States, where independence, competitiveness, and differentiation from the family as the goal of socialization is widespread. In Thailand, children and adolescents are referred for clinic treatment more often for "over-controlled syndrome" (fearfulness, sleep problems, somaticizing), whereas in the United States, referred children and adolescents are reported more often with "under-controlled syndrome" (disobedience, fighting, arguing). The same general pattern is discernable in an epidemiological study, although the culturally consistent trends are more marked in parents' decisions to refer for treatment than in their general ratings of their children (Weisz, Suwanlert, Chaiyasit, Weiss, Achenbach, & Walter, 1987). Another "over-controlled" society (Jamaican) has produced similar results (Lambert et al., 1992; Lambert, Weisz, & Knight, 1989).

Delinquent tendencies are associated with "hanging out in the mall" in Acosta's (op. cit.) Honolulu study. That association would be unlikely in a traditional community's market, where adolescents are in close proximity to family and adult members of their own neighborhood community members. Separating traditional market activity from its neighborhoods by converting markets into shopping malls is economical and convenient for Honolulu adults. However, a byproduct of the isolation of the mall from other community interactions is the distancing of appropriate supervising adults from idle youth groups.

Both of these features are richly illustrated in Yamamiya's (2003) study of juvenile delinquency and policing in Japan. Her palette of demographics, economics, history, and cultural analysis sketches a picture of increasing Japanese delinquency, appalling to the reader and frightening to Japanese adulthood. Most useful is her identification of Japanese cultural concepts that are implicated, violated, and distorted (but clearly and deeply involved) in juvenile delinquent activity. As in Acosta's Honolulu, youth in Japan – for all their homogeneous cultural history and identification – engage in joint activity in bands; find group solidarity, support, and meaning in psychosocial peer systems; and are alienated from adults of the home and school, where the psychosocial systems, if they still exist at all, are in alpha phase. Yamamiya (op. cit.), like Acosta, implicates the corruption of Japanese collectivism by Western individualism. Perhaps. But as with Polynesian delinquents, and with even more fervor, Japanese delinquent youth find their collectivist cultural valuation of authority, subservience, and obligation satisfied in power-stratified gangs. Yamamiya's descriptions suggest not a weakening or failure of traditional Japanese psychocultural values, but youth groups that have found satisfactions for those values greater than in the homes and schools from which they were alienated and rebelled against. Current delinquency is continuous with the developmental patterns characteristic of recruits to the *yakuza* – where these same traditional psychocultural needs continue to be met.

As for the specific actions of developing Japanese delinquency, youth society is "saturated with violence, often with erotic overtones," and it values explosive rage. In these descriptions, Yamamiya is clear, useful, and graphic, reporting for example that 50 percent of junior high school students read pornographic books. As an occasional traveler on the Tokyo-Kyoto trains, I notice that so do their fathers. In her analysis, Yamamiya does not discuss the traditional Japanese cultural elements of rage, violence, and Eros. In the restraints of poetry, pottery, tea, music, and dance, the sublime calm and patience of the self-disciplined and obedient Japanese is among the most admired of world images. Yet that image is foregrounded against an explosive potential of rage and cruelty that consistently erupts in Japanese film, drama, and entertainments of the demimonde, providing the stuff of tragedy, as in Mushima – but also with criminal ferocity in such settings as Nanking and World War II prisoner camps. A full understanding of the contents of Japanese delinquency will require considering this tension between the potential for violence and social and personal control. As Yamamiya says, Japan's traditional cultural values are pointed toward the social control of delinquency through regulation of social relationships. Though out of control in Japanese delinquents, these emotional elements are hardly unfamiliar to traditional society; what is alien is their inappropriate and unmodulated expression. Traditional supervision and socialization activities that have heretofore been adequate to the gradual transition to adult self-control and balance are becoming unreliable. Surely this is explained by the O'Donnell hypothesis: Weakening or absent adult membership in the psychosocial systems of youth is explained in the more general case by Delta Theory's view that familial systems that lose joint activity among youth and adults have phased down from delta to alpha, thus losing their capacity for influence.

If this is so, similar effects are developing in domains other than delinquency. The world's marginal youth – disappointed, frustrated, rejected, angered by school and home – are like the mine canaries in the new globalization of transportation, communication, commerce, and migration. Their symptoms alert us to the breakdown and toxicity that occurs when traditional cultures lose effective conditions for supervising youth into the self-control necessary for cultural socialization. Youth are most likely to go bad in the ways their culture has always feared, has always supervised against, and has always banded together to assist them to resist. Youth go bad in the ways of their own cultures, but – like canaries in the coalmine – show us poison in the air long before we notice that somewhere, something below the surface of culture is ruptured.

These fissures developing in the activity patterns shared by maturing youth and their adult supervisors can be due to language differences, cultural distances between generations expanded by schools, lack of time of hard-working immigrant families, or many other local conditions. Are these community problems the *cause* of delinquency? They are certainly contributive, but the causative chain is more complex.

Is it possible that in rapidly modernizing traditional societies or those of immigrated communities the ruptures of adult supervision and socialization increase the relative influence of peers? I suspect that a normal shift toward peer orientation is phylogenetically prepared as part of the differentiation of maturing youth from their families of origin. However, in conditions of lessening familial and community activity participation with youth, peer associations and activities tend to fill the relationship and support needs. Thus the activities of the peer psychosocial system – delinquent or nondelinquent – into which an adolescent moves will be the most potent and the proximal determinant of his or her own development.

This pattern is visible in Nghi Dong Thai's (2003) study of Vietnamese youth gangs in Honolulu. Adults consistently blame community disorganization and lack of parental supervision, communication, and support for their youth's gang activities. They are not wrong, certainly, but they do not recognize the proximal cause, which is peer influence in their psychosocial systems. Youth themselves attribute influence exclusively to peers, and they are correct, although they do not see that peers are more crucial when adult supervision is shrunken. An illuminating aspect of this study is the similar dynamic for nondelinquent Vietnamese youth. Peer influences are central for both, and association with delinquent peers is determinative for youth, whether or not they are alienated from their families and school. They, like youth in school everywhere, are more likely to encounter delinquent peers if they themselves are failing in school, have infrequent activity with their community adults, or are excluded and harassed by school associates. However, not all alienated youth are driven into association with delinquent peers, and if they are not, they do not become delinquent.

In light of the theory and data presented here, prevention of delinquency might be best directed toward those conditions more distal in the causal chain – toward improving opportunities for family and other adults to engage in activities with adolescents during which supervision/socialization can occur. Such prevention programs would reduce the attraction to, frequency of exposure to, and involvement in activity with already-delinquent peer psychosocial systems. These efforts might range from family counseling to organization of community-agency programs of youth activity in which adults are coparticipants – the best role for supervision.

School alienation is a specific risk factor for delinquency, particularly salient in recent-immigrant groups. Delta Theory provides both explanation and guidance for how this risk might be reduced, as in efforts to reform schooling through increasing cultural compatibility (Tharp & Gallimore, 1989). This argument states that culturally based secondary-socialization processes can be facilitated by activating the learners' cognitive and linguistic tools laid down by earlier primary socialization. Because joint activity is the nexus in which social values are influenced, competence in school-based activity is requisite for susceptibility to school influence. Positive academic and social outcomes are increased when school participation structures are congruent with those in the learners' repertoires. Such features as turn taking, wait time, observational learning versus trial and error, and various courtesies and conventions of conversation have characteristic features in each culture, and they differ from the conventions of schools of the common tradition. Interventions for school that radically increase joint activity among teachers and peers (resulting in increases in prosocial inclusion) have been described and evaluated by Tharp, Estrada, Dalton, and Yamauchi (2000) and Yamauchi (2003).

Correction programs for youth already involved in delinquent activity, according to both O'Donnell and Delta Theory, should focus on altering the composition, the patterns of association, and the activities of peer groups. Although theory and evidence overwhelmingly point to this as the appropriate locus for attention, vexing issues in program design remain. For example, Nghi Dong Thai (op. cit.) suggests that school and police authorities should not force association of new offenders with delinquent peers by gathering them all into punitive settings and activities. She suggests that an isolated or prosocial group-affiliated activity of public service is far more rational. Even this simple, persuasive policy suggestion quickly gets complex. In what proportion can these first offenders be absorbed into prosocial groups? Peer influence flows in every direction. Mixed groups of delinquents and their nondelinquent friends tend to alter their values toward the mean, as in the classic O'Donnell study (O'Donnell, Lydgate, & Fo, 1979; Fo & O'Donnell, 1974). What proportion, conditioned by which cultural, age, or gender variables, provides good odds for the desired social outcome?

At the other extreme is treatment of incarcerated groups, whose peer composition is necessarily homogeneous. Hopes in that setting for prosocial development lie with the adult authorities introduced into that community. Here theory does give guidance, suggesting that joint activity among the delinquents and supervising adults should be maximized if prosocial attitudinal development is to occur. For that, there is evidence: Once in detention and with supervising adults, school-avoiding delinquents introduced into their activity settings uniformly rate the school-detention activities as positive (Galbavy, 2003).

In an open rather than incarcerated community, the introduction of adults into youth-activity settings will founder unless cultural patterns of adult-youth relationship are incorporated. Consider adult-youth relationships normative for Polynesian cultures. Age-graded social organization is a well-known, well-nigh definitive characteristic of Polynesian societies (Gallimore, Boggs, & Jordan, 1974; D'Amato, 1987, 1988; Boggs, 1985). Young Hawaiian children are expected to organize themselves as independent-sibling and/or like age groups, closely monitored by the eldest sibling, who is often adolescent. When the performance of these groups breaks down, the supervising youth takes rapid and forceful action to discipline the children. That failing, the adolescent will feel the displeasure of the adults until the behavior of the children is corrected. Adults, however, intervene directly only when the age-appropriate supervision fails. Setting up "corrective" activity settings to incorporate adults must be organized in respect of these cultural patterns, or it will be sure to encounter stiff culturally based resistance from all parties.

We have already seen in Chapter 6 the historically determined preferences and attitudes toward the several means of influence. These preferences extend far beyond means of influence, however, and into the social structuring of activities themselves. For example, Hong Kong Chinese parents were trained to be mediators of behavior therapy for their own children, but the therapists reported severe culturally based reluctance arising from patterns of traditional family structure and interaction. These parents found it difficult to play with their children or respond contingently with praise or ignoring, as this violated their accustomed mode of childrearing, their beliefs about childhood problems, and their attitudes about the proper role of doctors. Thus Lieh-Mak, Lee, and Luk (1984) warned against importing treatment modality scripts from one culture to another. Activity settings can be designed using culturally appropriate interactions; but these need to be designed in collaboration with participants.

Here, in this example, we see the full complexity: cultural differences not only in means of influence, but also in tolerance of activity settings themselves. In Delta Theory, this is ultimately consequential, because all hinges on activity settings, through which influence is delivered and values are created. For activity settings to function, culturally appropriate values must be enacted. Here we find the heart of Delta Theory: biologically determined universals operating through culturally developed processes, intimately twined as blood and bone.

12

Challenges, Research, and Future Development

Many social scientists are wary of drawing on physical science once again for visions of theory and method. On the other hand, had we paid more attention to their science's development rather than on a fading Newtonian snapshot, all might have profited. My own use of physical science referents is intended as analogue, to allow a visual-conceptual alternative that illuminates certain key features of our domain. I do not suggest that we have – and I am agnostic as to whether we will have – any mathematical understanding equivalent to physical forces and their interplay. Biological rather than physical science models is a more relevant direct source of useful concepts and methods of inquiry.

Issues of Causation

Certainly lessons from the new physics, astronomy, and biology should give us comfort by their more complex view of causation. We have been well prepared for such a change by those in our own traditions, such as John Dewey, George Herbert Mead, and the symbolic interactionists, who decades ago held that causation is a process, and that in the long flow of events, variables and conditions alter their functions so that cause becomes outcome, and outcome cause. This view is indispensable to understanding a developmental process, and clearly influence and change is such.

In examining the force field of the stable beta system, the dominant explanatory analyses conducted by social scientists have been patterned by analogy to particle-to-particle "Newtonian" analysis. I have likened such analyses to *How does Mary influence John, and how does John influence*

Susan? Such individual-to-individual studies and interventions are of interest in a Delta Theory approach; they allow both analysis and intervention planning for such basic influence processes as the zone of proximal development and the provision of assistors within that zone. However, the psychosocial system itself *qua* system also influences and is influenced. Understanding of these system behaviors is vital for prediction of both naturally existent groups and of systems engineered for social influence and change. Indeed Mary and John can also be seen as a system, as can John and Susan, and from the point of view of John, they may all three constitute a system. How are these system behaviors to be comprehended?

As one example, we may examine an unanswered question in this current exposition of Delta Theory: What is the pattern of influence between and among social networks and psychosocial systems? The question arises from an absence of evidence, and also from the need for a more generous view of causation than is available from particle-to-particle analyses. In Chapter 2, *Psychosocial Systems and Influence*, the social organization of people was examined and seen to be orderly, resulting in social networks and psychosocial systems. In summary, we have seen that the force of influence by psychosocial systems on their members is foundational to change. Psychosocial systems are created and maintained by a dynamic relationship among propinquity, joint activity, intersubjectivity, affinity, and propinquity in recurring circular order. This force is powerful and predominant in the operations of human organization. I have drawn a clear distinction between psychosocial systems and social networks, the latter describing much looser links of acquaintance and activity. We know that social network members do influence one another, although with far less potency.

At this point, we face branching choices of hypothetical explanation of the relationships between psychosocial systems and social networks. If we look for useful ideas in natural science, we can draw metaphorical analogies – and I mean no more than metaphor – for possibilities of further inquiry. First, we could liken the power of psychosocial systems to some *strong force*, and that of social networks to some *weak force*. This would lead us to investigate whether or not there are different dynamic mechanisms in the two different kinds of force, as it were.

As a matter of evidence, we do not understand how network members influence one another, particularly at a distance. Thus a second choice might lead us to analogize to the concept from small-particle physics of *entanglement*. However, as electrifying as entanglement has been both to physicists and the general intellectual world, and even though the phenomenon is appearing in studies of macro-scale phenomena (e.g., Vedral, 2011), it as yet only labels an unexplained phenomenon.

The Example of Synchrony

As a third alternative analogy, there is available from natural science another theoretical system which treats phenomena of some similarity to those which perplex us. *Synchrony*, the emerging science of complex self-organizing systems, seems to provide one appropriate discipline for approaching the complex system phenomena central to Delta Theory. The signature studies of synchrony have been of the astonishing phenomenon of the rapid synchronization of the blinking lights of fireflies' swarms:

> Beyond serving as an inspiration to engineers, the group behavior of fireflies has broader significance for science as a whole. It represents one of the few tractable instances of a complex, self-organizing system, where millions of interactions occur simultaneously – when everyone changes the state of everyone else. Virtually all the major unsolved problems in science today have this intricate character.... Unfortunately, our minds are bad at grasping these kinds of problems. We're accustomed to thinking in terms of centralized control, clear chains of command, the straightforward logic of cause and effect. But in huge, interconnected systems, where every player ultimately affects every other, our standard ways of thinking fall apart (Strogatz, 2003, p. 34).

Interconnected systems, where every player ultimately affects every other is a fair description of psychosocial systems, and even before refinements of synchrony theory may be applied directly and mathematically to human social system analyses, it behooves students and practitioners of social influence and change to note how a propos synchrony concepts are to human-systems behavior: complex, self-organizing systems, where a multitude of interactions occur simultaneously – when everyone influences the behavior of everyone else, yielding emergent complex self-organized regularities. These insights are of enormous potential value to the study and practice of influence and change. For example, although the individual interactive effects of introducing William into the Mary-John-Susan system may be unpredictable, certain dynamics of the behavior of the system itself *are* predictable. For example, adjustments will follow, in propinquities, activity patterns, intersubjectivities, and affinities. William may be accepted or rejected, but the system will necessarily adjust itself toward stability, and the lights of all members will begin again to blink in synchrony.

On the other hand, in the developmental level of synchrony theory, we can see parallels to sociology's network studies as discussed in Chapter 2. That is, networks do produce a degree of change (sometimes dramatic), therefore influence is surely exerted. But how? Through what means? Synchrony theory itself has not as yet conducted studies of the dynamics of the synchronization it so usefully describes and predicts. That would require studies of, by analogy, how the individual firefly receives, processes, and responds to the behavior of others fireflies. Biologists or sociologists have not yet developed a methodology for such studies. Nevertheless, it cannot be denied that network members are in some kind of dynamic relationship, the effects of which are seen in increasingly varied and interesting empirical studies. Further advances in understanding network dynamics of influence will require analyses at the micro-level of interactions among members, and such studies can be helped by Delta.

What is the pattern of influence between and among social networks and psychosocial systems? In Delta Theory, we have a detailed micro-dynamic theoretical understanding of psychosocial systems' exertion of influence, a level of understanding that firefly synchrony studies lack. However, *we* lack an understanding at the intermediary level – the processes through which networks influence individuals. Yes, almost certainly through their constituent psychosocial systems, but how?

The fourth analogy we may draw is not from a new emerging concept, but one of science's oldest. Occam's Razor, or the law of parsimony, suggests that all else being equal among competing explanations, choose the hypothesis that introduces the fewest assumptions and postulates the fewest entities. This law of parsimony is a process of science dictum: Assert the simplest, and revise only when facts require. In the case of Delta Theory, therefore, I propose that the logical guiding hypothesis for further study is thus: *The influence of social networks operates through the network's partially overlapping constituent psychosocial systems.* Until that proposition is upset, no new force, physical or mystical, need be invoked; if the evidence is negative, then we must move.

Empirical studies and maps of these relationships would certainly facilitate the further development of Delta Theory. Such empirical study is entirely feasible, and if conducted, will forward a comprehensive understanding of how we humans synchronize.

FADS, FAILURES, AND FUTURES: PREDICTION AND POSTDICTION BY DELTA THEORY

Traditional Therapies

"New" influence-and-change programs sweep through society like seasonal weathers, often blown by set-breaking concepts that are more attractive than those of predecessors running low on evidence and energy. The fad phenomenon is often commercial, but even when not, popularity of influence-and-change programs is as unpredictable as that of new music and film. The fields of education, applied psychology, business management, and health improvement seem particularly susceptible to a plague of short-lived, low-evidence faddish programs. Yet a few prosper and enter the established canon. Alcoholics Anonymous, and the many descendant twelve-step programs are cases in point. In such programs, the psychosocial delta systems supporting influence and assistance in reducing addiction also provide the satisfactions of joint activity and intersubjectivity.

Many programs thrive because they satisfy needs broader than the original purpose. Psychoanalysis, purportedly designed for the relief of hysteria, although presenting no credible evidence for efficacy, swept conceptually victorious throughout the international intelligentsia almost certainly because it satisfied another need: the celebratory unmasking and freeing of the erotic in human discourse. For those individuals of sufficient means, "analysis" provided a dependable uncritical listener who from time to time engaged the Subject in some thoughtful retrospection.

Client Centered Therapy, the creation of Carl Rogers, offered even more personal satisfactions. He was a preternaturally intense listener, whom his followers emulated as best they could, thus meeting a human longing too seldom satisfied.

Fifty years ago, B. F. Skinner attempted a sort of overall theory by excluding as undependable and/or irrelevant any concepts or variables extralaboratory in source. He lost the contest for the hearts and minds of psychology to Albert Bandura, who incontrovertibly established observational learning as a major influence on human development. Both of these theoretical giants (along with their heritors) hauled psychology up from the philosophical and fanciful movements of psychoanalysis and existentialism. The methodological mechanisms of this hauling were in both cases empirical science.

In postdiction, none of the therapeutic programs growing from those sources is in full accord with the dynamics of influence and change as described in Delta Theory. In psychoanalysis, there is the occasional "interpretation," an attempt to influence through the means of cognitive structuring. There were undoubtedly effects of modeling, in which the patient became more like the emotionally cool analyst; and clients who emulated Rogers's listening and acceptance no doubt gained social skills and self-respect. Seldom were these effects pernicious. Yet the paucity of hard evidence for efficaciousness would have been predicted by Delta, although it is now accepted that Skinnerian behaviorism and Banduran observational learning are each one (but only one) of the means of influence.

Specific commercial programs will no doubt rise and fall, coursing through their histories, as do all companies, but the design of some commercial-influence plans is sound and can be expected to survive on the basis of efficacy. Behavior-change programs with goals of health and beautification (dieting and exercise, including commercial, public health, and informal settings) have clearly survived the fad stage, and may be expected to institutionalize and strengthen because the basic typical design of those influence plans is sound; they can be expected to survive on the basis of efficacy of their influence through social support.

Delta, a unified theory of influence and change, if it is valid, should provide criteria by which the reasonableness of new enterprises can be judged. For emerging new program proposals, it is a reasonable challenge to Delta Theory to make predictions of probable survival and effectiveness. Consumers and social scientists should be able to conduct this form of analysis on any emerging program, before it is known whether it be fad or efficacious.

Predictive Analysis: Tango Therapy

For several reasons,[1] I choose Tango Therapy as a demonstration of such an analysis and prediction. That the program sounds playful, even joyous, is no reason for Delta Theory to demur. At the time of this writing, Tango Therapy has enjoyed only a short life; empirical evidence for effects are just beginning to emerge, provoking interest and amusement in newsprint and blog postings. On the surface, it has all the marks of typical faddish programs, including the appropriation of words and activities with high positive emotional loading, a combination arousing hope and longing in potential Agents and Subjects. Tango Therapy's first International Conference has been held. All markers seem for a faddish short life.

Descriptively, the therapy is based on the tango, the romantic dramatic ballroom dance of Argentina, performed in pairs, ordinarily the man leading the woman[2] in a series of complex interlocked steps and body postures. Art, film, and literature attest to its addictive properties, whether in bursts of enthusiasm or lifetime dedication to the art. Perfection of tango is generally accepted as unachievable in one lifetime.

Tango therapy practitioners naturally are drawn from tango enthusiasts or teachers, who are likely to describe the pleasures and benefits of

---

[1] There are several reasons: Tango Therapy, as an idea, is provocative, unlikely, charming, seductive, easy to mock, and possessing excellent, if preliminary, efficacy data.

[2] Man/man and woman/woman pairs are acceptable in many venues; in all cases, one person leads and one follows.

the dance in such terms as the rousing of the libido, two hearts beating in unison, life at its basic core, the healing power of touch, the essence of play, and a dance for widening the body's smile. Audiences of artful tango will not find such language altogether hyperbolic.

Tango Therapy seems to be practiced in two settings. Tango studios may offer it as a kind of spiritual and biological tonic for rejuvenation of body and mind. Professional health providers are studying it as an adjunct treatment for Alzheimer's disease, Parkinson's disease, and depression, with comparison groups from the healthy elderly. These practitioners speak of the tango as offering improvement of functional mobility for Parkinson's disease patients, as exercises of cognitive complexity for Alzheimer's disease patients, and as an appealing exercise for the depressed. Secondary effects are being studied on diminution of social anxiety and increased feeling of well-being (e.g., McKinley et al., 2008 in press). Serious though still-small studies offer encouraging data on improvement in balance, posture, motor coordination, and the performance of complex cognitive tasks while multitasking in specific motoric performance.

As an example, a recent small study compared the effects of tango to those of traditional strength/flexibility exercise on functional mobility and quality of life in thirty-eight older individuals, half with Parkinson's disease. Twenty hour-long exercise or tango classes were completed within thirteen weeks. Balance, falls, and gaits were assessed pre- and post-treatment. All groups showed some gains in some measures. The Parkinson tango group improved on all measures and also felt more confident in their balance than the Parkinson exercise group:

> In psychosocial terms, both groups largely enjoyed their experiences because the classes fostered community involvement and became a source of social support for the members. Our results suggest that Argentine tango is an appropriate, enjoyable, and beneficial activity for the healthy elderly and those with Parkinson Disease and that tango may convey benefits not obtained with a more traditional exercise program. (Hackney, Kantorovich, & Earhart, 2007, p. 109)

To what are these effects attributable, should they prove reliable? The present analysis is an exercise in analyzing the correspondence of an emerging program to the tenets of Delta Theory. In Delta terms, tango therapy – despite stigmata of faddishness – offers many strong debating points:

(1) Prescribed activity settings will engage Subjects in desirable zones of proximal development. Tango is believed to provide optimum exercise without strain; the exercise of cognitively complex learning of

motion patterns and integration of joint performance; and intense strengthening of operations of balance, muscular control, and strength. It also has the intrinsic appeal of emotion and glamour that tango enthusiasts emphasize, making it more likely that Subjects will indeed dance, whereas walking and strength exercises have been known to pall.

(2) Provision of influence and assistance in the zone of proximal development by dance teachers, discussion leaders, primary Agents, personal coaches, and so forth appear integral to the practice.

(3) The regular activity settings of group dance sessions in which the new language of tango is taught and shared, together with the shared emotions roused by music and touch, should create intersubjectivities of interpretation and values, leading to increased affinities and resulting in

(4) Psychosocial systems composed of fellow members, who provide ongoing mutual influence and affinal solidarity, leading to continuation of the prescribed activity.[3]

Tango dancers wax poetic when they describe this phenomenon, often describing tango as ritual and ceremony, a celebration by the tango community, as well as a dance for two. Plausibly, tango would appeal to the healthy aging, as it offers participation once again in the movements and music of Eros and touch. In less poetic but corresponding language, the delta phases of tango therapy might well transform into sustaining beta psychosocial systems, allowing participants to dance as long as they are able.

On the basis of this theoretical analysis, *Tango Therapy clearly seems to warrant controlled feasibility studies.* I emphasize this recommendation because it is deserved, but also because of the caution it contains. Prior theoretical analysis is insufficient for unqualified prescription. However, Delta Theory alignment is certainly an appropriate criterion for continued investment of money, time, effort, feasibility studies, and, contingent on those results, wider-scale studies of efficacy.

The outcome of such studies cannot be predicted by theory alone. Vicissitudes of business plans for studios, difficulties of securing fidelity of implementation, finding and supervising competent tango therapist/ teachers, unanticipated interaction effects with multiple treatments:

---

[3] Hackney & Earhart (2010) compared the effects of partnered and nonpartnered tango dance on balance and mobility in mild to moderate Parkinson's disease patients. The nonpartnered class improved as much as the partnered. Partnered participants expressed more enjoyment and interest in continuing.

Randomized treatment trials in influence programs are not fully predictable by theory; that is why we conduct them.

Can Tango Therapy survive its fadlike beginnings and mature into a practical and respected form of influence and change? Tango therapists must avoid some temptations, particularly that of overclaiming. Some informally circulated discussions among enthusiasts extol tango as ameliorative for almost every distress, even schizophrenia. Enjoyable exercise is good for everyone, but in addition the actual activity settings of Tango Therapy map closely onto the changes needed for Parkinson's and Alzheimer's disease patients, as well as the depressed. My foregoing theoretical analysis is restricted to those populations.

EXPLORING THE COGNITIVE AND NEURAL BASES OF INFLUENCE THROUGH JOINT ACTIVITY

A central tenet of Delta Theory is thus: Joint activity leads to higher probability of intersubjectivity, which leads to a higher probability of affinity. Semiotic processes (especially language) have been emphasized in Cultural-Historical Activity Theory as the means by which values and emotions come to be shared during joint activity, thus building intersubjectivities. In Delta Theory, these processes lead to and maintain psychosocial units through which mutual influence is delivered. Current studies of cognition and psychoneurology are revealing another level of process, which reinforces and enriches our understanding of the Great Cycle.

Rapprochement among Delta Theory, cognitive studies, and psychoneurology is a possibility with the door already half open. In Chapter 2, discussion of Galantucci's (2005) findings showed that a task's requirement for interpersonal coordination between two experimental Subjects can drive the creation of nonverbal symbolic communication systems that then establish common ground between coactors. Articulation among Cultural-Historical Activity Theory, cognition, and neurology can offer mutual enlightenment and challenge. The fields of inquiry have already begun to overlap; now we need cross-discussion of those borderland findings. The following reports illustrate that Delta Theory, in its psychosocial bases, does not disconnect from neuroscience: "Progress in understanding the cognitive and neural processes involved in joint action has been slow and sparse, because cognitive neuroscientists have predominantly studied individual minds and brains in isolation. However, in recent years, major advances have been made by investigating perception and action in social context" (Sebanz, et al., 2006, p. 1).

Sebanz et al. (op. cit.) have published an excellent review of recent studies on joint attention, action observation, task sharing, and action coordination, and discuss them as contributions to the understanding of the cognitive and neural processes underlying joint action. They propose several mechanisms that allow sharing representations that predict actions of self and others, and those predictions can then be integrated. For example, when interaction partners direct attention to the same phenomenon, this creates a "perceptual common ground" allowing joint activity to begin and continue.

In general, a tendency to mimic and synchronize is facilitated by attending to one another (Richardson et al., 2005, 2007) and by visual coupling (Richardson et al., 2005; Schmidt, 1990). Even when coactors are instructed to synchronize, their success is heightened by being able to see the coactor and by attending. That is, interpersonal coupling is mediated by attention and the degree to which an individual is able to detect information about a coactor's movements.

Pairs of experimental Subjects working together on mental tasks such as solving puzzles mimic each other's actions nonconsciously and synchronize rhythmical movements. *Unintentional synchronization of movements* has been observed for the following: postural sway (Shockley et al., 2003); the swinging of hand-held pendulums by pairs of participants engaged in verbal problem-solving tasks (Schmidt, et al., 1990; Richardson, et al. 2005; 2007); and nonconscious synchronization of rocking chairs by Subject pairs sitting alongside one another, even though their instructions were to rock as they pleased, independently (Goodman, et al., 2005). Both the visual information available about the other person and the natural rocking frequency of the chairs was manipulated. When Subjects could see and attended to one another, they unintentionally adopted the same rocking frequency, even when Subjects rocked two chairs whose different eigenfrequencies militated against the chairs' natural tendency to desynchronize.

Postural synchronization was abetted by engaging in conversation (Shockley et al., 2003). Pairs of Subjects were found to share more postural locations in phase space where they were conversing with one another to solve a puzzle task as compared to conversing with others, illustrating interpersonal coordination of postural sway in the context of a cooperative verbal task. However, synchronization of rhythmic arm movements was not increased when coactors conversed to solve an interpersonal visual puzzle (Richardson, Marsh, & Schmidt, 2005), whereas they did increase by having each other in sight with no puzzle. Nontask-related general conversation between coactors did not facilitate mimicry in the study of Richardson et al. (2007).

These studies of nonconscious mimicry and synchronization support the emphasis in Delta Theory on shared, joint, and especially collaborative activity as the dynamic that increases intersubjectivity and thus affinity. These coordinations are achieved without semiotic mediation, suggesting that there are other and presumably more basic processes also in the intersubjectivity dynamic. However, Galantucci (2005) found that actors engaged in solving a common problem (although they cannot see each others' puzzle screens) will create symbolic representations of cognitive content; thus by citing the symbols, they enable a coactor to "see" their thinking.

Nonconscious mimicry of gestures, postures, and mannerisms not only enhances the smoothness of interactions, but also fosters *liking* between participants (Chartrand & Bargh, 1999) – effects experimentally supporting Delta propositions that link activity, intersubjectivity, and affinity.

Further studies of more general, unrestricted mimicry also connect in interesting ways to propositions in Delta. Chartrand and her associates have coined the phrase *chameleon effect* to label "nonconscious mimicry of the postures, mannerisms, facial expressions, and other behaviors of one's interaction partners, such that one's behavior passively and unintentionally changes to match that of others in one's current social environment" (Chartrand & Bargh, op. cit., p. 1). In a series of experiments, the motor behavior of Subjects unintentionally matched that of strangers with whom they shared a task. When confederates mimicked the posture and movements of participants, the smoothness of interactions with Subjects was facilitated and increased *liking* between interaction partners. Individuals more disposed to empathy exhibited the chameleon effect to a greater extent than did others, as did Subjects from a collectivist culture, who (in another study) were found more likely to perform nonconscious mimicry than those from an individualist culture (van Baaren, et al., 2003). Bailenson & Yee (2005) demonstrated that these social-influence effects are also elicited with a nonhuman, nonverbal mimicker in a setting of virtual reality.

Much intersubjectivity involves coactors feeling the same emotions in same situations. Coactors come actually to feel that they *share* emotions and motivations. Sociocultural theory emphasizes the role of semiotic mediation in transmitting these value reactions; psychoneurological studies add a more direct mechanism. Keysers and Gazzola (2006) review the evidence "that a single mechanism (shared circuits) applies to actions, sensations and emotions: witnessing the actions, sensations and emotions of other individuals activates brain areas normally involved in performing the same actions and feeling the same sensations and emotions" (p. 379). This provides the mechanism for translating what we see other people do and feel into what we ourselves feel and do.

Humans decode each other's emotions partly by a nonconscious simulating in their own facial musculature the expressions perceived in others' faces. This mechanism, presumed for decades by psychologists (e.g., Wallbott, 1991), has received further confirmation by demonstrations of an impairment of emotional understanding of others in those whose own facial musculature had been weakened by Botox injections (Neal and Chartrand, 2011). This microprocess – the imitation of facial expressions – offers further evidence for two core propositions of Delta Theory: the power of modeling/demonstration as a fundamental means of influence; and shared activity's status as the engine driving the development of intersubjectivity (and thus the entire Cycle of Sorting and maintenance of psychosocial systems). Agent and Subject, sharing actions and events, come to share facial expressions and thus emotions, providing powerful mutual conditioning of values and attitudes.

Do Subjects increase mimicry in order to create affiliation? Lakin and Chartrand (2003) gave research participants an affiliation goal, which increased nonconscious mimicry. Those participants who had been unsuccessful in previous attempts to create affiliation were subsequently more likely to engage in nonconscious mimicry than those who had not previously failed. The authors propose that behavioral mimicry is a part of an individual's natural repertoire, to be employed in a desire to create rapport.

In Delta Theory terms, does nonconscious mimicry function as a proffer of intersubjectivity/affinity? It being nonconscious disallows direct inquiry, but the repertoire of acts included in the chameleon effect – postures, mannerisms, facial expressions – are clearly outward signs of cognitive and emotional conditions, and thus the manifestations of subjectivity. At the Delta Theory level, the relationship between intersubjectivity and affinity is deep, both in evolutionary emergence and in contemporary effects. That signs of intersubjectivity are used unconsciously as signals of affinity enriches our understanding of the microprocesses of the Cycle of Social Sorting.

THE FUTURE DEVELOPMENT OF DELTA

The future cannot be fully seen, but some low-hanging fruit seem ready to blend with Delta principles. Delta needs further empirical testing for its predictive and analytic utility, especially if specific domains developing their new proposed interventions are to be sharpened by Delta dynamics. Two further lines of inquiry, introduced earlier, will surely reward effort: experimental studies of the cognitive and neurological bases of Delta processes and their preprimate evolution. Earlier in this chapter, I proposed empirical studies to discover the dynamics and distributions between psychosocial systems and social networks. If these inquiries mature, some outposts in the exploration of a true theory of everything will be secured.

Thus far, the connections among cognitive studies – psychoneurology, Cultural-Historical Activity Theory, psychology, sociology, and anthropology along with cross-species comparison – allow us a glimpse of unification. Enjoy it as we may, science is open ended and open sourced. Its moments of elegance are fated for disruption by new knowledge from new laboratories, and thus propositions will be revised.

Delta also aspires to be a universal theory. The Appendix to follow (§m), asserts a *Method of Universals*, mentioned several times in this book as William James's "one white crow" test. Surely this is the most demanding of methods: to continuously seek exceptions to one's propositions and revise accordingly. A universalist aspiration is always *Toward* ... and the daily discipline is to waken early and scan the skies for white crows, and if one be spotted, to revise.

APPENDIX

Criteria, Standards, and Guidelines Necessary
for a Unified, Universal Theory

A worthy unified theory must set criteria. Some are shared by any theory in any domain. Others are specific to social science, and another is particular to a unified theory of influence and change. These qualities may be expressed as propositions.

GENERAL REQUIREMENTS

§**a**. A unified social scientific theory, like any other comprehensive scientific theoretical structure, must be held to the standards of science, including generativity, testability, discomfirmability, simplicity, and elegance.

§**b**. It follows that the theory must be as parsimonious of concepts as pertinent phenomena will allow.

§**c**. A universal intellectual structure requires layered "subordinated" concepts, as in an outline or matrix. For example, some concepts will be posited as invariant and of strong force. Others will be considered as variables, present in degrees and thus variably potent. Another level – equally important in understanding or planning behavior change – will contain concepts whose efficacy is conditional on settings, such as professional roles, venues, and cultural expectations and values.

REQUIREMENTS SPECIFIC TO A UNIFIED THEORY

§**d**. A universal theory must preserve the knowledge bases and effective explanations achieved by the various disciplines. Rising in the pyramid or matrix of concepts does not imply that subordinated concepts are superseded, but rather that the phenomena can be understood at a level more general and less conditional. Only such a structure can unify existing knowledge, drawing varied scholars and practitioners into the enterprise of evolving a unified theory.

§e. A unified theory logically becomes a universal theory as it asserts its domain across cultures and across historical periods. Thus it must be plausibly grounded in species characteristics that are phylogenetically provided. At a minimum, there must be plausibility with respect to human morphology, function, and development as provided by phylogenesis, ethnogenesis, and ontogenesis.

Unified	*and*	*Universal*
⇑		⇑
all settings	and affects	all people

DESIRABLE QUALITIES

Other qualities are highly desirable and, indeed, necessary aspirations, although they constitute ideals that must be ever pursued and improved.

§f. For a unified theory to have utility, its language should be appealing across professions, each of which has developed from a body of practical knowledge and the disciplinary theories that have influenced them. A unified theory should serve as a lingua franca, allowing for communication and commerce across boundaries and institutions, but not attempting to replace or subordinate the several theories that it seeks to unite. This ideal would allow a criminologist, a teacher, and a community developer to readily comprehend the referents of the universal theory's lexicon. Although its scope was more modest, I have had the experience of such an integrating theory. At the long-lived Kamehameha Early Education Program (KEEP), our interdisciplinary research staff improved communication sharply when we agreed to use activity theory constructs as a lingua franca (Tharp & Gallimore, 1989). We did not ask anyone to abandon or subordinate their disciplinary theories, but only to reduce the quarrels over disciplinary superiority among linguistics, anthropology, education, and psychology. Consensual decisions were achieved more easily with a shared language, and most participants found the experience enriching rather than limiting. A *unified* theory should also be *unifying*.

§g. A unified theory should provide added value to those of the disciplines and professions. A fully developed universal theory should provide a conceptual structure to which any profession can repair, and there find templates to guide analysis and decision making. When considering a social program, individual treatment program, or political or advertising campaign, the theory should imply a check-list of basic processes to consider before implementation. Without that capacity, a unified theory would be an esoteric, abstract amusement.

§**h**. The explanatory power of a unified theory must lie at a level more general than those of the disciplines and professions. Paradoxically, this can be achieved by staying closer to the phenomenal surface. This means using a language that is close to the phenomena it seeks to explain, not unduly abstract, and insofar as possible a language that is comprehensible within our common-use vocabulary, so that all will understand the same referents when the theory speaks.

§**i**. A unified theory should not be reductionistic. The goal is not to reduce concepts to a presumably more elementary factor. For example, we know that emotional arousal during a learning experience will strengthen its impact. Although classical conditioning is certainly at play in such an event, attributing that specific causation is less useful in program design than is a theory that offers guidance for arranging the social conditions for appropriate emotional arousal on appropriate occasions. This does not invalidate the conditioning explanation; indeed, a universal theory would be invalid if it were inconsistent with basic psychophysical processes. The theoretical challenge is to find language and concepts that are valid, *and* authentic, *and* transparent to the phenomena of interest.

METHODOLOGICAL IMPLICATIONS OF A UNIFIED THEORY

§**j**. The unified theory must generate hypotheses testable at each level. This testability criterion is of particular importance in a conceptually layered and subordinated theory.

§**k**. A universal theory will require units of analysis appropriate to each level of concept and to the nature of specific inquiries. However, those units of analysis must link, so their relationships across levels can be investigated.

§**l**. Testability changes with the level of generality of the conceptual layers. As conditionality increases, probability designs become indispensable to test specific causal hypotheses. However, when generality rises finally to propositions of universality, they cannot be tested by probability mathematics. Universality is properly tested by the method of *analytic deduction*, or "the Method of Universals."

§**m**. The indispensable method for testing the validity of universal claims is the method of analytic deduction, also known as the Method of Universals. Previously used in studies of disease causation (see Rhodes, 1999), opiate addiction (Lindesmith, 1957), dangerous criminality (Athens, 1997; 1992), and education (Tharp & Dalton, 2007), analytic deduction "requires the researcher to attempt to formulate propositions which apply to all instances without exception. Crystallized, the advantages of this method are 1) theories can be disproved and compared against evidence; 2) knowledge can grow as old propositions are revised in the light of negative evidence; and 3) investigators are required to closely link theory and fact, as exceptions demand revision" (Znaniecki, 1934, quoted in Lindesmith, 1957, p. 19). The logic of the method is that of William James's white crow test: "[I]f you wish to upset the law that all crows are black, you must not seek to show that no crows are; it is enough if you prove one single crow to be white" (1890/1969, p. 41):

> This methodology establishes causality by identifying what is unique in the background of an exemplary population … its requirement that all members of a class but no nonmembers exhibit a complete set of the identified unique features provides for falsification. Models derived by analytic induction, unlike models derived by quantitative statistical methodologies, are logically unaffected by the n of the population studied (an n of 1 has been sufficient historically in medical research to identify the cause of a disease) but their universality is tested by every new case. (Rhodes, 2003, p. 93)

Surely the most unforgiving of methods, it imposes discipline on theorists/researchers: to diligently seek exceptions to our propositions, thus striving to prove ourselves wrong; we thereby enable the formulation of more refined, more accurately phrased propositions.[1]

---

[1] An undergraduate in my class once opined that the best response to one white crow would be to shoot it. The students' applauded her wit; my laughter was wry, because her approach is the standard response to experiments that "did not turn out." Crows reported in social science journals are black.

REFERENCES

Acosta, J. (2003). The effects of cultural differences on peer group relationships. In: C. R. O'Donnell (Ed.), *Culture, peers and delinquency* (pp. 13–26). Binghamton, NY: Haworth Press. (Published simultaneously as a special issue of the *Journal of Prevention & Intervention in the Community*).

Adcock, F. (2000). *Poems 1960–2000.* Tarset, Northumberland, UK NE48 1RP: Bloodaxe Books Ltd.

Ainslee, G. (1992). *Picoeconomics: The strategic interaction of successive motivational states within the person.* New York: Cambridge University Press.

Allport, G. (1954). *The nature of prejudice.* Cambridge, MA: Addison Wesley.

Athens, L. H. (1992). *The creation of dangerous violent criminals.* Urbana: University of Illinois Press.

(1997). *Violent criminal acts and actors revisited.* Urbana: University of Illinois Press.

Athens, L. & Starr, R. (2003). One man's story: How I became a "disorganized" dangerous violent criminal. In: Athens, L. & Ulmer, J. T. (Eds.). *Violent acts and violentization: Assessing, applying and developing Lonnie Athens' theories.* Series Volume 4: Sociology of Crime, Law and Deviance (pp. 53–76). JAI, Oxford, UK.

Athens, L. & Ulmer, J. T. (Eds.). *Violent acts and violentization: Assessing, applying and developing Lonnie Athens' theories.* Series Volume 4: Sociology of Crime, Law and Deviance. JAI, Oxford, UK.

Au, K. H., Tharp, R. G., Crowell, D. C., Jordan, C., Speidel, G. E., & Calkins, R. P. (1985). The role of research in the development of a successful reading program. In: J. Osborn, P. Wilson, & R. Anderson (Eds.), *Reading education: Foundations for a literate America* (pp. 275–292). Lexington, MA: D. C. Heath & Co.

Axtell, J. (1981). *The European and the Indian: Essays in the ethnohistory of colonial North America.* New York: Oxford University Press.

Back, M. D., Schmukle, S. C., & Egloff, B. (2008). Becoming friends by chance. *Psychological Science, 19,* 439–440.

Bailenson, J. N. & Yee, N. (2005). Digital chameleons automatic assimilation of nonverbal gestures in immersive virtual environments. *Psychological Science, 16* (10), 814–819.

Bakhtin, M. M. (1981). *The dialogic imagination: Four essays.* Austin: The University of Texas Press.

Bandura, A. (1969). *Principles of behavior modification.* New York: Holt, Rinehart, & Winston.

(1977). *Social learning theory.* Englewood Cliffs, NJ: Prentice-Hall, Inc.

Barnes, B. E. (2007). Conflict resolution across cultures: A Hawaii perspective and a Pacific mediation model. *Conflict Resolution Quarterly, 12* (2), 117–133.

Bates, E., Elman, J., Johnson, M., Karmiloff-Smith, A., Parisi, D., & Plunkett, K. (1998). Innateness and emergentism. In: William Bechtel & George Graham (Eds.), *A companion to cognitive science* (pp. 590–601). Oxford: Basil Blackwell.

Bolívar, J. & Chrispeels, J. H. (2011). Enhancing parent leadership through building social and intellectual capital. *American Educational Research Journal, 48* (1), 4–38.

Bourdieu, P. (1977). *Outline of a theory of practice.* Cambridge University Press.

Bronfenbrenner, U. (1979). *The ecology of human development.* Cambridge, MA: Harvard University Press.

Byrne, D. S. (1998). *Complexity and the social sciences.* New York: Routledge.

Callon, M. & Latour, B. (1986). Unscrewing the big Leviathan: How actors macro-structure reality and how sociologists help them to do so. In: K. Knorr-Cetina & A. V. Cicourel (Eds.), *Advances in social theory and methodology.* New York: Routledge.

Caro, T. & Hauser. M. D. (1992). Is there teaching in nonhuman animals? *Quarterly Review of Biology, 67* (June), 151–174.

Cazden, C. B. & John, V. P. (1971). Learning in American Indian children. In: M. L. Wax, S. Diamond, & F. O. Gearing, (Eds.) *Anthropological perspectives on education* (pp. 252–272). New York: Basic Books.

Chartrand, T. L. & Bargh, J. (1999) The chameleon effect: the perception-behavior link and social interaction. *Journal of Personality and Social Psychology, 76,* 893–910.

Christakis, M. D. & Fowler, J. H. (2007). The spread of obesity in a large social network over 32 years. *New England Journal of Medicine, 357,* 370–379.

Cohen, E. G. (1994a). *Designing groupwork: Strategies for the heterogeneous classroom,* 2nd Ed. New York: Teacher's College Press.

(1994b). Restructuring the classroom: Conditions for productive small groups. *Review of Educational Research, 64* (1), 1–35.

Cohen, E. G. & Lotan, R. A. (1995). Producing equal status interaction in the heterogeneous classroom. *American Educational Research Journal, 32,* 99–120.

(1997). *Working for equity in heterogeneous classrooms.* New York: Teachers College Press.

Cohen, E. G., Lotan, R. A., & Leechor, C. (1989). Can classrooms learn? *Sociology of Education, 62,* 75–94.

Cohen, S. & Lichtenstein, E. (1990). Perceived stress, quitting smoking and smoking relapse. *Health Psychology, 9,* 466–478.

Cole, M. (1985). The zone of proximal development: Where culture and cognition create each other. In: J. V. Wertsch (Ed.), *Culture, communication and cognition: Vygotskian perspectives* (pp. 146–161). Cambridge University Press.

(1998). *Cultural Psychology: A Once and Future Discipline.* (Reprint edition). Cambridge, MA: Belknap Press of Harvard University Press.

Cooley, C. (1962). *Social Organization.* New York: Schocken (originally published 1909).

Cooper, C. R. & Denner, J. (1998). Theories linking culture and psychology: Universal and community-specific processes. *Annual Review of Psychology, 49,* 559–584.

Crespo, N. (1997). *The recruitment of Oahu's female youth into commercial sex.* Unpublished master's thesis, Department of Psychology, University of Hawaii, Honolulu: May.

(2007, June). *The recruitment of Oahu's female youth into commercial sexual exploitation.* Paper presented at the biennial conference of the Society for Community Research and Action, Anaheim CA.

Crespo, N. & Dowrick, P. (2007). Features worth investigating in commercial sexual exploitation of youth. *Community Psychologist, 40* (1), 47–49.

Dalton, S. S. (2007). *Five standards for effective teaching: How to succeed with all learners, grades K-8.* San Francisco: Jossey-Bass.

Dalton, S.S. & Youpa, D. (1998). School reform in Zuni Pueblo middle and high schools. *Journal of Equity and Excellence in Education, 31* (1), 55–68.

Darnell, F., & A. Höem, A. (1996). *Taken to extremes: Education in the far north.* Cambridge, MA: Scandinavian University Press North America.

Davis, T. (2009). "The dynamics of the universe ... ": Ask the experts. *Scientific American, 300* (4) April, p. 84.

Dennison, J. (2005). Spiritual perspectives. The Navajo Enemy Way ceremony. *The Gallup Independent,* June 25. Gallup, New Mexico. [Electronic version]: http://www.gallupindependent.com/2005/june/062505spenway.html

Derounian-Stodola, K. Z. (Ed.). (1998). *Women's Indian captivity narratives.* New York: Penguin Books.

Drimmer, F. (Ed.) (1961). *Captured by the Indians: 15 firsthand accounts, 1750–1870.* New York: Dover Publications, Inc.

Elman, J. L., Bates, E.A., Johnson, M., Karmiloff-Smith, A., Parisi, D., & Plunkett, K. (1996). *Rethinking Innateness: A Connectionist Perspective on Development.* Cambridge, MA: MIT Press.

Emmelkamp, P.M.G. (1990). Anxiety and fear. In: A. S. Bellack, M. Hersen, & A. E. Kazdin (Eds.) *International handbook of behavior modification and therapy* (pp. 283–306). NY: Plenum.

Engeström, Y. (2008). *From teams to knots: Activity-theoretical studies of collaboration and learning at work.* Cambridge: Cambridge University Press.

Engeström, Y. & Middleton, D. (Eds.) (1996). *Cognition and Communication at Work.* Cambridge: Cambridge University Press.

Epstein, J. L. (1989). The selection of friends. In: *Peer relationships in child development,* edited by G. Ladd & T. Berndt. New York: John Wiley & Sons.

(1983). Selection of friends in differently organized schools and classrooms. In: J. L. Epstein & N. Karweit (Eds.), *Friends in school: Patterns of selection and influence in secondary schools* (pp. 73–92). New York: Academic Press.

Estrada, P. (1997). *Patterns of social organization in a sample of nine culturally and linguistically diverse schools.* Santa Cruz, CA: Center for Research on Education, Diversity & Excellence, University of California at Santa Cruz.

(2005). The courage to grow: A researcher and teacher linking professional development with small-group reading instruction and student achievement. *Research in the Teaching of English, 39*, 320–364.

Festinger, L., Schachter, S., & Back, I. (1950). *Social pressures in informal groups: A study of human factors in housing.* Stanford, CA: Stanford University Press.]

Fisher, E. B., Jr., Lowe, M. R., Levenkron, J. C., & Newman, A. (1982). Reinforcement and structural support of maintained risk reduction. In: R. B. Stuart (Ed.), *Adherence, compliance and generalization in behavioral medicine* (pp. 145–168). New York: Brunner/Mazel.

Foreman, G. (1938). *Sequoyah.* Norman: University of Oklahoma Press.

Freed, S. A. & Freed, R. S. (1983). Clark Wissler and the development of anthropology in the United States. *American Anthropologist, 85* (4), 800–825.

Frenzen, J. K. & Davis, H. L. (1990). Purchasing behavior in embedded markets. *The Journal of Consumer Research, 17*, (1), 1–12.

Galantucci, B. (2005) An experimental study of the emergence of human communication systems. *Cognitive Science, 29*, 737–767.

Galbavy, R. J. (2003) Juvenile delinquency: An examination of peer influences, gender differences and prevention. In: C. R. O'Donnell, Ed., *Culture, peers and delinquency* (pp. 65–78). Binghamton, NY: Haworth Press. (Published simultaneously as a special issue of the *Journal of Prevention & Intervention in the Community.*)

Gallimore, R. Bernheimer, L., & Weisner, T. (1999). Family life is more than managing crisis: Broadening the agenda of research on families adapting to childhood disability. In: R. Gallimore, et al. (Eds.) *Developmental perspectives on high incidence handicapping conditions: Papers in honor of Barbara K. Keogh* (pp. 55–80). Mahwah, NJ: Erlbaum & Associates.

Gallimore, R., Boggs, J. W., & Jordan, C. (1974). *Culture, behavior and education: A study of Hawaiian-Americans.* Beverly Hills, CA: Sage Publications.

Gallimore, R. & Goldenberg, C. (2001). Analyzing cultural models and settings to connect minority achievement and school improvement research. *Educational Psychologist, 36*, (1), 45–56.

Gallimore, R., Goldenberg, C., & Weisner, T. S. (1993). The social construction and subjective reality of activity settings: Implications for community psychology. *American Journal of Community Psychology, 21* (4), 537–559.

Gallimore, R., Keogh, B. K., & Bernheimer, C. (1999). The nature and long-term implications of early developmental delays: A summary of evidence from two longitudinal studies. *International Review of Research in Mental Retardation, 22*, 105–135.

Gallimore, R. & Tharp, R. (2004). What a coach can teach a teacher 1975–2004: Reflections and reanalysis of John Wooden's teaching practices. *The Sport Psychologist, 18* (2), 119–137.

Gallimore, R., Tharp, R. G., & Kemp, B. (1969). Positive reinforcing function of "negative attention." *Journal of Experimental Child Psychology, 8*, 140–146.

Gallimore, R., Tharp, R. G., & John Steiner, V. (1992). The developmental and sociohistorical foundations of mentoring. In: C. Herrington, (Ed). *Mentoring.* New York: Columbia University, Institute For Urban Minority Education. ERIC ED354292.

Givvin, K.B., Hiebert, J., Jacobs, J.K., Hollingsworth, H., & Gallimore, R. (2005). Are there national patterns of teaching? Evidence from the TIMSS 1999 Video Study. *Comparative Education Review 49* (3), 311–343.

Goh, S. S. (n.d.) *Supporting children and families of women prisoners and drug inmates.* Save the Children Singapore, Ltd., % Singapore Prison Service, Singapore 499936.

Goldenberg, C., Gallimore, R., & Reese, L. (2005). Using mixed methods to explore Latino children's literacy development. In: T. S. Weisner, Ed. *Discovering Successful Pathways in Children's Development: New Methods in the Study of Childhood and Family Life* (pp. 21–46.) Chicago: University of Chicago Press.

Gonzalez, M. C., Hidalgo, C. A., & Barbási, A.-L. (2008). Understanding individual human mobility patterns. *Nature, 453,* June 5, 779–782.

Goodman, J.R.L. et al. (2005) The interpersonal phase entrainment of rocking chair movements. In: Heft, H. & Marsh, K.L., Eds. *Studies in Perception and Action VIII: Thirteenth International Conference on Perception and Action,* (pp. 49–53), Erlbaum.

Grandin, T. & Johnson, C. (2006). *Animals in translation.* New York: Harcourt Group (Harvest).

Hackney, M. E. & Earhart, G. M. (2010). Effects of dance on gait and balance in Parkinson's disease: A comparison of partnered and nonpartnered dance movement. *Neurorehabiliton and Neural Repair, 24,* 384–392.

Hackney, M. E., Kantorovich, S., & Earhart, G. M. (2007). A study on the effects of Argentine tango as a form of partnered dance for those with Parkinson disease and the healthy elderly. *American Journal of Dance Therapy, 29* (2), 109–127.

Hackney, M. E., Kantorovich, S., Levin, R., Earhart, G. M. (2007). Effects of tango on functional mobility in Parkinson's disease: A preliminary study. *Journal of Neurologic Physical Therapy, 31* (4), 173–179.

Hammond, R. A. (2010). Social influence and obesity. *Current Opinion in Endocrinology, Diabetes & Obesity, 17,* 467–471.

Harrison, D. (2008). Music teachers advised not to touch children to avoid abuse claims. *Sunday Telegraph,* 09 November. UK.

Hart, B. & Risley, T. R. (1995). *Meaningful differences in the everyday experience of young American children.* Baltimore, MD: Paul H Brookes Publishing Co.

Hart, R. (1997). *Beginning a long journey.* Ottawa, Ontario, Canada: Minister of Public Works and Government Services; Health Canada, National Clearinghouse on Family Violence, Family Violence Prevention Division.

Hatfield, E., Cacioppo, F. T., & Rapson, R. L. (1994). *Emotional contagion.* Cambridge University Press.

Hebbeler, K. M. & Gerlach-Downie, S. G. (2002). Inside the black box of home visiting: A qualitative analysis of why intended outcomes were not achieved. *Early Childhood Research Quarterly, 17,* 28–51.

Heinzelman, E. & Bagley, R. W. (1970). Response to physical activity programs and their effects on health behavior. *Public Health Reports, 85,* 905–911.

Hiebert, J., Gallimore, R., Garnier, H., Givvin, K.B., Hollingsworth, H., Jacobs, J., Chui, A. M., Wearne, D., Smith, M., Kersting, N., Manaster, A., Tseng, E., Etterbeek, W., Manaster, C., Gonzales, P., & Stigler, J.W. (2003). Understanding and improving mathematics teaching: Highlights from the TIMSS 1999 Video Study. *Phi Delta Kappa, 84,*10, 768–775.

Hilgers, T. & Molloy, M. (1981). "Your Holiness, what's your favorite color?": Talking with the Dalai Lama. *American Benedictine Review, 32,* 189–199.

Israel, A. C. & Saccone, A. J. (1979). Follow-up of effects of choice of mediator and target of reinforcement on weight loss. *Behavior Therapy, 10,* 260–265.

James, W. (1969). What psychical research has accomplished. In: G. Murphy & R. O. Ballou, (Eds.), *William James on psychical research* (pp. 25–47). New York: Viking. (Original work published 1890).

Jarjoura, G. R. & Triplett, R. (2003). From violent juvenile offenders to dangerous violent criminals: A test of Athens' theory. In: Athens, L. & Ulmer, J. T. (Eds.). *Violent acts and violentization: Assessing, applying and developing Lonnie Athens' theories.* Series Volume 4: *Sociology of Crime, Law and Deviance* (pp. 147–174). JAI, Oxford, UK.

John-Steiner, V. P. & Oesterreich, H. (1975). *Learning styles among Pueblo children: Final report to National Institute of Education.* Albuquerque: University of New Mexico, College of Education.

Jordan, C. (1985). Translating culture: From ethnographic information to educational program. *Anthropology & Education Quarterly, 16,* 105–123.

Jordan, C. & Tharp, R. G. (1979). Culture and education. In: A. J. Marsella, R. G. Tharp, & T. Ciborowski (Eds.), *Perspectives in cross-cultural psychology* (pp. 265–285). New York: Academic Press.

Kana'iaupuni, S. M. & Malone, N. (2006). This land is my land: The role of place in Native Hawaiian identity. *Hulili, 3* (1), 281–307.

Keysers, C. & Gazzola, V. (2006). Towards a unifying neural theory of social cognition. In: Anders, S., Ende, G., Junghöfer, M., Kissler, J., & Wildgruber, D. (Eds.) *Progress in Brain Research, 156,* 379–400. Amsterdam: Elsevier B.V.

Kluckhohn, C. (1949). *Mirror for Man.* New York: McGraw-Hill.

LaFromboise, T. D. & Bigfoot, D. (1988). Cultural and cognitive considerations in the prevention of American Indian adolescent suicide. *Journal of Adolescence, 11,* 139–153.

LaFromboise, T. D. & Low, K. G. (1989). American Indian children and adolescents. In: Gibbs, J. T. & Huang, L. N. & Associates (Eds.) *Children of Color: Psychological intervention with minority youth* (pp. 114–147). San Francisco: Jossey-Bass.

LaFromboise, T. D., Trimble, J. E., & Mohatt, G. V. (1990). Counseling intervention and American Indian tradition: An integrative approach. *Counseling Psychologist, 18,* 628–654.

Lakin, J. L. & Chartrand, T. L. (2003). Using nonconscious behavioral mimicry to create affiliation and rapport. *Psychological Science, 14* (4), 334–339

Lambert, M. C., Weisz, J. R., & Knight, F. (1989). Over- and under-controlled clinic referral problems of Jamaican and American children and adolescents: The cultural general and the culture specific. *Journal of Consulting and Clinical Psychology, 57,* 467–472.

Lambert, M. C., Weisz, J. R ; Knight, F., Desrosiers, M. F., Overly, K., & Thesiger, C. (1992). Jamaican and American adult perspectives on child psychopathology: Further exploration of the threshold model. *Journal of Consulting and Clinical Psychology 60,* 146–149.

Lawson, D. M. & Rhodes, E. C. (1981, November). Behavioral self-control and maintenance of aerobic exercise: A retrospective study of self-initiated attempts to improve physical fitness. Paper presented at the annual meeting of the Association for the Advancement of Behavior Therapy, Toronto.

Lehman, D.R., Chiu, C., & Schaller, M. (2004). Psychology and Culture. *Annual. Rev. Psychol., 55,* 689–714.

Leont'ev, A. N. (1981). The problem of activity in psychology. In J. V. Wertsch (Ed.). *The concept of activity in Soviet psychology* (pp. 37–71). Armonk, NY: M. E. Sharpe.

(1989). Joint activity, communication, and interaction (toward well-grounded "Pedagogy of Cooperation"). *Journal of Russian & East European Psychology 30* (2): 43–58.

LeTendre, G. K., Baker, D. P., Akiba, M., Goesling, B., & Wiseman, A. (2001). Teachers' work: Institutional isomorphism and cultural variation in the U.S., Germany, and Japan. *Educational Researcher, 30* (6), 3–15.

Lieh-Mak, F., Lee, P. W. H., & Luk, S. L. (1984). Problems encountered in teaching Chinese parents to be behavior therapists. *Psychologia, 27,* 56–64.

Lindesmith, A. R. (1957). *Opiate addiction.* Evanston: Principia Press of Illinois.

Lisi, A. G. & Weatherall, J. O. (2010). A geometric theory of everything. *Scientific American, 303,* (6), 54–61.

Marzluff, J. M., Walls, J., Cornell, H. N., Withey, J. C., & Craig, J. P. (2010). Lasting recognition of threatening people by wild American crows. *Animal Behaviour, 79,* 3, 699–707.

Maynard, A. E. (2005) Child development and changing behavior in diverse societies: An activity settings approach. In: C. R. O'Donnell & L. Yamauchi (Eds.). *Culture and context in human behavior change: Theory, research, and applications. Papers in Honor of Roland G. Tharp* (pp. 41–62). NY: Peter Lang.

McKinley, P., Jacobson, A., Leroux, A., Bednarczyk, V., Rossignol, M., & Fung, J. (2008). A community-based Argentine tango dance program improves functional balance and confidence in at-risk older people: A randomized control feasibility study. *Journal of Aging and Physical Activity, 16* (4), 435–453.

McNarie, A. D. (2005). No place of refuge. Hawai'i Island Journal. *http://hawaiiislandjournal.com/2005/01a05b.html,* January 1–15.

Milgram, S. (1974). *Obedience to Authority.* New York: Harper & Row Publishers.

Miller, D. B. & Beer, S. (1977). Patterns of friendship among patients in a nursing home setting. *The Gerontologist, 17* (3) 269–275.

Miltenburg, R. & Singer, E. (1999). Culturally mediated learning and the development of self-regulation by survivors of child abuse: A Vygotskian approach to the support of survivors of child abuse. *Human Development, 42,* 1–17.

Mokuau, N. (2002). Culturally based interventions among Native Hawaiians. *Public Health Reports, 117,* Supplement (pp. S82–S87).

(1990). A family centered approach to Native Hawaiian culture. *Families in Society: Journal of Contemporary Human Services, 71,* 607–613.

Monteith, C. L. (1984). Literacy among the Cherokee in the early nineteenth century. *Journal of Cherokee Studies, 9* (2), 56–75.

Moodley, R. & West, W. (Eds.) (2005). *Integrating traditional healing practices into counseling and psychotherapy.* Thousand Oaks, California: Sage Publications.

Müller, C. A. & Cant, M. A. (2010) Imitation and traditions in wild Banded Mongooses. *Current Biology*, 03 June 2010; on line, 10.1016/j.cub.2010.04.037

Neal, D. & Chartrand, T. (2011). Embodied emotion perception: Amplifying and dampening facial feedback modulates emotion perception accuracy. *Social Psychological and Personality Science.* Abstract published online before print April 21, 2011, http://spp.sagepub.com/content/early/2011/04/21/194855061140 6138

Nsamenang, A. B. (1992a). *Human development in cultural context: A third-world perspective.* Beverly Hills, CA: Sage.

   (1992b). Early childhood care and education in Cameroon. In: M. E. Lamb, K. J. Sternberg, C. P. Hwant, & A. G. Broberg (Eds.), *Child care in context: Cross-cultural perspectives* (pp. 419–439). Hillsdale, NJ: Lawrence Erlbaum Associates.

Nsamenang, A. B. & Lamb, M. E. (1994). Socialization of Nso children in the Bamenda Grassfields of Northwest Cameroon. In: P. Greenfield & R. Cocking, Eds. *Cross-cultural roots of minority child development* (pp. 133–146). Hillsdale, NJ: Lawrence Erlbaum Associates.

Nater, S. & Gallimore, R. (2005). *You haven't taught until they have learned: John Wooden's teaching principles and practices.* Morganstown, West Virginia: Fitness International Technology, Inc.

O'Donnell, C. (Ed.), *Culture, peers and delinquency.* Binghamton, NY: Haworth Press. Co-published simultaneously as Journal of Prevention & Intervention in the Community, 25 (2).

O'Donnell, C. R., Lydgate, T., & Fo, W. S. O. (1979). The Buddy System: Review and follow-up. *Child Behavior Therapy, 1,* 161–169.

O'Donnell, C. R. & Tharp, R. G. (1982). Community intervention and the use of multi-disciplinary knowledge. In: A. S. Bellack, M. Hersen, & A. E. Kazdin (Eds.), *International handbook of behavior modification and therapy.* New York: Plenum.

   (1990). Community intervention guided by theoretical development. In: Bellack, A. S., Hersen, M., & Kazdin, A. E. (Eds.), *International handbook of behavior modification and therapy,* 2nd Ed. (pp. 251–266). New York: Plenum Press.

O'Donnell, C. R., Tharp, R. G., & Wilson, K. (1993). Activity settings as the unit of analysis: A theoretical basis for community intervention and development. *American Journal of Community Psychology, 21,* 501–520.

O'Donnell, C. R., Wilson, K., & Tharp, R. G. (2001). The Cross-cultural context: What can be learned from community development projects. In: Melton, G. B., Thompson, R. A., & Small, M. A. (Eds.). *Toward a child-centered, neighborhood-based child protection system* (pp. 104–114). Westport, CT: Praeger.

Olsen, K. K. & Tharp, R. G. (in press). Indigenous education in Greenland: Effective Pedagogy and the struggles of decolonization. In: Craven, R. G., Bodkin-Andrews, G., & Mooney, J. (Eds). *International Advances in Education: Global Initiatives for Equity and Social Justice.* Information Age Press, USA.

Parker, S. T. (2004). The cognitive complexity of social organization and socialization in wild baboons and chimpanzees: Guided participation, socializing interactions, and event representation. In: Russon, A. E. & Begun, D. R.

(Eds.). *The evolution of thought: evolutionary origins of Great Ape intelligence* (pp. 45–60). Cambridge University Press.

Poonwassie, A. & Charter, A. (2005). Aboriginal worldview of healing: Inclusion, blending and bridging. In: Moodley, R. & West, W. *Integrating traditional healing practices into counseling and psychotherapy* (pp. 15–25). Thousand Oaks, California: Sage Publications.

Portes, P. R. (1999, April). *CHAT and the Practice of Psychology and Counseling.* Presented at the annual meeting of the American Educational Research Association, Montreal.

Powell, E. A. (2009). Sequoyah was here. *From the trenches, 62,* #4, July–August. Retrieved March 1, 2011. www.archaeology.org/0907/trenches/cherokee.html

Red Horse, Y. (1982). A cultural network model: Perspectives for adolescent services and paraprofessional training. In: S. M. Manson, Ed., *New directions in prevention among American Indian and Alaska native communities* (pp. 173–184). Portland, OR: Oregon Health Sciences University.

Red Horse, J., Lewis, R. G., Feit, M., & Decker, J. (1978). Family behavior of urban American Indians. *Social Casework, 59,* 67–72.

Remerowski, T. (Writer) & Fleming, S. (Director). (2010) A murder of crows. [Television series episode]. In: F. Kaufman (Producer), *Nature.* New York: WNET.

Rhodes, G., Allen, G. J., Nowinski, J, & Cillessen, A. H. N. The violent socialization scale: Development and initial validation. In: Athens, L. & Ulmer, J.T. (Eds.). *Violent acts and violentization: Assessing, applying and developing Lonnie Athens' theories. Series Volume 4: Sociology of Crime, Law and Deviance* (pp. 125–146). JAI, Oxford, UK.

Rhodes, R. (1986). *The Making of the Atomic Bomb.* New York: Simon and Schuster (1999). *Why they kill: The discoveries of a maverick criminologist.* New York: Knopf.

(2002). *Masters of death: The SS-Einsatzgruppen and the invention of the Holocaust.* New York: Knopf.

(2003). Violent socialization and the SS-Einsatzgruppen. In: Athens, L. & Ulmer, J.T. (Eds.). *Violent acts and violentization: Assessing, applying and developing Lonnie Athens' theories.* Series Volume 4: Sociology of Crime, Law and Deviance (pp. 93–106). JAI: Oxford, UK.

Richardson, M. J., Marsh, K. L., Isenhower, R. W., Goodman, J. R. L., & Schmidt, R. C. (2007). Rocking together: Dynamics of intentional and unintentional interpersonal coordination. *Human Movement Science, 26* (6), 867–891.

Richardson, M. J., Marsh, K. L., & Schmidt, R. C. (2005). Effects of visual and verbal interaction on unintentional interpersonal coordination. *Journal of Experimental Psychology: Human Perception and Performance Vol. 31* (1), 62–79.

Rilling, J. K., Gutman, D. A., Zeh, T. R., Pagnoni, G., Berns, G. S., & Kilts, C. D. (2002). A neural basis for social cooperation. *Neuron, 35,* 395–405.

Rivera, H. & Tharp, R. (2006). A Native American community involvement and empowerment to guide their children's development in the school setting. *Journal of Community Psychology, 34* (4), 435–451.

Rivera, H. H., Tharp, R. G., Youpa, D., Dalton, S. S., Guardino, G. M., & Lasky, S. (1999). *ASOS: Activity Setting Observation System Coding & Rule Book.* 54

pp. Center for Research on Education, Diversity & Excellence, University of California, Santa Cruz CA 95064. http://repositories.cdlib.org/crede/rsrchrpts/ ASOS

Roberts, R. N. (2005). Community: The ties that bind. In: C. R. O'Donnell & L. Yamauchi (Eds.). *Culture and context in human behavior change: Theory, research, and applications. Papers in Honor of Roland G. Tharp* (pp. 63–84). NY: Peter Lang.

Rogoff, B. (1989). The joint socialization of development by young children and adults. In: L. M. & S. Feinman (Eds.), *Social influences and behavior* (pp. 253–280). New York: Plenum Press.

Rueda, R. (2006). Motivational and cognitive aspects of culturally accommodated instruction: The case of reading comprehension. In: D. M. McInerney, M. Dowson, & Van Etten, S. (Eds.) *Effective Schools* (pp. 129–150). Greenwich CT: Information Age.

Ryle, A. (Ed.). (1995). *Cognitive analytic therapy: Developments in theory and practice.* Chichester, England: John Wiley & Sons.

Sanborn, J. (2003). The short course for murder: How soldiers and criminals learn to kill. In: Athens, L. & Ulmer, J.T. (Vol. Eds.) *Violent acts and violentization: Assessing, applying and developing Lonnie Athens' theories. Vol. 4, Sociology of Crime, Law and Deviance* (pp. 107–124). JAI: Oxford, UK.

Saxe, G. B., Gearhart, M., & Guberman, S. R. (1984). The social organization of early number development. In: B. Rogoff & J. V. Wertsch (Vol. Eds.) *Children's learning in the "zone of proximal development." New directions for child development*, (Vol. 23, pp. 19–30). San Francisco: Jossey-Bass.

Schmidt, R.C., Carello, C., & Turvey, M. T. (1990) Phase transitions and critical fluctuations in the visual coordination of rhythmic movements between people. *Journal of Experimental Psychology: Human Perception and Performance, 16* (2), 227–247.

Schramek, T. A. (2006). Tango anyone? *Geronto-McGill: Bulletin of the McGill Center for Studies in Aging 22* (1), January–February, p. 3.

Scribner, S. & Cole, M. (1973). Cognitive consequences of formal and informal education. *Science, 182*, 553–559.

Searle, J. R. (1983). *Intentionality: An essay in the philosophy of mind.* New York: Cambridge University Press.

(1995). *The Construction of social reality.* New York: The Free Press.

(1998). *Mind, Language and Society.* New York: Basic Books.

Sebanz, N., Bekkering, H., & Knoblich, G. (2006). Joint action: Bodies and minds moving together. *Trends in Cognitive Science, 10* (2), 70–76.

Shepardson, M. & Hammond, B. (1970). *The Navajo Mountain community: Social organization and kinship terminology.* Berkeley: University of California Press.

Shockley, K. D., Baker, A. A., Richardson, M. J., & Fowler, C. A. (2007). Verbal constraints on interpersonal postural coordination. *Journal of Experimental Psychology: Human Perception and Performance, 33*, 201–208.

Shockley, K., Santana, M. V., & Fowler, C. A. (2003). Mutual interpersonal postural constraints are involved in cooperative conversation. *Journal of Experimental Psychology: Human Perception and Performance, 29*, 326–332.

Slavin, R. E. 1979. Effects of biracial learning teams on cross-racial friendships. *Journal of Educational Psychology 71* (3) 381–387.

1985. Cooperative learning: Applying classroom organization. *Journal of Social Issues 41* (1), 45–62.

1987. A theory of school and classroom organization. *Educational Psychologist*, 22 (1), 89–108.

1996. Research for the future: Research on cooperative learning and achievement: What we know, what we need to know. *Contemporary Educational Psychology 21* (1), 43–69.

Shockley, K., Santana, M-V. & Fowler, C.A. (2003) Mutual interpersonal postural constraints are involved in cooperative conversation. *Journal of Experimental Psychology: Human Perception and Performance*, 29 (2), 326–332.

Shweder, R. A. & Goldstein, J. L. (1995). Who sleeps by whom revisited: A method for extracting the moral goods implicit in practice. In: J. J. Goodnow, P. J. Miller, & F. Kessel (Vol. Eds.), *Cultural Practices as contexts for development. New Directions for child development* (Vol. 67, pp. 21–39). San Francisco, Jossey-Bass.

Smith, D. P. (2005). The sweat lodge as psychotherapy: Congruence between traditional and modern healing. In: R. Moodley & W. West, (Eds.). *Integrating traditional healing practices into counseling and psychotherapy* (pp. 196–209). Thousand Oaks, California: Sage Publications.

Staats, A. W. (1968). *Learning, language, and cognition.* New York: Holt, Reinhart, & Winston.

Steward, J. H. (1972) *Theory of Culture Change: The Methodology of Multilinear Evolution*: University of Illinois Press.

Stigler, J. W., & Hiebert, J. (1998). Teaching is a cultural activity. *American Educator*, 22 (4), 4–11.

(1999). *The teaching gap: Best ideas from the world's teachers for improving education in the classroom.* New York: Free Press.

Strogatz, S. (2003). *Sync: The emerging science of spontaneous order.* New York: Hyperion/Theia.

Sweller, J. (2007). Human cognitive architecture. In: J. M. Spector, M. D. Merrill, J. J. G. van Merriënboer, & M. P. Driscoll (Eds.). *Handbook of Research on Educational Communications and Technology* (3rd ed., pp. 1117–1160). London: Routledge.

Thai, N. D. (2003). Vietnamese youth gangs in Honolulu. In: C. R. O'Donnell, Ed. *Culture, Peers and Delinquency* (pp. 47–64). Binghamton, NY: Haworth Press. (Published simultaneously as a special issue of the *Journal of Prevention & Intervention in the Community*).

Tharp, R. G. (1975). The triadic model of consultation: Current considerations. In: C. A. Parker (Ed.), *Psychological consultation: Helping teachers meet special needs.* University of Minnesota and the Council for Exceptional Children (pp. 135–151). Reston, VA.

(1977). *Highland Station.* Poetry Texas Press, Texas City.

(1984). The triadic model. In: J. A. Tucker (Ed.), *School psychology in the classroom: A case study tutorial.* Minneapolis, MN: National School Psychology In-service Training Network, University of Minnesota.

(1991). Cultural diversity and treatment of children. *Journal of Consulting and Clinical Psychology, 59*, 799–812.

(1993). The institutional and social context of educational practice and reform. In: E. A. Forman, N. Minick, & C. A. Stone (Eds.), *Contexts for learning: Sociocultural dynamics in children's development* (pp. 269–282). Cambridge: Cambridge University Press.

(1994). Intergroup differences among Native Americans in socialization and child cognition: An ethnogenetic analysis. In: P. Greenfield & R. Cocking, Eds. *Cross-cultural roots of minority child development* (pp. 87–105). Hillsdale, NJ: Lawrence Erlbaum Associates.

(1999). Therapist as teacher. *Human Development, 42*, 18–25.

(2003). Juvenile delinquency: Culture and community, person and society, theory and research. In: C. O'Donnell, Ed., *Culture, Peers and Delinquency* (pp. 1–11). Binghamton, NY: Haworth Press. (Published simultaneously as a special issue of the *Journal of Prevention & Intervention in the Community*.)

(2005, February). *Alpha: Toward a Universal Theory of Behavior Influence and Change.* Paper delivered at the Congress of Psychology and Education in Times of Change, Universitat Ramon Llull, Barcelona.

(2006). Four hundred years of evidence: Culture, pedagogy and Native America. *Journal of American Indian Education, 45* (2), 8–25.

(2007). A Perspective on unifying culture and psychology: Some philosophical and scientific issues. *Journal of Theoretical and Philosophical Psychology, 27* (2), 801–821.

(2010). *Mad with flowers and tears: Selected Poems, 1950–2010.* Baltimore: PublishAmerica.

Tharp, R. G. & Dalton, S. S. (2007). Orthodoxy, cultural compatibility, and universals in education. *Comparative Education, 43* (1), 53–70.

Tharp, R. G., Estrada, P., Dalton, S. S., & Yamauchi, L.A. (2000). *Teaching transformed: Achieving excellence, fairness, inclusion and harmony.* Boulder, CO: Westview Press.

Tharp, R. G. & Gallimore, R. (1976). What a coach can teach a teacher. *Psychology Today, 9* (8), 74–78.

(1989). *Rousing minds to life: Teaching and learning in social context.* New York: Cambridge University Press.

(1991). A theory of teaching as assisted performance. In: *Learning to think: Child development in social context.* Paul Light, Sue Sheldon, & Martin Woodhead, (Vol. Eds.) (Vol. 2, pp. 42–61). Routledge: London.

Tharp, R. G., Jordan, C., Speidel, G. E., Au, K. H., Klein, T. W., Calkins, R. P., Sloat, K. C. M., & Gallimore, R. (2007). Product and process in applied developmental research: Education and the children of a minority. *Hulili: Multidisciplinary Research on Hawaiian Well-Being* 4, 269–317. Reprinted, with new foreword and current reflections, from: M. E. Lamb, A. L., Brown, & B. Rogoff (Eds.), *Advances in developmental psychology, Vol. III, 1984*, pp. 91–141. Hillsdale, NJ: Lawrence Erlbaum & Associates, Inc.

Tharp, R. G. & Note, M. (1988). The triadic model of consultation: New developments. In: F. West (Ed.), *School consultation: Interdisciplinary perspectives on theory, research, training, and practice*, (pp. 35–51). Austin, TX: Research and

Training Project on School Consultation, The University of Texas at Austin, & The Association of Educational and Psychological Consultants, Austin TX 78705.

Tharp, R. G. & Otis, D. (1966). Toward a theory for therapeutic intervention in families. *Journal of Consulting Psychology, 30,* 426–434.

Tharp, R. G. & Wetzel, R. (1969). *Behavior modification in the natural environment.* New York: Academic Press.

Tharp, R. G. (with various contributors). (2004). *Research Evidence: Five Standards for Effective Pedagogy and Student Outcomes.* Technical Report No. G1, March 2004. Center for Research on Education, Diversity & Excellence. www.crede edu.

Thornton, A. & McAuliffe, K. (2006) Teaching in wild meerkats. *Science, 313,* July 14, 227–229.

Thornton, A., Raihani, N. J., & Radford, A. R. (2007). Teachers in the wild: Some clarification. *Trends in Cognitive Sciences 11:* 272–273.

Ulmer, J. T. (2003). Afterword: Where does violentization go from here? In: Athens, L. & Ulmer, J. T. (Eds.), *Violent acts and violentization: Assessing, applying and developing Lonnie Athens' theories,* Volume 4 in the series Sociology of Crime, Law and Deviance (pp. 178–179). JAI: Oxford, UK.

van Baaren, R. B., Maddux, W. W., Chartrand, T.L., de Bouter, C., & van Knippenberg, A. (2003). It takes two to mimic: Behavioral consequences of self-construals. *Journal of Personality and Social Psychology, 84* (5), 1093–1102.

Vedral, V. (2011). Living in a quantum world. *Scientific American.* June, pp. 38–43.

Vogt, L. A., Jordan, C., & Tharp, R. G. (1987). Explaining school failure, producing school success: Two cases. *Anthropology & Education Quarterly, 18,* 276–286.

Vygotsky, L. S. (1978). *Mind in society: The development of higher psychological processes.* (M. Cole, V. John-Steiner S. Scribner, & E. Souberman, Eds. & Trans.). Cambridge MA: Harvard University Press.

(1978). *Mind in society: The development of higher psychological processes* (M. Cole, V. John-Steiner, S. Scribner, & E. Souberman, Eds. & Trans.). Cambridge, MA: Harvard University Press.

(1960). *Razvitie vysshikh psikhicheskikh funktsii.* (The development of higher mental functions.) Moscow: Izdatel'stvo Akademii Pedagogicheskikh Nauk.

Walker, W. (1969). Notes on native writing systems and the design of native literacy programs. *Anthropological Linguistics, 11* (5), 148–166. Available online at http://www.jstor.org/stable/30029223

Walker, W. (1984). The Design of native literacy programs and how literacy came to the Cherokees. *Anthropological Linguistics, 26* (2), 161–169. Available online at http://www.jstor.org/stable/30027501

Walker, W. & Sarbaugh, J. (1993). The Early history of the Cherokee syllabary. *Ethnohistory, 40* (1), 70–94. Available online at http://www.jstor.org/stable/482159

Wallbott, H. G. (1991). Recognition of emotion from facial expression via imitation? Some indirect evidence for an old theory. *British Journal of Social Psychology, 30* (3), 207–219.

Watson, D. R. & Tharp, R. G. (2006). *Self-directed behavior* (9th ed.) Monterey, CA: Brooks/Cole.

Weisner, T. (1984). Ecocultural niches of middle childhood: A cross-cultural perspective. In: W. A. Collins (Ed.), *Development during middle childhood: The years from six to twelve* (pp. 335–369). Washington, DC: National Academy of Sciences Press.

Weisner, T. S. & Gallimore, R. (1985). *The Convergence of Ecocultural and Activity*. Paper read at the Annual Meetings of the American Psychological Association, Washington, DC, December.

Weisz, J. R., Suwanlert, S., Chaiyasit, W, & Walter, B. R. (1987). Over- and under-controlled referral problems among children and adolescents from Thailand and the United States: The *vat* and *wai* of cultural differences. *Journal of Consulting and Clinical Psychology, 55,* 719–726.

Weisz, J. R., Suwanlert, S., Chaiyasit, W., Weiss, B., Achenbach, T. M, & Walter, B. R. (1987). Epidemiology of behavioral and emotional problems among Thai and American children: Parent reports for ages 6 to 11. *Journal of the American Academy of Child and Adolescent Psychiatry, 26,* 890–897.

Wertsch, J. V. & Stone, C. A. (1985). The concept of internalization in Vygotsky's account of the genesis of higher mental functions. In: J. V. Wertsch (Ed.), *Culture, communication, and cognition: Vygotskian perspectives* (pp. 162–179). New York: Cambridge University Press.

White, L. (2007). Culture. In *Encyclopædia Britannica*. Retrieved January 10, 2007, from *Encyclopædia Britannica Online*: http://www.britannica.com/eb/article-68814

White, S., Tharp, R. G., Jordan, C., & Vogt, L. (1989). Cultural patterns of cognition reflected in the questioning styles of Anglo and Navajo teachers. In: D. Topping, V. Kobayashi, & D. C. Crowell (Eds.), *Thinking Across Cultures: The Third International Conference on Thinking* (pp. 79–91). Hillsdale, NJ: Lawrence Erlbaum Associates.

Wissler, C. (1923). *Man and Culture*. NY: Thomas Y. Crowell.

Witherspoon, G. (1977). *Language and art in the Navajo universe*. Ann Arbor: University of Michigan Press.

Wittgenstein, L. (1969). *On Certainty*. Oxford: Basil Blackwell.

Wyatt, T. R. (2009). The Role of culture in culturally compatible education. *Journal of American Indian Education, 48* (3), 47–63.

Wyatt, T. R. & Lyberth, N. (in press) Addressing systematic oppression in Greenland's preschools: The adaptation of a coaching model, *Journal of Equity & Excellence in Education, 44* (2), 221–232.

Yamamiya, Y. (2003). Juvenile delinquency in Japan. In: C. R. O'Donnell, Ed. *Culture, peers and delinquency* (pp. 27–46). Binghamton, NY: Haworth Press. (Published simultaneously as a special issue of the *Journal of Prevention & Intervention in the Community*).

Yamauchi, L. A. (2003). Making school relevant for at-risk students: The Wai'anae high school Hawaiian Studies Program. *Journal of Education For Students Placed At Risk, 8,* 379–390.

Zesch, S. (2004). *The Captured: A true story of abduction by Indians on the Texas frontier*. New York: St. Martin's Press.

Znaniecki, F. (1934). *The Method of Sociology*. New York: Rinehart & Co.

INDEX

Aboriginal Americans, 90–94, *See also* Native
    Americans
  healing ceremonies, 104–06, 139–41,
    See also ho'o'ponopono; Navajo,
    healing 'sings'
activity
  as engine of change, 54, 58
  joint, 14–17, 19, 20, 54　55, 73, 78, 86, 94,
    96, 101, 107, 110, 121–22, 127–28, 129, 137,
    143–44, 146, 153, 157–59
  organization of, 54–58, 111–22, 123–26
  virtual, 12n2
activity settings
  activity itself in, 120–22
  concept of , 55–56
  cultures and, 43, 74–79, 91–93, 139–48
  motive and meaning in, 55–58
  office-bound, 129
  persons in, 121–22
  as unit of analysis, 55–56, 125
Adcock, F., 110, 131
advertising, 88, 93, 164–65
affinity, 13–19, 96, 107, 157–60
Agents and Agencies, 86
Agents and Subjects of influence, 4–6, 22–23,
    34, 49, 54–55, 98, 112–15, 127–28, 132,
    140–41, 154–56, *See also* Dyadic Model of
    Influence; Triadic Model of Influence
Agents, Mediators and Subjects of Influence,
    109, 113–14, 118–20, 127, 131–38, 147–48
alcohol cessation, 86
Allport, G., 107
Alzheimer's Disease, 155, 157
analytic deduction, method of, 161, 165
Aristotle, 6n1
assistance as influence, 28, 38–39

assortative mating , 12–13, 68
Athens, L., 10, 97, 98, 99, 100–03, 141, 166
automatization, 34–35

Background (Searle's philosophical concept),
    69　74, 75, 77, 79, 141
  cultural influences on, 75, 79
  deep Background, 71, 72–73
  and emotions, 77
  and primary socialization, 72　73
Bakhtin, M. M., 74
Bandura, A., 46, 47, 48, 153
behavior therapy, 129, 147
belligerency, 97–100
bílá, 78
Bronfenbrenner, U., 17
Brown v. Board of Education, 107–08
brutalization, 97–100, 102

Cai, L. 52n6
captives converted, 93–94
causation, 66, 149–50, 165
chameleon effect. *See* mimicry, studies of
CHAT. *See* Cultural-Historical-Activity-
    Theory
Cherokee, 91–93, *See also* syllabary
choreographer and dancers, 52n6
Client Centered Therapy, 49, 153
coaching, 7, 29, 31, 33, 88, 98–99, 112
  athletic, 43, 47, 49, 135
  life- or personal-, 126, 129, 156
cognition studies, 42, 69, 157–59
cognitive behavior therapies, 115n1, 129
Cognitive Structuring (as Means of Influence),
    41–43, 48, 50–51, 75, 118, 153
Cole, M., 39, 43, 46, 57, 66, 75

Comanche, 94n4
competence before performance principle, 78
contact theory, 107–08
Contingency Management, (as Means of
　　Influence), 41–42, 48–49, 52, 57, 76, 96,
　　116, 135
cooperative learning, 107–08
Creation of Dangerous Violent Criminals,
　　97–101, *See also* Athens, L.
CREDE, 136n4
Crespo, N., 95n5
crows, 72
cults, 133
Cultural-Historical-Activity-Theory (CHAT),
　　5, 16, 24, 25, 38, 157, 161
Culture(s)
　　and anthropology, 59–60, 61–64
　　and Background, 69–79
　　collectivist/individualist, 121, 130, 143, 159
　　cultural psychology, 64–65
　　defining, 69–70, 73–74
　　development of, 79
　　and ecology, 61, 79–82
　　and formal activities of influence, 74–79,
　　　121, 139–48
　　indigenous, 139–41
　　and means of influence, 41–43, 52, 74–79, 143
　　as pattern, 69–73
　　and phases of psychosocial systems, 75
　　studies, 61–65
　　traits and complexes, 62, *See also* Wissler, C.
cybernetics, 51
Cycle of Social Sorting, 12–19, 89, 160
　　diagram, 13
　　microprocesses, 160

Dalton, S. S., 16, 37, 45n4, 81, 107, 108, 123, 124,
　　136n4, 138, 146, 166
dance therapy. *See* Tango Therapy
degrees of separation, 85, 121
Delta Theory, aspects
　　and Athen's Violentization Theory, 98
　　and Background. *See* Background
　　challenges to, 59–60
　　future development, 160–61
　　and O'Donnell theory of delinquency,
　　　141–48
　　overview, 7–9
　　relationship to other sciences, 149–52
　　scope of, 7
　　social influence on development,
　　　overview, 27–28

standards and guidelines, 163–66
sub-primate correspondence to, 71–72
summary, 25–28, 148
Delta Theory of Practice
　　activity settings, 129
　　goals, basic 126–27
　　tactics, basic types, 127–38
　　tactics, multiple, 135–38
demonstration. *See* Modeling
Denmark, 79–81, 136n4
desensitization, 129
Dewey, J., 12
discomfirmability, 163
dogs, 72
domain knowledge, 32–33
Dyadic Model of Influence, 111–13, 118, 132

Effective Pedagogy, 80, 81, 108, 136n4
emotional contagion, 17, 67–68
Engeström, Y., 24, 66, 123

Feeding-back Against a Standard
　　(as Means of Influence), 41, 51–52
　　video playback effects, 52n6
feral children, 30
field-vectored deltas, 114–15
fireflies, 171–72
fossilization, 35
Franklin, B., 93–94

Gallimore, R., 3, 29, 37, 38, 43, 44n3, 47, 49, 50,
　　51, 52, 55, 57, 58, 75, 76, 81n10, 104, 109, 118,
　　123–24, 135, 136n4, 146, 147, 164
Greenland, 79–82, 136n4
guided reinvention, 26

habitus, concept of, 70
Hawaiians, Native, 52, 75–77, 81n10, 93, 103–04,
　　109–10, 121, 132, 134, 139, 147
health improvement, 86, 117, 153, 154, 155
Himmler, Heinrich, 102
Hitler, Adolph, 102
home-based treatments, 7, 124, 129, 131, 132
hoʻoponopono 103–04, 121, 132, 140
Hume, David, 70

identity, 10, 68, 74, 86, 91, 92, 93, 94, 109,
　　121, 141
Ijoga, 104n10
imitation, 45–48, 72, 160, *See also* Modeling
　　and mimicry
inertia, 5, 8, 125

Influence
  adventitious, 3, 86, 87
  Agent and Subject of, 6
  and assistance, 28–29
  history of the theoretical term, 38
  inadvertent, 3, 90, 91
  intended, 3, 87
  limits of the term, 39n1
  and regulation, 28–29, 38
  sources of, 18, 90, 127
  unintended consequences, law of, 3
  and zone of proximal development, 28–37
Instructing (as Means of Assistance), 40–41,
    48–52, 75–77, 109, 115n2, 119, 132
Instructional Conversation, 76, 81, 137
internalization, 26, 29, 34, 42, 47
intersubjectivity, 12–17, 18–20, 34, 54, 68, 73, 86,
    88, 93–94, 96, 100, 101, 106–07, 109, 115,
    128, 134, 137, 142, 150, 153, 157–60
  psychoneurological processes of, 157–60

Jordan, C., 58, 75, 76, 78, 81, 109, 147
juvenile delinquency, 123, 141–48
  in Honolulu, 142–43, 145
  in Japan, 143–44
  in Vietnamese gangs, 145–47
  theory of. *See* Delta Theory, aspects, and
    O'Donnell theory of delinquency

Kamehameha Early Education Program
    (KEEP), 75–6, 134, 136n4, 164
KEEP. *See* Kamehameha Early Education
    Program

LaFromboise, T. D., 121
law of parsimony, 152
levels of development, 6–7, 66–69, 164
  ethnogenesis, 66n4, 71, 81–82
  microgenesis, 28, 109–11, 126
  ontogenesis, 6, 28
  phylogenesis, 68, 71
literacy, 75, 91–93, 123

malign-purposed influence, 6, 7, 8, 49, 95, 103
  examples, 95–102
'maverick criminologist'. *See* Athens, L.
Mead, G. H., 149
Means of Influence, 38–53
  case examples, 74–79, 96–97, 100, 135
  criterion for listing, 41
  cultural preferences for, 52–53, 74–79,
    104, 109

intertwined, 45
linguistic/verbal, 40, 48–53
list, as open-ended, 4
list, the current 40–43
non-verbal, 40–41
organizational use, 117–18
phylogenetically provided, 40–41
self-applied, 115
meerkats, 41, 43–45
method of universals, 97, 161, 165–67,
  See also One White Crow Test
military training, 49, 101, 102, 134
mimicry, studies of, 159–60
Modeling (as Means of Influence) 30–31,
  41–42, 43, 45–49, 52, 77–78, 94, 109, 113,
  116, 117, 119, 132, 135, 153, 160
mongooses, banded, 72
multivocalities, 73–74

Native Americans. *See* Aboriginal Americans,
    Comanche, Cherokee, Hawaiians,
    Navajo, Zuni
Navajo, 52, 76–78, 81n10
  healing 'sings', 104–06, 132, 140
Nazi Germany, 101–02
Newton, Issac's First Law of Motion 6, 8, 125,
    See also inertia
Nietzsche, Friedrich, 70
Nso people (Northwest Cameroon).
    See primary socialization of children

observational learning. *See* Modeling
observational learning complex, 78
Occam's Razor. *See* law of parsimony
occupational therapy, 7, 32, 88, 124
O'Donnell, C. R., 55, 123, 141, 142, 144, 146
'ohana, 103
One White Crow Test, 17, 98, 161, 166, 247
organizational structures for
    influence, 117–19

Parkinson's Disease, 155, 156n3, 157
parsimony, law of, 25, 152, 163
persuasion, 6n1, 93
phases. *See* Psychosocial Systems
philosophical issues, 65–66, 70–71, 72–74
physical fitness, 86
pimps, 95–97, 135–36
plane(s) of consciousness, 26
Plato, 49
pool of eligibles, 12–13, 18
pre-commitment, 116

primary socialization of children, 7, 24, 73–75, 77, 102, 108–10, 131, 146
  Germany, early 20th century, 102
  non-human primate, 108
  Nso (Northwest Cameroon), traditional/current, 108–09
  Scotland, contemporary 110
product parties, 132–33
propinquity
  case example, 95–96
  defined, 12–13
  effects, 13–14, 18
  virtual, 12n2
Propping/Nudging (as Means of Assistance), 41, 44–45, 52
  subprimate use of, 44
prostitutes, recruitment and socialization of, 6n1, 95–97, 133, 134–36
psychoanalysis, 129, 153
psychoneurology studies, 157–59, 161
Psychosocial System(s)
  Agent and Subject as, 128–31
  dynamics of formation and change, 12–19
  extraction from, 4, 133, 136
  introduced and defined, 7–8
  as Mediator of influence, 119
  overview, 5, 6, 8–9, 12–15
  phase Alpha, 21
  phase Beta, 21
  phase Delta, 21–23, 30
  phases introduced, 8, 20–22
  as 'primary group', 10
  and schools, 22n4, 136–38
  and social networks, 6, 121, 136–38, 149–52, 161
  as Subject of influence, 126, 131–33, 137–38
  unifying the psychological and social, 10–11, 125
  as unit of analysis, 125–26
psychotherapy, 4, 22, 88, 123, 128–29, 152, 154, 160

Questioning (as Means of Influence) 49–50

rehabilitation, practice of, 7, 52, 88, 114, 115, 124
Reichstag Death Squadrons, 101–02
reinforcement. *See* Contingency Management, (as Means of Influence)
Rhodes, R., 97, 98n8, 101, 102, 103, 165, 166
Rogers, C., 153

Rogoff, B. 31n1, 43, 46
Rueda, R. 69

Samoa. *See Ijoga*
Save the Children Singapore (SCS), 114–15
Save Our Sisters (SOS), 136
scaffolding, 39–40
schools, 18–19, 22n4, 80, 91–92, 123–24
  as beta phase organizations, 22n4, 124
  and cultures, 75–77, 146
  Delta classroom, 136–38
  and desegregation, 107–08
  in Greenland. *See* Greenland.
  in Native America, 75–77, 136n4
  and psychosocial systems, 22–23
  students as Mediators, 137–38
  teacher as Agent, 137–38
  transnational culture of, 75, 81, 123–24
Searle, J., 65, 70–72, 79
Sebanz, N., 157–58
self assistance (self influence) 29, 32, 33–35, 36–37, 49, 51, 115–17, 123
semiotics, 16, 42, 72, 73, 78, 92, 108, 109, 157, 159
Sequoia, 91–93
sibling caretaking, 109, 147
Skinner, B. F., 68, 153
Slavin, R., 107–08
smoking cessation, 86, 117
social class, 11, 13, 18, 19
social distance. *See* degrees of separation
social networks, 6, 82, 85–88, 102, 109, 120, 121, 124, 150–52, 161
  relation to psychosocial systems, 150–52, 161
  therapies for, 121–22, *See also* Navajo, healing 'sings'; *Ho'o'ponopono*
sociocultural theory. *See* Cultural-Historical-Activity-Theory
sociolinguistic patterns, 76
Socrates, 49, 50
SS-Einsatzgruppen. *See* Reichstag Death Squadrons
Strogatz, S., 66, 151
"subject to", 88–89, 93
sweat lodges, 140
syllabary, Cherokee, 91–92
symbolic interactionists, 149
synchronization studies, 158–59
Synchrony Theory, 66, 151–52

Tango Therapy, 154–57
Task Structuring (as Means of Assistance), 31–33, 43–45, 49
testability, 9, 163, 165
Tharp, R. G., 3, 4, 12, 24, 29, 34n2, 37, 43, 44n, 47, 48, 49, 50, 51, 52, 55, 57, 58, 59n1, 66n3, 67, 75, 76, 77, 78, 80, 81, 104, 107, 108, 109, 116, 118, 120n2, 123, 124, 129, 135, 136n4, 138, 141, 142, 146, 164, 166
TIMSS, 123–24n1
Triadic Model of Influence, 113–14, 116, 118–19
'Tupperware'. *See* product parties
teaching, 19, 37, 45, 49–50, 68, 88, 92, 94, 104, 110, 117, 118, 123n1, 136–38, *See also* schools
    definitions, 44n3, 76
    in lower species, 43–44, 44n3, 45, 72
    music, 47, 52

unified theory, 3, 5, 7, 10–11, 15, 25, 27, 28, 29, 32, 42, 60–61, 63, 65, 69, 74, 79, 95, 98, 129, 163–66
    as *lingua franca*, 164
    requirements and criteria, 163–65
units of analysis, 55, 125–26, 165

universal theory, 7, 9, 10–11, 20, 21, 25, 32–33, 41, 59–64, 73, 74, 76, 78–79, 88, 95, 101, 103, 141–42, 148, 163–66
    method for testing, 98, 161, 165–66, *See also* analytic deduction, method of; One White Crow Test

violentization , 98n8, 101–02, 141
virulency, 97, 99–101
Vygotsky, L., 16, 24–30, 33–35, 40, 42, 66–67, 76

Watson, D. W., 34n2, 88, 177–78, 187
weight loss, 135, 205
'white Indians', 144–45
White, L., 61
Wittgenstein, L., 70
Wetzel, R. J., 4, 84, 217
Wissler, C., 101–04, 111, 113, 116
Wooden, John, 207

Zone of Proximal Development (ZPD), 28–37, 77n13, 89, 92, 94, 120, 122, 139, 165, 171, 197, 207
    case examples, 96, 100, 108–09
    defined, 27
    stages of, 29–37
Zuni, 81n10, 139

Made in the USA
Monee, IL
24 February 2023

28555111R00116